Cacti 0.8
Beginner's Guide

Learn Cacti and design a robust Network Operations Center

Thomas Urban

BIRMINGHAM - MUMBAI

Cacti 0.8
Beginner's Guide

First published: March 2011

Production Reference: 1110311

Published by Packt Publishing Ltd.
32 Lincoln Road
Olton
Birmingham, B27 6PA, UK.

ISBN 978-1-849513-92-0

www.packtpub.com

Cover Image by Ed Maclean (edmaclean@gmail.com)

Credits

Author
Thomas Urban

Reviewers
Michael Bouma
Mark Cutting

Acquisition Editor
Tarun Singh

Development Editor
Kartikey Pandey

Technical Editor
Kavita Iyer

Copy Editor
Neha Shetty

Indexers
Hemangini Bari
Tejal Daruwale

Editorial Team Leader
Akshara Aware

Project Team Leader
Ashwin Shetty

Project Coordinator
Poorvi Nair

Proofreader
Bernadette Watkins

Graphics
Nilesh Mohite

Production Coordinator
Aparna Bhagat

Cover Work
Aparna Bhagat

About the Author

Thomas Urban is the owner of Urban-Software.de, a software and consulting services company providing add-ons, plugins, and services for the Cacti and Zenoss Network Monitoring systems. He has been programming web applications for over 15 years, building reporting interfaces, network management software, asset management sites, and more.

I would like to thank the team at Packt Publishing—most of all for giving me this opportunity to write a book and also for taking care of schedules, providing support, guidance and feedback, and keeping me on track the whole way.

I would also like to thank all of the reviewers for taking the time to read, correct, and provide valuable feedback to the book throughout the writing process.

Lastly, I want to thank Despina—for making sure I never ran out of coffee on the countless evenings I spent sitting in front of the keyboard instead of with her and the children. I dedicate this book to her.

About the Reviewers

Michael Bouma in the IT business since 1990, starting as a programmer in assembly and Pascal.

He worked for more than 10 years in satellite communications, where he developed an interest for networks and network monitoring. Michael has worked with Cacti since 2001 and has introduced Cacti as the main monitoring product in three different companies. In his last two companies, he was also involved in writing several plugins for Cacti.

Michael is currently working as a network engineer at Atos Origin in the Netherlands. Here he is developing plugins for customers and setting up tooling and monitoring.

In his spare time he is active with Sloop Rowing races.

http://www.sterkesietze.nl

Mark Cutting has been working in the IT arena for the last 20 years. During this time, he has worked in a variety of areas including manufacturing, commodity-based trading, and finance.

In these positions, he has been involved in numerous network and application builds/ rollouts, projects, design standards, and day-to-day operations. He currently manages a network consisting of 10 sites globally where he supports the core network infrastructure and the applications that are key to the business functions.

These technologies include SQL, Windows 2003/2008, Cisco, Juniper, Citrix, and numerous others. He also supports a wide range of global MPLS networks, and has designed and developed a network fail-over strategy that provides minimum down time for critical business applications and voice traffic.

In addition to the activities above, Mark is a member of the Cacti forums, under the name of "mcutting". He is also a keen developer, working with technologies such as PHP, MySQL, Bash, AutoIT, and of course, Cacti.

www.PacktPub.com

Support files, eBooks, discount offers and more

You might want to visit www.PacktPub.com for support files and downloads related to your book.

Did you know that Packt offers eBook versions of every book published, with PDF and ePub files available? You can upgrade to the eBook version at www.PacktPub.com and, as a print book customer, you are entitled to a discount on the eBook copy. Get in touch with us at service@packtpub.com for more details.

At www.PacktPub.com, you can also read a collection of free technical articles, sign up for a range of free newsletters, and receive exclusive discounts and offers on Packt books and eBooks.

http://PacktLib.PacktPub.com

Do you need instant solutions to your IT questions? PacktLib is Packt's online digital book library. Here, you can access, read, and search across Packt's entire library of books.

Why Subscribe?

- Fully searchable across every book published by Packt
- Copy and paste, print and bookmark content
- On demand and accessible via your web browser

Free Access for Packt account holders

If you have an account with Packt at www.PacktPub.com, you can use this to access PacktLib today and view nine entirely free books. Simply use your login credentials for immediate access.

Table of Contents

Preface

Generally speaking, network management refers to the tasks associated with running a network, along with the software, tools, and technology required to support these tasks. One major part of running a network is to monitor the devices on it in order to know what is happening.

One definition of network management from the ISO Telecommunications Management Network model and framework for network management is known as FCAPS. It divides network management into five disciplines: Fault, Configuration, Accounting, Performance, and Security. Most network management tools can be assigned to one of these disciplines and, out of the box, Cacti is generally more of a performance measurement tool than a management tool, but it can be enhanced to also perform additional tasks.

What is Cacti?

Cacti is an open source performance measurement and graphing application. The first version of Cacti was published on 23rd September, 2001, and provided a complete web-based frontend to RRDtool, the high performance data logging and graphing system created by Tobias Oetiker, two years earlier. Cacti stores all of the information required to gather this data and create the graphs in a MySQL database, all of which is completely configurable via its web interface.

For data gathering, Cacti uses external scripts and commands, as well as all 3 SNMP versions.

Even in its initial release, Cacti included much of the functionality needed for an enterprise class performance measurement tool:

- Complete web-based RRD and RRA management
- Complete RRD Graph configuration and generation
- With external Script/Command and SNMP support
- With easy configuration for SNMP interface data graphing
- With granular user rights management

System architecture of Cacti

From an architectural point of view, Cacti uses a cron/at-based poller to gather data from different sources, Round Robin Database (RRD) files to store the polled data, and a MySQL database to store the systems configuration. The primary user interface is a PHP web application that allows for easy management of all aspects of the system, as well as automatic display mechanisms for viewing the graphs.

Cacti is available for different operating systems such as Windows, Linux, and Solaris.

Cacti is more than performance measurement

Although the main area for which Cacti is used is performance measurement, it can be extended to do much more! With the introduction of the Plugin Architecture, Cacti can be extended to include tasks such as:

- Threshold alerting
- Real-time monitoring of specific data sources
- Creating and sending scheduled reports
- System logging and analysis
- Performing network configuration backups
- Integration of other network management software
- Tracking network hardware

Many of these extensions or plugins are actively maintained and supported by the Cacti Group itself, while others are maintained by the Cacti community and the developer of each extension.

What this book covers

Chapter 1, Installing Cacti, will take you through the installation and configuration of Cacti. You will also learn how to upgrade an existing installation. The final part of the chapter will get you familiar with the different features of Cacti.

Chapter 2, Using Graphs to Monitor Networks and Devices, will teach you how to create graphs using RRDtool. Cacti uses RRDtool to store the polled data. In addition to storing data, RRDtool is also used to create performance graphs. This chapter also shows you how to add new devices and performance measurement graphs to them. Then you'll learn how to group devices using the Cacti tree. Cacti provides a facility to create templates for data, graphs, and hosts.

Chapter 3, Creating and Using Templates, will teach you how to create data templates and apply them to devices. You will create a threshold-based graph template and change the appearance of the graph depending on the data value. This chapter will also teach you how to create a selection of SNMP-based graphs and data queries, and how to import a template from the template repository and export our own host template.

Chapter 4, User Management, teaches you how to create a user and apply basic settings to it. Then we discuss different kinds of permissions, user authentication, and how to import a list of users through the command line interface.

Chapter 5, Data Management, will teach you about retrieving data for graphing with Cacti, which is more than just pulling SNMP data. Cacti allows several different methods for data retrieval. This chapter teaches you how to create your own data input methods and create custom scripts to gather remote data. After you complete this chapter, you will be comfortably able to manage a Cacti system.

Chapter 6, Cacti Maintenance, shows you how to create backups of your Cacti installation and how to restore it, as well as providing information on how to keep your Cacti instance clean of dead hosts and files. This chapter is dedicated to Cacti management.

Chapter 7, Network and Server Monitoring, will teach you how to set up Cisco network devices and prepare Windows systems to be monitored using the WMI interface. You will be provided with several instructions to configure your network devices, windows servers, and VMware ESX servers. Each of the different systems requires different methods and configuration tasks in order to poll the performance data.

Chapter 8, Plugin Architecture, shows you how to extend the capabilities of your Cacti instance with the available Plugin Architecture. Plugins allow end-users to implement missing features or create specific enhancements needed for internal corporate usage. At the end of this chapter, you will be able to add new features and functionality to your Cacti instance using external plugins.

Chapter 9, Plugins, provides an overview of the general plugin design based on the ntop plugin. It describes commonly used plugins and also helps you create your first plugin.

Chapter 10, Threshold Monitoring with Thold, provides an overview of the Thold plugin. It describes the different threshold types available. It shows you how to create a threshold and also helps you to build a threshold template and assign it to a data source.

Chapter 11, Enterprise Reporting, shows you how to define reports with the free Nectar and the commercially supported CereusReporting plugins.

Chapter 12, Cacti Automation for NOC, provides an overview of Cacti automation. It describes the process of using the CLI to add permissions, devices, and trees. It also guides you through the process of installation and usage of Autom8.

Appendix A, Mobile Access / Administration, gives some further information on how to access your Cacti installation with mobile devices.

Appendix B, Online Resources, gives more information on the other online resources available.

Appendix C, Further Information, gives more information on RRDtool, SNMP, and Cacti forums.

Appendix D, Pop Quiz Answers, gives answers to the pop-quizzes which appear at the end of each chapter.

What you need for this book

- A Windows- or Linux-based system (CentOS is preferred)
- A code or text editor
- A browser
- The code download for the book

Who this book is for

This book is for anyone who wants to implement performance measurement for trending, troubleshooting, and reporting purposes. The book also explains how to extend Cacti by implementing and creating your own plugins. If you are a network operator and know the basics of network management and SNMP, then this book is for you.

Conventions

In this book, you will find several headings appearing frequently.

To give clear instructions of how to complete a procedure or task, we use:

Time for action – heading

1. Action 1
2. Action 2
3. Action 3

Instructions often need some extra explanation so that they make sense, so they are followed with:

What just happened?

This heading explains the working of tasks or instructions that you have just completed.

You will also find some other learning aids in the book, including:

Pop quiz – heading

These are short multiple choice questions intended to help you test your own understanding.

Have a go hero – heading

These set practical challenges and give you ideas for experimenting with what you have learned.

You will also find a number of styles of text that distinguish between different kinds of information. Here are some examples of these styles, and an explanation of their meaning.

Code words in text are shown as follows: "We can include other contexts through the use of the `include` directive."

A block of code is set as follows:

```
/usr/bin/rrdtool graph -
--imgformat=PNG
--start=-86400
--end=-300
```

When we wish to draw your attention to a particular part of a code block, the relevant lines or items are set in bold:

```
$temp = array(
    "ntop_header" => array(
        "friendly_name" => "NTop",
        "method" => "spacer",
        ),
```

Any command-line input or output is written as follows:

```
perl create_rrdfile_linux.pl test.rrd
```

New terms and **important words** are shown in bold. Words that you see on the screen, in menus or dialog boxes, for example, appear in the text like this: "Go back to the device overview page by clicking on the **Devices** link under the **Management** menu".

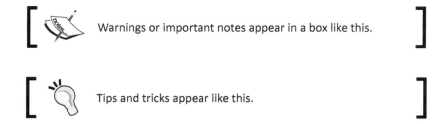

Warnings or important notes appear in a box like this.

Tips and tricks appear like this.

Reader feedback

Feedback from our readers is always welcome. Let us know what you think about this book—what you liked or may have disliked. Reader feedback is important for us to develop titles that you really get the most out of.

To send us general feedback, simply send an e-mail to feedback@packtpub.com, and mention the book title via the subject of your message.

If there is a book that you need and would like to see us publish, please send us a note in the **SUGGEST A TITLE** form on www.packtpub.com or e-mail suggest@packtpub.com.

If there is a topic that you have expertise in and you are interested in either writing or contributing to a book, see our author guide on www.packtpub.com/authors.

Customer support

Now that you are the proud owner of a Packt book, we have a number of things to help you to get the most from your purchase.

Downloading the example code for the book

You can download the example code files for all Packt books you have purchased from your account at http://www.packtpub.com. If you purchased this book elsewhere, you can visit http://www.packtpub.com/support and register to have the files e-mailed directly to you.

Errata

Although we have taken every care to ensure the accuracy of our content, mistakes do happen. If you find a mistake in one of our books—maybe a mistake in the text or the code—we would be grateful if you would report this to us. By doing so, you can save other readers from frustration and help us improve subsequent versions of this book. If you find any errata, please report them by visiting http://www.packtpub.com/support, selecting your book, clicking on the **errata submission form** link, and entering the details of your errata. Once your errata are verified, your submission will be accepted and the errata will be uploaded on our website, or added to any list of existing errata, under the Errata section of that title. Any existing errata can be viewed by selecting your title from http://www.packtpub.com/support.

Piracy

Piracy of copyright material on the Internet is an ongoing problem across all media. At Packt, we take the protection of our copyright and licenses very seriously. If you come across any illegal copies of our works, in any form, on the Internet, please provide us with the location address or website name immediately so that we can pursue a remedy.

Please contact us at copyright@packtpub.com with a link to the suspected pirated material.

We appreciate your help in protecting our authors, and our ability to bring you valuable content.

Questions

You can contact us at questions@packtpub.com if you are having a problem with any aspect of the book, and we will do our best to address it.

1
Installing Cacti

Let's get right on with setting up Cacti. Take a look at what we will do next.

In this chapter, we are going to:

- ◆ Install Cacti's prerequisites
- ◆ Install Cacti on both a CentOS and a Windows system
- ◆ Compile and install the spine poller
- ◆ Upgrade an existing Cacti installation
- ◆ Run Cacti for the first time
- ◆ Provide a quick overview on the Cacti web frontend

Here we go....

Preparing the system—basic prerequisites

In order to install and run Cacti, we need to make sure that all system prerequisites are met. Here we'll give an overview of the different components needed.

Web server

As most of Cacti is built as a web interface, a web server is needed. This can be Apache's httpd or Microsoft's Internet Information Server (IIS) if installing on Windows, but in fact, any PHP-capable web server can be used to run the web interface. For optimal support, the use of Apache or IIS is suggested.

PHP

Cacti is built with the PHP programming language and therefore needs PHP to be installed on the system. Most Linux distributions already have a base PHP environment installed, but some might need additional packages for Cacti to function properly. In particular, the LDAP, SNMP, and MySQL extensions should be installed.

MySQL database

Cacti uses the freely available MySQL database engine as its database server and it is available on most operating systems. One should note that the database server does not need to be installed on the same host as Cacti. For best performance, MySQL version 5 should be used.

NET-SNMP package

The NET-SNMP package provides the SNMP binaries used by Cacti and supports SNMPv1, SNMPv2c, and SNMPv3.

The NET-SNMP package also provides the SNMP daemon for Linux.

Installing Cacti on a CentOS 5 system

You're now going to install Cacti from source on a CentOS 5 system. You should use at least Centos 5.5 as it is 100% binary compatible with RedHat Enterprise Linux 5, but in fact you can follow most of the installation processes on other Linux distributions, such as Ubuntu or SuSe Linux, as well. By installing from source you'll get some insight into the inner workings of Cacti, and it will also provide you with a system which most Cacti and plugin developers are used to. There are differences between a source installation and a Yum/APT installation, but they will be described later on. Let's get started.

Preparing the system

Assume that the CentOS system has been installed with only the "Server Package" selected and there is no graphical user interface installed.

This is the default installation for a CentOS system with no manual package selection.

Time for action – installing the missing packages

The default CentOS installation is missing several important packages. So, we are now going to install these.

1. Install the RPMForge repository. For a 32bit CentOS installation this can be achieved by executing the following command (all on one line):

```
rpm -Uhv http://apt.sw.be/redhat/el5/en/i386/rpmforge/RPMS/
rpmforge-release-0.3.6-1.el5.rf.i386.rpm
```

2. The RPMForge repository includes an RRDtool version for CentOS.

3. Issue the following command to install all required packages:

```
yum install mysql-server php-mysql net-snmp-utils rrdtool php-snmp
```

What just happened?

You just gave the system a location to find the remaining packages needed for the Cacti installation and then installed them; therefore, you are now ready to start the next installation phase.

Downloading and extracting Cacti

Go to `http://www.cacti.net` and download the latest version of Cacti. In the top-left corner, under **Latest Files**, right-click on the `tar.gz` file and save the link address to the clipboard. You are going to need this link later. For simplicity we're assuming that your server has an Internet connection.

Time for action – downloading Cacti

It's now time to download the latest version of Cacti to your server. You will need your system username and password to login to your CentOS installation. If you have installed your CentOS system with the default settings, you should already have an SSH server running. If you're already logged on to the machine, you can ignore the first step.

1. From a Windows machine, logon to your system using an SSH client such as Putty. If this is the first time you have connected to the server, Putty will display a security alert and ask you to accept the RSA key. By doing so, Putty will display the logon prompt where you can logon to the system.

2. Maximize the window, so that long text lines do not break at the end of the line. This will make things easier.

3. You'll need to become the root user in order to be able to setup Cacti properly. Should that not be an option, performing these steps with sudo should achieve the same results.

4. Navigate to /var/www/html. This is the document root for Apache.

5. To download Cacti you can use the wget command. Enter the following command to download Cacti. After entering the wget command, right-clicking into the window client using Putty will paste the URL you copied earlier after the command:

   wget http://www.cacti.net/downloads/cacti-0.8.7g.tar.gz

   You should see the following output on your screen:

```
# wget http://www.cacti.net/downloads/cacti-0.8.7g.tar.gz
--2011-01-02 19:57:22--  http://www.cacti.net/downloads/cacti-0.8.7g.tar.gz
Resolving www.cacti.net... 209.242.232.5, 140.211.167.231, 173.225.179.10
Connecting to www.cacti.net|209.242.232.5|:80... connected.
HTTP request sent, awaiting response... 200 OK
Length: 2236916 (2.1M) [application/x-gzip]
Saving to: `cacti-0.8.7g.tar.gz'

43% [================>                    ] 974,037     157K/s   eta 9s
```

6. You now have the tar.gz file on your system, so let's move on and extract it. To do this, enter the following command:

   tar-xzvf cacti-0.8.7g.tar.gz

7. This will extract the files and directories contained in the archive to the current directory.

8. Finally you are going to create a symbolic link to this new Cacti directory. This will allow you to easily switch between different Cacti versions later, for example, when upgrading Cacti. To create a symbolic link, enter the following command:

   ln -s cacti-0.8.7g cacti

9. This will create a link named cacti which points to the cacti-0.8.7g directory:

```
# ls
cacti-0.8.7g  cacti-0.8.7g.tar.gz
# ln -s cacti-0.8.7g cacti
# ls
cacti   cacti-0.8.7g   cacti-0.8.7g.tar.gz
#
```

What just happened?

You downloaded the latest Cacti version to the root directory of the web server and created a symbolic link to the extracted directory. With the Cacti files in place, you are now ready for the next phase of the installation process.

Creating the database

The database isn't automatically created during the installation of Cacti. Therefore, you need to create it here. At the same time, a database user for Cacti should be created to allow it to access the database. It's also a good idea to secure the MySQL database server by using one of the included CentOS tools.

Time for action – creating the database

To keep it simple let's assume that you're going to host the database on the same server as Cacti.

1. Execute the following command to logon to the MySQL CLI:

    ```
    mysql -u root mysql
    ```

2. The default MySQL root account does not have a password set, so you can set one as follows:

    ```
    SET PASSWORD FOR root@localhost = PASSWORD('MyN3wpassw0rd');
    ```

3. You can now also remove the example database, as it is not needed:

    ```
    DROP DATABASE test;
    ```

4. Together with the example database, some example users may have been created. You can remove these with the following command:

    ```
    DELETE FROM user WHERE NOT (host = "localhost" AND user = "mydbadmin");
    ```

5. On a CentOS distribution you can use the following command to guide you through the above steps:

    ```
    /usr/bin/mysql_secure_installation
    ```

6. Now that MySQL is secured, let's create the Cacti database. Enter the following command:

    ```
    mysqladmin -u root -p create cacti
    ```

    This will ask for the MySQL root password which you provided in Setup Step 1. When finished, you will have an empty database called cacti.

7. As the database is still empty, you need to create the tables and fill it with the initial data that comes with Cacti. The following command will do just that:

```
mysql -p cacti < /var/www/html/cacti/cacti.sql
```

8. Again it will ask for the MySQL root password. Once the command finishes you'll have a working Cacti database. Unfortunately Cacti is still unable to access it, therefore you are now going to create a database user for Cacti.

9. Enter the following command:

```
mysql -u root -p mysql
```

10. You'll see the following on the screen:

```
# mysql -u root -p
Enter password:
Welcome to the MySQL monitor.  Commands end with ; or \g.
Your MySQL connection id is 5682
Server version: 5.0.77 Source distribution

Type 'help;' or '\h' for help. Type '\c' to clear the buffer.

mysql>
```

11. Type the next few lines in the MySQL prompt to create the user. Make sure to choose a strong password:

```
GRANT ALL ON cacti.* TO cactiuser@localhost IDENTIFIED BY
'MyV3ryStr0ngPassword';
flush privileges;
exit
```

What just happened?

You used some tools to secure the MySQL server and created a database. You also filled the Cacti database with the initial data and created a MySQL user for Cacti. However, Cacti still needs to know how to access the database, so let's move on to the next step.

In case you are not using CentOS to install Cacti, you can use some MySQL internal functions to secure your installation.

Configuring Cacti

You need to tell Cacti where to find the database and which credentials it should use to access it. This is done by editing the `config.php` file in the `include` directory.

Time for action – configuring Cacti

The database and some other special configuration tasks are done by editing the information in the `config.php` file.

1. Navigate to the `cacti` directory:

   `cd /var/www/html/cacti/include`

2. Edit `config.php` with `vi`:

   `vi config.php`

```
<?php
/*
 +-------------------------------------------------------------------------+
 | Copyright (C) 2004-2010 The Cacti Group                                 |
 +-------------------------------------------------------------------------+
 | http://www.cacti.net/                                                   |
 +-------------------------------------------------------------------------+
*/

/* make sure these values refect your actual database/host/user/password */
$database_type = "mysql";
$database_default = "cacti";
$database_hostname = "localhost";
$database_username = "cactiuser";
$database_password = "MyV3ryStr0ngPassword";
$database_port = "3306";

/* Default session name - Session name must contain alpha characters */
#$cacti_session_name = "Cacti";

$config['url_path'] = '/cacti/';
?>
```

3. Change the `$database_username` and `$database_password` fields to the previously created username and password.

4. Change the line `$config['url_path'] = '/'` to `$config['url_path'] = '/cacti/'`

What just happened?

You changed the database configuration for Cacti to the username and password that you created earlier. These settings will tell Cacti where to find the database and what credentials it needs to use to connect to it. You also changed the default URL path to fit your installation. As you install Cacti to `/var/www/html/cacti`, a sub-directory of the document root, you need to change this setting to `/cacti/`, otherwise Cacti will not work correctly.

Creating the poller cron entry and Cacti's system user

For the poller to work correctly, Cacti needs a system user account. You are going to create one now and also set up the poller's cron entry.

Time for action – creating the poller's cron entry and Cacti's system account

1. To create a Cacti system user called `cactiuser`, issue the following command as root:

   ```
   adduser cactiuser
   ```

2. Navigate to the `cacti` directory:

   ```
   cd /var/www/html/cacti
   ```

3. Change the ownership of the `rra` and `log` directory to the newly created user:

   ```
   chown -R cactiuser rra/ log/
   ```

4. Add the poller cron entry. Edit the file `cacti` in `/etc/cron.d`:

   ```
   vi /etc/cron.d/cacti
   ```

5. Add the following line to the file:

   ```
   */5 * * * * cactiuser /usr/bin/php /var/www/html/cacti/poller.php
   > /dev/null 2>&1
   ```

6. Save the file.

What just happened?

You just created a system user which runs the Cacti poller and scheduled the poller to run every 5 minutes. Five minutes is the default interval, but it can be changed to 1 minute if needed. For more information on how to do so, go the following post in the Cacti forums: `http://forums.cacti.net/viewtopic.php?p=116403`.

Installing the Spine poller

By default, Cacti comes with a poller written in PHP. For small-to-medium installations, this poller does its job just fine, but for larger installations, an alternative poller, spine, needs to be used. It is written in C and is much faster than the original poller, as it makes use of the multi-tasking capabilities of modern operating systems and hardware.

Here we will deep-dive into installing and configuring the spine poller.

Time for action – installing Spine

1. You now need to prepare the development environment for Spine. On CentOS you can do this by issuing the following command:

```
yum install gcc mysql-devel net-snmp-devel autoconf automake
libtool
```

```
Transaction Summary
===============================================================================
Install      20 Package(s)
Upgrade      13 Package(s)

Total download size: 20 M
Is this ok [y/N]: y
Downloading Packages:
(1/33): elfutils-libelf-devel-0.137-3.el5.i386.rpm           |   24 kB    00:00
(2/33): keyutils-libs-devel-1.2-1.el5.i386.rpm               |   27 kB    00:00
(3/33): rpm-python-4.4.2.3-20.el5_5.1.i386.rpm               |   60 kB    00:00
(4/33): elfutils-devel-0.137-3.el5.i386.rpm                  |   61 kB    00:00
(5/33): elfutils-libelf-devel-static-0.137-3.el5.i386.rpm    |   66 kB    00:00
(6/33): popt-1.10.2.3-20.el5_5.1.i386.rpm                    |   74 kB    00:00
(7/33): lm_sensors-devel-2.10.7-9.el5.i386.rpm               |   77 kB    00:00
```

2. Download the spine source code. For this, go to http://www.cacti.net and click on **Download** under the **Spine (Cactid)** section. Right-click on **Spine Source** in the tar.gz format and copy the link address.

3. Navigate to /tmp/ and issue the following command:

```
wget http://www.cacti.net/downloads/spine/cacti-spine-0.8.7g.tar.gz
```

4. Extract the file:

```
tar -xzvf cacti-spine-0.8.7g.tar.gz
```

5. Navigate to the newly created cacti-spine-0.8.7g directory.

6. Prepare the directory for compilation. Please note that this step may not work on other distributions, or additional steps need to be taken to accomplish it:

```
./bootstrap
```

7. Configure the compiling environment:

```
./configure
```

8. Compile Spine:

```
make
```

9. Once the make command finishes, install Spine:

```
make install
```

10. You now have Spine installed, but it needs to be configured. Therefore, copy the sample configuration file to a location where Spine will find it:

```
cp /usr/local/spine/etc/spine.conf.dist /etc/spine.conf
```

11. Edit the file in `vi`:

```
vi /etc/spine.conf
```

12. Change the database configuration to match the settings from earlier.

13. Create a symbolic link in `/sbin` to the spine binary:

```
ln -s /usr/local/spine/bin/spine /sbin/spine
```

What just happened?

You just set up a basic development environment for compiling Spine, compiled it, and then installed it. You also configured Spine to use the correct database information.

Compiling Spine on other Linux distributions

When compiling Spine on other Linux distributions such as Ubuntu, you will have to go through some additional steps. Look at the following URL for more information on how to do so:

```
http://docs.cacti.net/manual:087:1_installation.1_
install_unix.6_install_and_configure_spine.
```

Differences between source and APT/Yum installations

The main difference between installing Cacti from source and using APT/Yum-based installations is the location of configuration files and availability of patches. Cacti, by default, does not follow the **Filesystem Hierarchy Standard (FHS)** defined for the Linux operating systems. The FHS defines directories where applications should add their configuration or log files. APT/Yum-based installations usually follow this standard. Due to this, add-ons such as the Plugin Architecture may not be available on all platforms using APT/Yum.

The main advantage of using APT/Yum-based installations is the ease of installation but as we've just seen, installing Cacti isn't very difficult.

However, the disadvantage of using APT or Yum is the availability of newer Cacti versions. Source-based Cacti installations can be upgraded to the latest version as soon as it is available on the Cacti website, while APT/Yum-based installations might need to wait until the package maintainers update their repositories.

Have a go hero – remote server for database hosting

Here is a little challenge for you. It's not difficult but it will allow you to alter the installation to suit your needs. What if you want to use a remote database server? Maybe you want to use an existing dedicated MySQL server, instead of hosting the database on the same system as Cacti, or you want to separate the roles to allow more growth. Can you figure out what to change?

Solution: Create the MySQL database on the remote system using the same command as if you were installing it locally, but this time use the `-h <hostname>` option to specify the remote server. When creating the user and granting it permissions, use the following command, assuming the Cacti server has the IP '192.168.0.10':

```
GRANT ALL ON cacti.* TO cactiuser@'192.168.0.10' IDENTIFIED BY
'MyV3ryStr0ngPassword';
flush privileges;
exit
```

This will allow the Cacti user access to the database from the Cacti server. Now change `$database_hostname` in `config.php` and `DB_Host` in `spine.conf` on the Cacti server to point to your remote database server.

Installing Cacti on a Windows system

The installation of Cacti on a Windows system is quite different from Linux. Most of the prerequisites that are already available on a Linux platform need to be installed on a Windows system. The MySQL database is an example of such a prerequisite. In the following sections you can find more information about the Windows installation and how you can overcome most of the manual installation procedures by making use of the community-built Windows Installer.

The community-built Windows Installer

Instead of installing every prerequisite individually, the community-built Windows Installer provides a convenient way of installing them together with Cacti.

Time for action – starting the Windows setup

1. Download the Windows Installer to the system on which you want to install Cacti. To retrieve the latest version, go to `http://forums.cacti.net/viewtopic.php?t=14946` and click on the download link at the end of the first post. Save the installer to your desktop.

2. Double-click on the setup file. The installer will check what has already been installed and give you a report. Click **Next >** after you have read the information.

3. The next screen shows the GPL license. Accept it and click on **Next >**.

4. Next comes the selection of the web server to be used. If you have IIS installed, you can select it here, otherwise Apache will be installed.

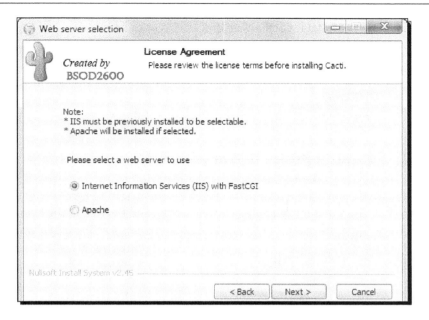

5. In the next step you can choose the components to install. For now, you will only install the Cacti Core Files, so click on **Next >** without adding any additional components.

6. Keep the defaults for the installation locations and click on **Next >**.

7. The final step provides an overview of the paths to be created. Click on **Install** to start the installation process.

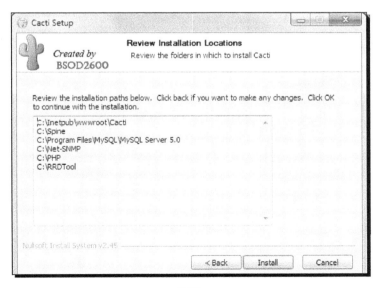

8. Please note the default Cacti admin and MySQL root passwords.

9. Open the Post-Install Instructions and follow the tasks.

What just happened?

You installed Cacti on Windows along with all the prerequisites.

Installing the Spine poller under Windows

Unlike Linux, where compilation from source is the preferred method, Cacti has pre-compiled binaries for Windows. You can download the latest versions from `http://www.cacti.net`. Click on **Download** under the **Spine (Cactid)** section and download the latest Windows binary from there. Extract the archive to the computer running Cacti and edit `spine.conf` to fit your database settings. In case you want to compile spine yourself, you will have to install a working copy of Cygwin. The following URL will provide you with some information on how to compile Spine using Cygwin:

`http://www.cacti.net/spine_install_wincyg.php`.

Upgrading Cacti

Upgrading Cacti involves several steps, one of which is backing up the database. As you have created a symbolic link to the Cacti directory, you don't need to back up any files, but instead you can copy or move them from the old version over to the new one.

Time for action – upgrading Cacti

1. Create a backup of the database:
   ```
   mysqldump -u root -p --lock-tables --add-drop-table cacti > /root/
   cacti_backup.sql
   ```

2. This will back up the Cacti database to a file called `cacti_backup.sql`. You will be asked for the MySQL root password.

3. Change to the `/var/www/html` directory. From `http://www.cacti.net` download the source of the version to which you want to upgrade.

4. Extract the file:

```
tar -xzvf cacti-0.8.7g.tar.gz
```

5. You will have a new directory named `cacti-0.8.7g`.

6. Change to the newly created directory and edit `include/config.php`. Change the database entries in there to match your installation.

7. Before copying the files, you should stop the poller using the web interface. Go to the **Configuration | Settings** and change to the **Poller** tab. Disable the poller by unchecking it.

8. Copy the files from your existing installation to the new one. Execute the following commands, replacing `0.8.x` with the new version:

```
cp /var/www/html/cacti/rra/* /var/www/html/cacti-0.8.x/rra/

cp -u /var/www/html/cacti/scripts/* /var/www/html/cacti-0.8.x/
scripts/

cp -u -R /var/www/html/cacti/resource/* /var/www/html/cacti-0.8.x/
resource/
```

9. Set the permissions on the log and `rra` folders:

```
cd /var/www/html/cacti-0.8.7g/
chown -R cactiuser log/ rra/
```

10. Change the symbolic link so that it points to the new directory:

```
cd /var/www/html/
ln -fs cacti-0.8.x cacti
```

11. The final upgrade process is done using the web interface. Point your browser to `http://<yourserver>/cacti/install` and follow the steps. Make sure you select **Upgrade** on the second page.

12. You can now enable the poller again using the Cacti web interface.

13. Once you have made sure that everything is working fine, you can remove or archive the original Cacti directory.

What just happened?

You upgraded Cacti to a newer version. As a safety net, you created a backup of the database so you can revert back to the old version in case of an error. You copied the RRD files and other resources to the new installation and switched over by changing the symbolic link to point to the new location. You finished the upgrade process by going to the install URL which provided the final web-based upgrade process.

Using Cacti for the first time

After the installation of the database and files, there are still several additional configuration tasks left. For these tasks you are going to use the web interface provided with Cacti to guide you through the final part of the setup. The following steps are almost identical for Windows and Linux.

Time for action – configuring Cacti

1. Go to the installation URL `http://<yourserver>/cacti/install`. Read the license agreement and click on **Next >>**.

2. The next page asks if you are installing a new system, or upgrading an existing one. Choose **New Install** then click on **Next >>**.

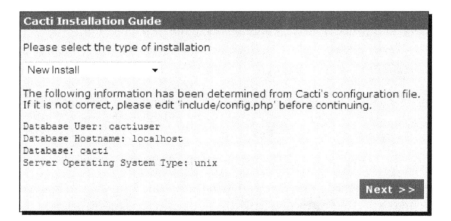

3. The last page provides an overview of all required binaries and paths. If you have followed the installation steps correctly, all fields should be **green**:

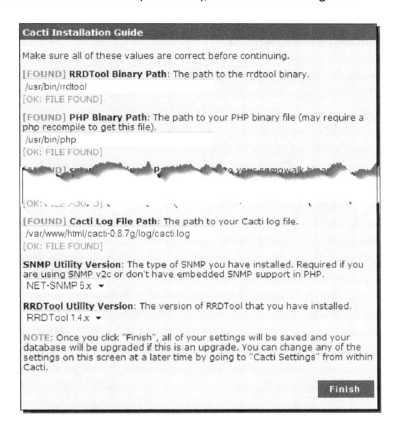

4. Click on **Finish** and you should be redirected to the Cacti login screen.

What just happened?

You finalized your Cacti installation by running the included web-based installer. If you have been following the instructions correctly, you will now have a working Cacti installation.

The installation will leave you with the default `cmd.php` poller. If you want to use Spine, you will now have to logon to the Cacti web interface and set the **Spine Poller File Path** in the **Paths** section of the **Settings** page. You also have to change the **Poller Type** to **Spine** in the **Poller** section.

The Cacti web interface explained

The first time you login, use the username **admin** and password **admin** (for Linux) or **cactipw** (for Windows). You will be forced to change the **admin** password but, after doing so, you will be presented with the Cacti web interface:

The initial page is called the **Console** and only administrators and users with special access rights are able to see it. From here you can fully administer Cacti.

The Console tab

The **Console** tab is where you manage your Cacti installation. From here you can add devices and users or create graphs and assign them to a tree. We're going to explain each of the menu sections next.

Create section

The **Create** section provides an easy access for new graph creations for specific devices. It's a shortcut to the **Create Graphs** link within each device.

Management section

The **Management** section, as its name suggests, allows the management of graphs, devices, data sources, and graph trees. Within this section you can add/edit or delete devices, delete graphs, add devices to trees, and much more.

Collection methods section

The **Collection Methods** section describes the different ways in which Cacti retrieves data from devices or systems. Here you can manage data queries such as SNMP retrieve methods, or manage the different input methods which are used by external scripts called from the poller.

Templates section

The **Templates** section provides an easy way of combining data templates into a graph (graph templates), graphs, and data queries for a specific type of host (host templates), or different data source items (data templates). Many graph, data, and host templates are available on the Cacti forums.

Import/export section

The **Import/Export** section allows the import and export of templates. This is especially useful for providing templates of exotic devices to the Cacti community, or to import them from one of the many provided on the Cacti forum.

Cacti doesn't yet provide a method for importing or exporting other data (for example, device lists) from within the web interface.

Configuration section

Within the **Configuration** section we can change the settings of Cacti. These settings include:

- General settings (for example, logging levels)
- Paths settings (similar to the paths page from the installer)
- Poller settings (number of threads, or poller type to use)
- Graph export settings (graphs can be exported to a local path or remote FTP server)
- Visual settings (size of the graphs, font size to use)
- Authentication settings (local authentication, LDAP, or HTTP Basic)

Utilities section

The **Utilities** section provides access to some basic system tools such as log or poller cache management and also hosts the user management interface.

The Graphs tab

The **Graphs** tab is the main screen for end users. Here they can view the graphs for their devices and systems and also change some personal settings:

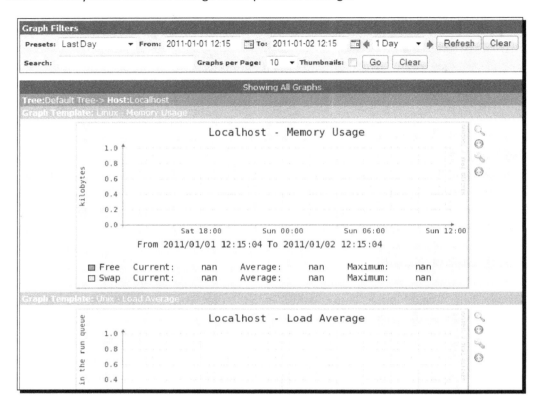

The **Graphs** tab contains a hierarchical tree to the left containing all of the devices which a user is allowed to view. The main part of the page contains the graphs and a filtering system which can be used to customize the timeframe or to search for specific graphs.

Before we continue

You now have a rough overview of the Cacti web interface and how it interacts with the database. You're going to dive a bit deeper into the details in the next few chapters so it is not important at this stage to know in detail where everything is or how it works.

Pop quiz – a few questions about Chapter 1

1. If you are using a remote database server, which configuration files do you need to change?

   a. The `config.php` file and `spine.conf`

   b. The `global.php` file and `config.php`

   c. The `global.php` file only

2. Which section on the Console tab allows you to change the path to the Cacti log file?

   a. The System Utilities section

   b. The Path tab within the Configuration Section

   c. The General tab within the Configuration Section

3. On a CentOS system, how can you configure the MySQL server to start automatically during system startup?

   a. You can use the `enableservice` command

   b. The `setstartup` command allows you to do so

   c. You can use the `chkconfig` command

Summary

You learned a lot in this chapter about installing Cacti.

We covered:

◆ Obtaining and installing Cacti—where to download it and how to set up the files

◆ MySQL database setup—how to create a database and fill it with the base Cacti data

◆ Configuring Cacti—how to tell Cacti where to find its database and how to access it

◆ Configuring the system components—how to add a Cacti system user and create the poller's cron entry

◆ Spine poller—how to download, compile, and install the spine poller

◆ Upgrading Cacti—how to upgrade an existing Cacti installation

◆ The Cacti web interface—a brief look at the different sections of the web interface

You're now ready to create your first few devices and graphs. In the next chapter, you're going to create your own graphs using the RRDtool as well as add your first devices to Cacti.

2
Using Graphs to Monitor Networks and Devices

After having installed and configured Cacti, you will now be able to add your first devices and graphs to the system. This chapter will show you how to add new devices and how to add some performance measurement graphs to them. You will also learn how to group devices using the Cacti tree.

This chapter is going to cover the following topics:

- ◆ Introduction to graph creation with RRDtool
- ◆ Adding devices to Cacti
- ◆ Adding graphs to a device
- ◆ Assigning host templates to a device
- ◆ Adding a device to the Cacti tree

So let's get started...

An introduction to Cacti graphs and the RRDtool

You can learn more about how RRDtool stores data in Appendix C. Now, you'll be looking into the actual graph creation process and what features Cacti supports.

Creating graphs with the RRDtool

Cacti uses the RRDtool to store the polled data. In addition to just storing the data, the RRDtool is also used to create the actual performance graphs.

If you now expect to see a fully-featured charting application, you will be disappointed. The RRDtool graph functionality offers only a very limited range of chart types. They can either be line charts, area charts, or a combination of both. There is no 3D option available, nor are there any other types of charts such as Pie or Scatter charts. This may be a disadvantage for some at first, but concentrating on only a few basic chart types makes it a fast specialized rendering engine for these. Being fast in displaying the raw RRD data is the main focus of the RRDtool graphing engine.

There are several graphing features available for plotting the data. The most commonly used types are:

- LINE: The data is drawn as a line which can be formatted by width and type (for example, dashed line)
- VRULE: A fixed vertical line is drawn at a defined value
- HRULE: A fixed horizontal line is drawn at a predefined value (for example, threshold limits)
- AREA: A solid filled area chart is drawn. Several area charts can be stacked together

Each of these graph types can be combined together to build the final chart image.

Let us dive into the graph creation process here to get a better understanding of the RRDtool graphing capabilities.

You need to have the RRDtool in your path for the following commands to work.

Basic RRDtool graph creation

Let's begin with the RRD example which you can find in Appendix C and use that RRD file as the basis for our graphs.

A note for Windows users

The following examples also work for Windows. Simply replace the RRDtool command with the full path to the RRDtool binary, for example, use `C:\rrdtool\rrdtool.exe` instead of `rrdtool`.

You will also have to copy the DejaVu font from the `RRDtool` directory to your Windows fonts directory.

I have created a Perl script which will help in the creation of the RRD file and its automatic update with random data. In order to create the test RRD file, use the following command:

```
perl create_rrdfile_linux.pl test.rrd
```

If you have installed the RRDtool to `C:\rrdtool` you can use the following command for Windows:

```
perl create_rrdfile_windows.pl test.rrd
```

Having created the test data, you can now start to generate your first RRDtool-based graph. It is going to be a very simple graph displaying only the pure data.

Execute the following code at the command line interface (CLI):

```
rrdtool graph data_image.png \
--start 1282413600 \
--end 1282468500 \
DEF:intspeed=test.rrd:data:AVERAGE \
LINE2:intspeed#FF0000
```

This will create the following graph:

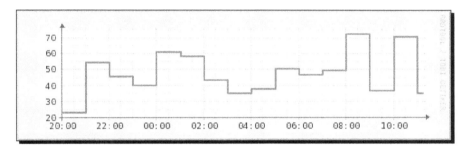

So what does this command actually do? Using the command, you defined a start and end time in the Unix time format and defined the RRD file and data set you wanted to plot. You also told RRDtool to draw a two-pixel line (LINE2) using this data set and stored the resulting graph as `data_image.png`. The RRDtool automatically creates the X- and Y-axis for you and also inserts the time and value description. This is the most basic way of creating an RRDtool-based graph.

Advanced RRDtool graph creation

Although this basic graph image already has a lot of information in it, it is still missing some important features. It neither describes what is being graphed, nor does it provide additional information such as threshold breaches or MAX/MIN values. So, let's go back to this basic graph and look at how you can enhance it step-by-step using some of the advanced RRDtool features.

Adding a label and title to the graph

The first enhancement to our graph will be the addition of a label and a graph title. For this you can use the `--vertical-label` and `--title` parameters:

```
rrdtool graph data_image.png \
--start 1282413600 \
--end 1282468500 \
--vertical-label bps \
--title "Interface Speed" \
DEF:intspeed=test.rrd:data:AVERAGE \
LINE2:intspeed#FF0000
```

The resulting graph now has a title at the top and a description to the left as can be seen in the following image:

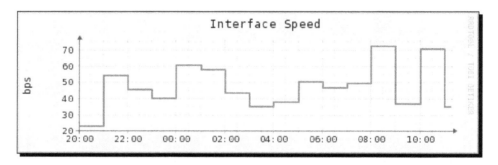

As you can see, the RRDtool command added a rotated description to the Y-axis and also added the title at the top of the graph. The graph is now bigger in dimensions than the first one. The RRDtool uses only the width and height information to set the actual chart size. Everything else must be added to the graph separately. You can see more about how this works in the following examples.

Adding a legend to the graph

Now that you have added some description to the graph, you can also add a legend to it. For this, you are going to use the LAST, AVERAGE, and MAX poller values. The function of the `GPRINT` item is to add additional graph information to the legend. You are also going to add a description field to the `LINE2` item. Adding a description to the `LINE` or `AREA` items will automatically create a legend entry for you.

The LAST, AVERAGE, and MAX values are always calculated using the data limited by the start and end time. Therefore they directly relate to the chart being displayed.

Let's look at the following command:

```
rrdtool graph data_image.png --start 1282413600 --end 1282468500 \
--vertical-label bps --title "Interface Speed" \
DEF:intspeed=test.rrd:data:AVERAGE \
LINE2:intspeed#FF0000:"Interface eth0" \
GPRINT:intspeed:LAST:"Current\:%8.01f" \
GPRINT:intspeed:AVERAGE:"Average\:%8.01f" \
GPRINT:intspeed:MAX:"Maximum\:%8.01f\n"
```

The resulting image now also contains a small legend at the bottom:

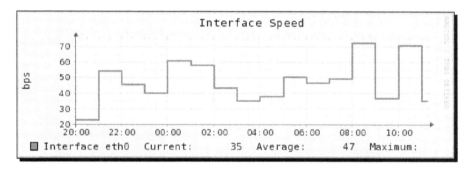

As you can see, the legend was added to the bottom of the graph, expanding its height. By adding a description to the LINE2 line (**Interface eth0**) the description was automatically placed at the bottom along with the color being used to draw that line. The GPRINT text and values have then been added right after the description. If you want to add some more text to the next line, you need to make sure that the last GPRINT value contains a \n (newline) string at the end.

In this example, you can also see that the RRDtool did not increase the width of the graph to fit the legend in it. The Maximum value has been silently dropped. GPRINT statements do not automatically increase the graph width, so you will need to increase the width yourself. This can be done by using the -width parameter.

Adding a threshold line to the graph

Now let's also set a threshold and display a line on the graph marking the threshold. This can be achieved by using the HRULE item. You are going to set a threshold at 50 and use a light grey color to display it on the graph. The following command creates this line and also adds an additional entry to the legend. In addition, you are also going to change the LINE2 item to an AREA item, so the data being displayed is shown as a filled area:

```
rrdtool graph data_image.png --start 1282413600 --end 1282468500 \
--vertical-label bps --title "Interface Speed" \
DEF:intspeed=test.rrd:data:AVERAGE \
HRULE:50#C0C0C0FF:"Threshold ( 50 )\n"   \
AREA:intspeed#FF0000:"Interface eth0" \
GPRINT:intspeed:LAST:"Current\:%8.01f" \
GPRINT:intspeed:AVERAGE:"Average\:%8.01f" \
GPRINT:intspeed:MAX:"Maximum\:%8.01f\n"
```

You can see the light gray line being printed horizontally in the image, providing a good overview of when the data exceeds the threshold:

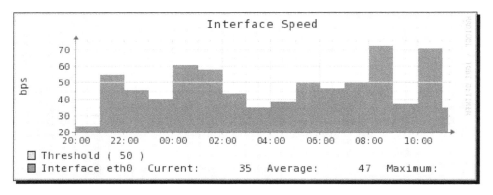

Note the usage of the newline string \n in the description string for the HRULE item. As you can see in the graph, the following text items are added to the next line.

Adding threshold breaches to the graph

You have now seen how you can add a threshold line to the graph, but you probably also want to change the color of the data every time the threshold is breached. Let us assume that you want to have the color go red at or above the threshold and go green once it is below. This can be achieved by using a **Computed DEFinition (CDEF)** and the LIMIT statement.

You define a CDEF named isGreen which returns a number as long as the value of intspeed is between 0 and 50, otherwise no value is returned. You are going to use this CDEF to change the color of the displayed area.

Instead of using the `intspeed` value you assign this new `CDEF` `isGreen` to the `AREA` item and change the color of the `AREA` to green (`RGB: 00FF00`). You also create a new `AREA` entry, to which you now assign the `intspeed` value, set the color to red, and give it a description `Over Threshold\n`. For this to work correctly, you need to place this new `AREA` above the old `AREA` statement.

Why are there two AREA statements? In fact, changing the color of one `AREA` as it is displayed is not possible, so you need to do a little trick here. The first `AREA` statement will graph all values in red, also the ones which are below the threshold, as you have seen in the preceding example. With the second `AREA` statement a green area will be drawn at all data values which are below the threshold. As the color is not transparent, the red area will disappear. You can see the total red area when you remove the second `AREA` statement.

The complete code now looks like the following:

```
rrdtool graph data_image.png --start 1282413600 --end 1282468500 \
--vertical-label bps --title "Interface Speed" \
DEF:intspeed=test.rrd:data:AVERAGE \
CDEF:isGreen=intspeed,0,50,LIMIT \
HRULE:50#C0C0C0FF:"Threshold ( 50 )\n"  \
AREA:intspeed#FF0000:"Over Threshold\n" \
AREA:isGreen#00FF00:"Interface eth0" \
GPRINT:intspeed:LAST:"Current\:%8.01f" \
GPRINT:intspeed:AVERAGE:"Average\:%8.01f" \
GPRINT:intspeed:MAX:"Maximum\:%8.01f\n"
```

Run this code from the command line and you will see the resulting graph:

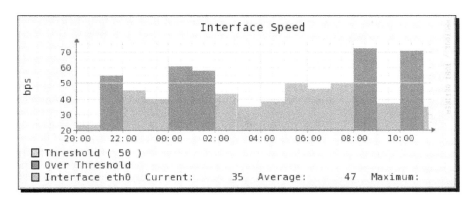

All of the graphs you have just created can be created in Cacti using the Cacti web interface. This section provides a small and very limited overview of the capabilities of the RRDtool graphing functions, but should give you enough ideas to start playing around with it to create your own graphs.

Further reading

The RRDtool webpage provides some very good documentation on the RRDtool and the graphing functions. The features you have seen here are only a small set of what is possible with the RRDtool. Unfortunately, providing information on all of the features is beyond the scope of this book, but it is recommended that you especially look at the gallery at `http://oss.oetiker.ch/rrdtool/` for some further ideas on the graphs.

Please remember that, although Cacti does provide many of the functions of the RRDtool, there are some which may not yet be available.

Have a go hero – creating a yellow warning area

Let's assume green and red areas are not granular enough, and you also want to have a yellow area where you can immediately see that the threshold is about to be breached. This yellow warning area should be displayed between the values of 45 and 50.

Have a look at the following image:

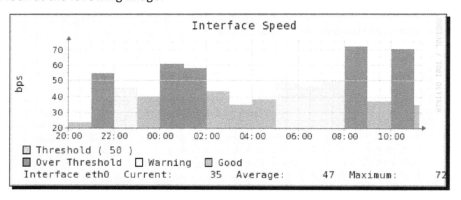

What would you need to change in the above RRDtool command line to get this image?

Solution: You need to add one additional `CDEF` and another `AREA` for this to work. You also need to change the `isGreen CDEF`. The following command line will create and display the yellow warning area and the appropriate legend:

```
rrdtool graph data_image.png --start 1282413600 --end 1282468500 \
--vertical-label bps --title "Interface Speed" \
DEF:intspeed=test.rrd:data:AVERAGE \
```

```
CDEF:isGreen=intspeed,0,44,LIMIT \
CDEF:isYellow=intspeed,45,50,LIMIT \
HRULE:50#C0C0C0FF:"Threshold ( 50 )\n"  \
AREA:intspeed#FF0000:"Over Threshold" \
AREA:isYellow#FFFF00:"Warning" \
AREA:isGreen#00FF00:"Good\n" \
COMMENT:"Interface eth0" \
GPRINT:intspeed:LAST:"Current\:%8.0lf" \
GPRINT:intspeed:AVERAGE:"Average\:%8.0lf" \
GPRINT:intspeed:MAX:"Maximum\:%8.0lf\n"
```

Note that we use a COMMENT item to add the Interface eth0 text at the beginning of the graph legend.

Adding devices to Cacti

A device in Cacti can be anything which can be monitored remotely or locally. This can include storage devices, Windows or UNIX servers, and of course network devices. For Cacti to be able to monitor a device, it needs to be reachable by ping or SNMP, but the actual data retrieval can also be done using scripts and commands, or a set of SNMP queries.

Creating a device

Creating a device in Cacti can be achieved by using the Cacti web interface. You are going to add your first device here. While looking at the different steps it takes to add a device, you are not going too much into the details of every field, as most of the user interface is self-explanatory and provides a detailed description of each field.

Before you start: Create a naming standard

If you have not already done so, you should now think about a naming standard for your devices. Creating and keeping to a naming standard is the first step to automation. Later in this book you will go through some device and graph creation automation, where it is assumed that you have in place a naming standard for your devices.

Time for action – creating a new device in Cacti

1. Login as an admin user to your new Cacti installation.

2. Click on the **Devices** link under the **Management** menu. This will open a table with all devices added so far. For a new installation there should only be the **localhost** device showing its status as **Up**.

3. On the top right of the new page click on **Add**. This is the default position for this **Add** link.

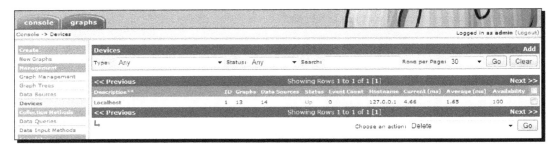

4. You will now be presented with the **Devices [new]** screen. Have a look at this screen and make yourself comfortable with the different fields.

5. Enter a **Description** and **Hostname** (or IP address).

6. If you add an SNMP-enabled device, select **SNMP** as the **Downed Device Detection** method. Otherwise select **Ping.** When selecting **Ping** you can choose the protocol type and port to use.

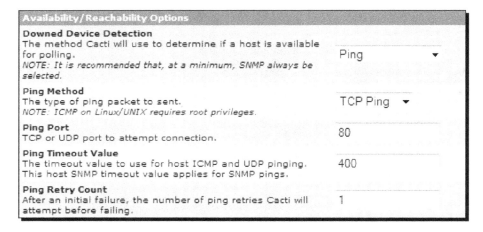

7. Enter the SNMP community and select the correct version (some additional fields will show up when you choose SNMP **Version 3**). If the device is not SNMP compatible, you can select **Not used**.

8. You can also add some notes. Click on the **Create** button once you are finished.

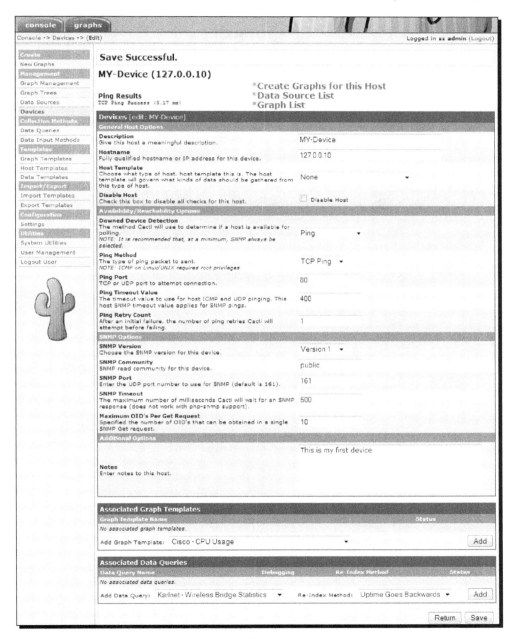

What just happened?

You just created your first device within Cacti by providing some basic information such as an IP address and SNMP management options. With this information Cacti is now able to poll the device. However, it still does not have any graphs associated with it.

Selecting host templates for the device

You may have noticed the **Host Templates** field, but what is a host template? A host template is a predefined package of graphs or data queries which can be assigned to a device. Using a template for complex devices reduces the administrative task for adding devices. Here you are going to assign a template to the device. Host templates can also be selected once the device has been created. Cacti comes with some very basic host templates such as Cisco Router Windows 2000/XP Host or Generic SNMP-enabled Host. All of these contain predefined graphs or data queries for these hosts.

Time for action – adding a host template to the device

1. Go back to the device overview page by clicking on the **Devices** link under the **Management** menu.

2. Click on the device (the description) you have just created.

3. In the **Host Template** drop-down box, select a template that fits your device best.

4. Click on the **Save** button.

5. Note the additional entries in the **Associated Graph Templates** and **Associated Data Queries** fields.

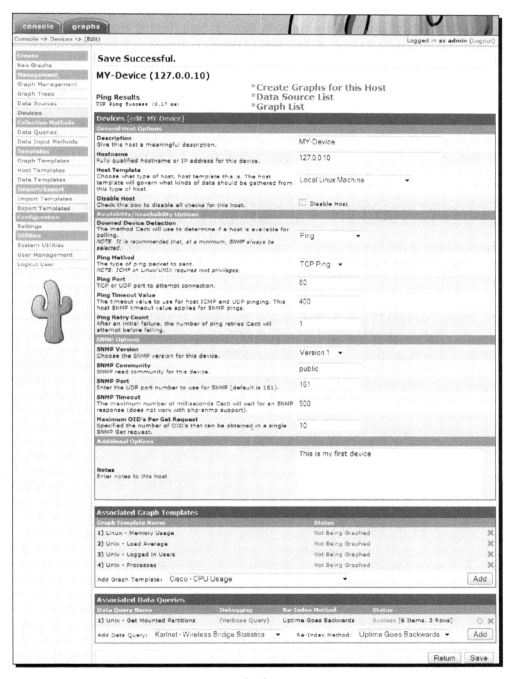

What just happened?

By selecting a host template for the device, you have added a predefined package of graph templates and data queries to the host. This is a convenient way of reducing the administrative tasks of adding these manually through the provided drop-down lists. You will come back to templates later in the book, so you do not have to fully understand these right now.

Adding graphs to the device

Cacti displays performance data as graphs, therefore we are now going to add some basic graphs to the device which we have just added. The first graph which you are going to add is a simple ping graph. Let's go ahead and add the ping template to the host and later add the associated graph to the device.

Time for action – adding graphs to the device

1. Go back to the device overview page by clicking on the **Devices** link under the **Management** menu.

2. Click on the device you have just created.

3. In the **Associated Graph Templates** section select the **Unix - Ping Latency** from the drop-down list and click on the **Add** button.

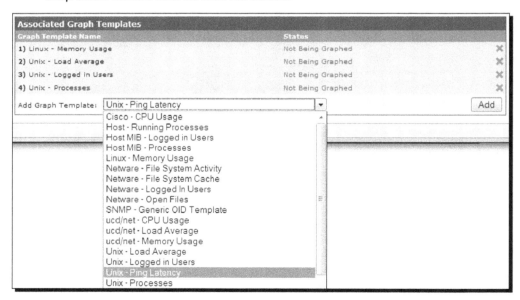

4. Click on the **Save** button at the bottom of the page.

5. Go to the top of the page and click on, **Create Graphs for this Host**.

6. Select **Create: Unix - Ping Latency**.

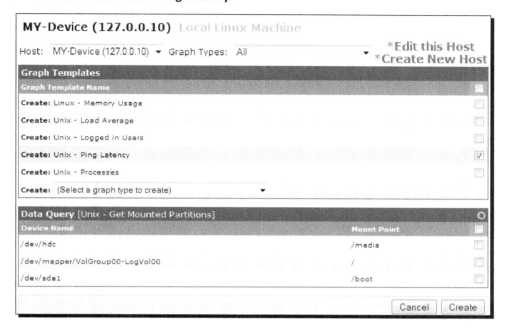

7. Click on the **Create** button.

8. A new screen will appear, where you can choose a legend color and text, but for now, just click on **Create**.

9. You will be redirected back to the graphs selection screen with the entry we selected being greyed out.

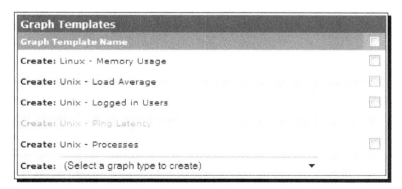

What just happened?

You just added your first graph to a Cacti device by adding a graph template to the device and selecting it during the graph creation screen. Cacti will now start to poll the data for this graph and generate the associated RRD file for it.

The Unix templates

Except for the Ping Latency template, all other Unix templates are for the localhost only and will not provide any information for remote systems.

Adding interface graphs to a device

Adding interface graphs is a little different from adding a generic one such as the ping graph. Normal network devices have several network interfaces, all of which can be polled for performance data. Cacti provides a nice interface for selecting the different network interfaces using the web interface. In the following section you are going to look into this kind of graph selection.

Time for action – adding interface graphs to a device

1. Go back to the device overview page by clicking on the **Devices** link under the **Management** menu.

2. Click on the device you have just created or create any other SNMP capable device having network interfaces.

3. Configure the device to use SNMP and click on the **Save** or **Create** button.

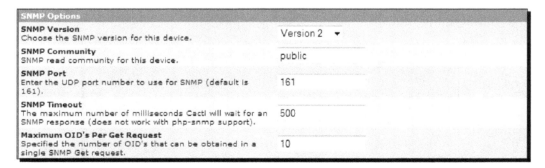

4. Make sure that the following information appears at the top of the page. This will show that the device is SNMP capable.

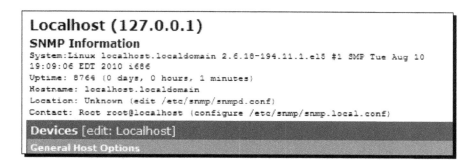

5. In the **Associated Data Queries** section select the **SNMP – Interface Statistics** from the drop-down list and click on the **Add** button. If it is already there, then skip this step.

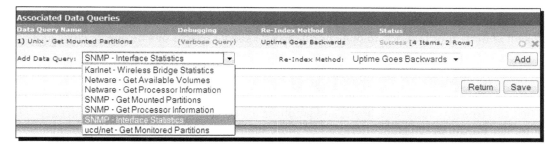

6. Click on the **Save** button at the bottom of the page.

7. Go to the top of the page and click on **Create Graphs for this Host**.

8. On the new page which appears, select the interfaces you want to monitor and select a **Graph type** from the drop-down list.

9. Click on the **Create** button.

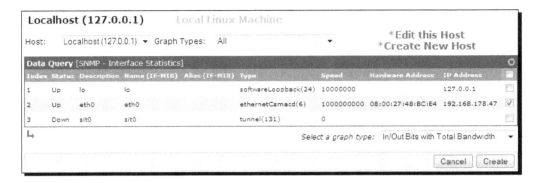

What just happened?

You added the SNMP – Interface data query to the device and selected some interfaces from the interfaces list.

The SNMP – Interface data query is a special package, containing the graph definitions and a kind of blue-print for Cacti to poll information for the interfaces of a device.

Adding devices to the Cacti tree

The Cacti tree lists sub-trees, hosts, and graphs in a tree-like interface. It is the main user interface for the **Graphs** tab. There can be more than one tree which allows for a granular definition of the tree structure.

 Before creating the Cacti tree, think about a good structure for it. Changing the tree later is going to involve quite some manual work, so it is better to have this set up correctly beforehand, so it is better to have this set up correctly beforehand.

Creating a tree

Cacti already has a default tree defined which holds the localhost. You are going to leave this default tree empty and create your very own tree.

Time for action – creating a Cacti tree

1. Click on **Graph Trees** under the **Management** menu.

2. You will see the **Default Tree**. Click on the **Add** link to the top right of that table.

3. Enter a name, for example, **Customer A**.

4. Click on the **Create** button.

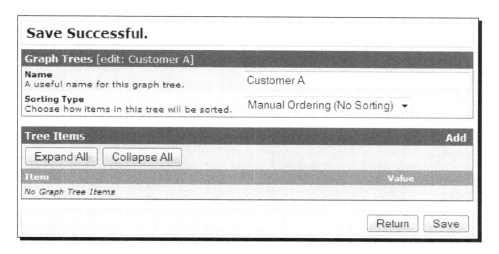

What just happened?

You created a new Cacti Tree called **Customer A** which you can now use to add all **Customer A**-specific entries. Using separate trees for customers or business units will enable you to better allow or deny access to these for specific users. You are going to see the interaction between a tree and the users later in the book.

Sub-tree items

A sub-tree item enables the creation of sub-entries to the Cacti tree. These can be entries such as "Country", "Site", or a "Business Unit". Creating sub-tree items allows end users to easily find their devices on the Cacti Tree.

Time for action – adding a sub-tree

1. Click on **Add** at the top right of the **Tree Items** table.

2. Select **Header** as the **Tree Item Type**.

3. Enter **Country A** as the title.

4. Click on the **Create** button.

5. Click on the **(Add)** link next to the new **Country A** entry.

6. Keep the **Parent Item** to **Country A** and the **Tree Item Type** to **Header**.

7. Enter **Site A** as the title.

8. Click on the **Create** button.

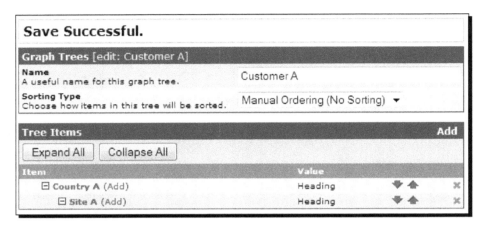

What just happened?

You created your first site for **Customer A**. You can now use this tree to fit all countries, sites, and buildings into a nice manageable tree structure. Your end users will immediately recognize the structure and will be able to quickly find the necessary information.

Adding a device to the tree

Now that you have created a tree and its sub-tree items, you can move on and add a device to the tree.

Time for action – adding a device to the Cacti tree

1. Click on the **(Add)** link next to the **Site A** entry.

2. Select **Host** as **Tree Item Type**.

3. From the **Host** drop-down list, select the host which you created earlier. There should also be a **Localhost** listed. This is the Cacti server.

4. Leave all the others to their defaults.

5. Click on the **Create** button.

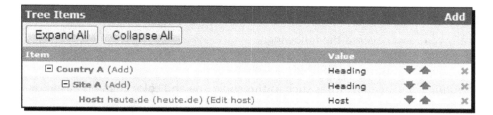

What just happened?

You just added your first device to your newly created Cacti tree. You can also add single graphs to the tree by changing the **Tree Item** type.

Before we continue

You now have a basic knowledge of the RRDtool graph functionality and have also added your first device to Cacti.

Pop quiz – a few questions about Chapter 2

1. If you want to add an additional threshold line, what do you need to add?

    a. A `LINE2` item

    b. A `THRESHOLD` item

    c. An `HRULE` item

2. What information will be displayed when you create an SNMP-enabled device?

    a. The hardware configuration of the device

    b. A message of the day

    c. The contact information and hostname of the device

3. Where do you add the "Cisco - CPU Usage" graph?

    a. At the Cacti tree

    b. At the RRDtool command prompt

    c. At the Device screen

Summary

In this chapter you have learned quite a bit about the RRDtool graph generation features.

Specifically you have covered the following:

- Creating some basic graphs using the RRDtool
- Adding advanced features such as threshold line and color changes based on the threshold
- Adding a device to Cacti
- Assigning graphs and interface graphs to a device
- Creating a new Cacti tree containing sub-tree items and devices

You now have a running Cacti server, which is capable of polling and graphing at least one device.

In the next chapter, you are going to learn more on creating and using graph and device templates.

3
Creating and Using Templates

Cacti provides a facility to create templates for data, graphs, and hosts. This chapter is going to explain how to create these templates and apply them to the devices.

This chapter is going to cover the following topics:

- ◆ An introduction to templates
- ◆ Defining a data template
- ◆ Defining a graph template
- ◆ Defining a host template
- ◆ Assigning a host template to a device
- ◆ Importing/exporting templates
- ◆ References to the template repository

So let's get started...

An introduction to templates

Cacti has templates which can be used to simplify the process of creating and administering graphs, as well as assigning them to specific types of hosts. There are three different types of templates: graph, host, and data.

Data templates

Data templates describe the data which Cacti is going to store in the RRD files. This basically comes down to the RRDtool `create` command. Having a template for the RRDtool `create` command issued internally by Cacti assures you that RRD files based on this template are always created in a common way.

Please note that once a data template is being used to create an RRD file, changes to the data template will not be reflected on that RRD file.

Data input methods

Data templates are based on "Data Input Methods". Data input methods describe different methods for Cacti to retrieve data to be inserted into the data sources. There are different methods available to retrieve data. The most common ones are through executing external scripts or using SNMP.

Graph templates

Graph templates define the look and feel of a graph. They also provide the skeleton to the RRDtool graph function, defining the data sources to use and the graph items to display. Changes to a graph template get propagated to all graphs based on that template.

Host templates

Host templates are like shopping baskets for graph templates and data queries. Let's assume a specific device type should contain several different graphs. Instead of adding each single graph template and data query to each single device, you can simply define these within a host template and assign that host template to the device.

Unfortunately, changes to a host template do not get propagated down to the single devices.

Data queries

We just heard about "Data Queries", but what is it? A data query is a special way of retrieving indexed data such as a list of network interfaces or running processes on a Linux server. It consists of an XML file defining the location of the data to be retrieved and the actual method for retrieving it. In addition to the XML file, a data query also needs to be defined in Cacti in order for Cacti to map the data to an associated graph template.

Defining a data template

You are now going to define a data template for the host `MIB hrSystemProcesses`. Although a data template already exists for this, this task provides a good example of how to create SNMP-based data templates. For this to work, let's assume that your

CentOS-based Cacti server is already configured with an SNMP daemon. You can check your box with the following command:

```
[root@localhost ~]# snmpwalk -On -c public -v 2c localhost HOST-
RESOURCES-MIB::hrSystemProcesses.0

.1.3.6.1.2.1.25.1.6.0 = Gauge32: 101
```

Time for action – defining a data template

The hrSystemProcesses MIB provides information on the current number of running processes on a system supporting the host resource MIB. This MIB is a collection of system-specific data such as logged in users, disk space, installed software packages, and other valuable information which can be retrieved using SNMP.

1. Log on to your Cacti system and go to **Templates | Data Templates**.

2. Click on the **Add** link at the top-right of the list. This will open a new page where you can define your data template.

3. Enter **Host-Resource-Mib: Running Processes** in the **Name** field.

4. Enter **|host_description| - Running Processes** as the **Name** for the data source. The **|host_description|** text is a special Cacti variable which will be replaced with the actual host description of the device where this data template will be added. You can find a list of these Cacti variables at the following link: `http://docs.cacti.net/manual:087:6_reference.variables#variables`.

5. Select **Get SNMP Data** as the **Data Input Method**.

6. Deselect the **Hourly (1 Minute Average)** RRA, as the polling interval will be 5 minutes anyway and breaking this down to a 1 minute average does not provide more details.

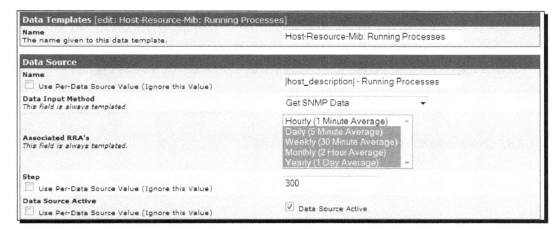

7. Enter **runProcesses** as the **Internal Data Source Name** of the **Data Source Item**.

8. Enter **1000** as the **Maximum Value**. There should never be 1000 processes running at the same time.

9. The **Data Source Type** should be **Gauge**, as this is what the `snmpwalk` example from above returns.

10. Keep everything else to the default values and click on **Create**.

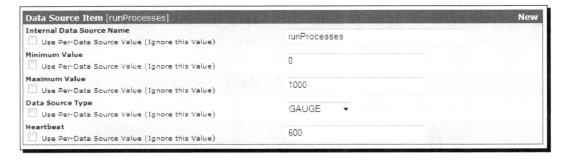

11. You're not done yet. Clicking on the **Create** button should have added some additional fields to the end of the page. Here you can add the SNMP-specific **Custom Data**.

12. As you are going to retrieve the active processes, enter **.1.3.6.1.2.1.25.1.6.0** as the OID.

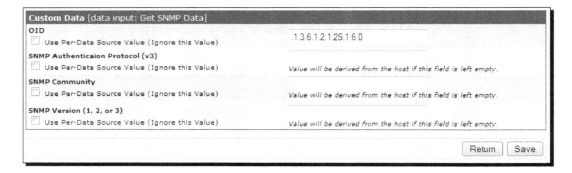

13. Click on the **Save** button and you're done.

What just happened?

You just created your first SNMP-based data template. SNMP-based data templates are the most common templates used within Cacti. In the example you used the `hrSystemProcesses` MIB to template a **Get SNMP data** input method in order to get the actual running processes on a system. You also defined a **Maximum Value** so Cacti knows the range of values which the returned data is allowed to fall within.

> **Always define a good maximum value**
>
> If the value is defined as **0**, the SNMP poller will always fail with an error message of **WARNING: Result from SNMP not valid. Partial Result: U**, so make sure to set a good maximum value.

This basic example can be adapted to create a data template for any kind of SNMP. A good webpage to find SNMP OIDs/MIBs to poll is the `www.mibdepot.com` site. The site provides free information on almost any SNMP data that can be queried.

Have a go hero – template for currently established TCP connections

Let's assume that you have a server with performance issues. Maybe users are unable to connect to it at a specific time of the day. Wouldn't it be good to have some data on the server which will provide some valuable information for further troubleshooting or even letting us identify a problem before the users are aware of it? In this special case, we want to know the number of currently established TCP connections on a system to identify a possible build up of connections to a point where no more connections can be created. What does the data template for this look like? A small hint: Look for the **TCP-MIB**.

Solution: Take the data template example and duplicate it. Go to **Templates | Data Templates** and select it. From the drop-down box at the bottom select **Duplicate** and then **Go**. In the following page, enter **TCP-MIB: Established TCP Connections** as the title then click on **Continue**. Edit the template again and change the name fields to fit the new data. Enter **tcpCurrEstab** as the **Internal Data Source Name** and use **.1.3.6.1.2.1.6.9.0** as the OID. Click on **Save** and you're done.

Defining a graph template

Remember the "Have a go hero" challenge from Chapter 2? The graph showed a yellow area reaching a defined threshold and a red one once the threshold was breached. Now you're going to define the same type of graph template for a running processes graph template.

CDEF definition

As a prerequisite you're first going to create your two CDEFs, one for the green area and one for the yellow area. The threshold is set at 50, but you can change this to fit your needs. Let's have a look at the two CDEFs you're going to create shortly:

```
CDEF:isGreen=intspeed,0,44,LIMIT
```

```
CDEF:isYellow=intspeed,45,50,LIMIT
```

Cacti does not use named variables like `intspeed` but defines them according to the alphabet from a to z, so your definition from a Cacti view actually looks like:

```
CDEF:cdefa=a,0,44,LIMIT
```

```
CDEF:cdefb=a,45,50,LIMIT
```

`isGreen` and `isYellow` have also been changed. Don't worry, Cacti takes care of this automatically. Just remember that your green area will go from 0 to 44, the yellow area will show up once the number of process are between 45 and 50 and the red area will show above 50.

Time for action – defining a CDEF in Cacti

1. Go to **Management | Graph Management** and click on the **CDEFs** submenu.

2. On the usual screen, click on the **Add** link to the top right.

3. Now you can give the new `CDEF` a useful name. Enter **isGreen_0-44** and click on **Create**.

4. Another table will appear. Click on the **Add** link.

5. For **CDEF Item Type**, select **Custom String** from the drop-down box.

6. Enter **a,0,44,LIMIT** into the **CDEF Item Value** field and click on **Create**. The first `CDEF` is created and you will see your `CDEF` definition together with a **Save Successful** message at the top.

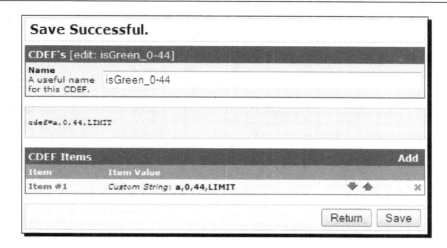

7. Repeat the steps and create a new CDEF called **isYellow_45-50** and the **Item Value** of **a,45,50,LIMIT**.

8. Now that you have defined your two CDEF items, you can proceed with the graph template creation.

What just happened?

You have created the two CDEF items which you are going to use to change the appearance of your running processes graph to go yellow before reaching a threshold, and stay green when it is way below the threshold.

Defining the graph template

Now that you have created your CDEFs, you can create your special graph template. The graph will have the green, yellow, and red areas defined, as well as the HRULE item showing the threshold. The threshold is set at 50.

Time for action – defining the graph template

1. Go to **Templates | Graph Templates** and click on the **Add** link to the upper right of the page.

2. Enter **Host - Running Processes** as the name of the graph.

3. Enter **|host_description| - Running Processes** as the **Title** of the graph template.

4. Enter **processes** as the **Vertical Label**.

5. Leave everything else as default and click on the **Create** button. This will create the base graph template for you to work with. As you can see in the following screenshot, some additional fields have been added:

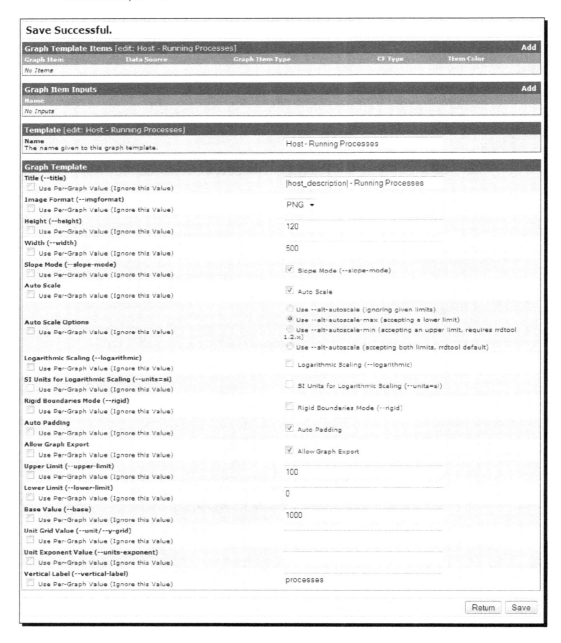

Chapter 3

What just happened?

You created your first graph template. There will be two new sections showing up, **Graph Template Items**, and **Graph Item Inputs**.

Adding the threshold line

The threshold line will immediately show viewers the value at which the threshold is set and whether the graph is breaching it somewhere. Let's create your new graph template and add this line to it.

Time for action – defining a graph template

1. At the **Graph Template Items** section, click on the **Add** link.

2. Select **None** as the **Data Source.**

3. Select a light grey color (for example, **C0C0C0**).

4. Set the **Graph Item Type** to **HRULE** and enter **50** as the **Value.**

5. Enter **Threshold (50)** as the **Text Format** and check the **Insert Hard Return** box.

6. Click on **Create.**

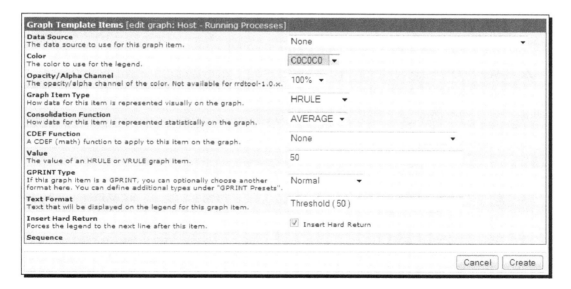

What just happened?

You just added your first item, an HRULE graph item, to your graph representing your threshold line. HRULE items are based on a fixed value, therefore you did not choose any data source, but instead entered your threshold **Value** into the value field. Now all of your graphs based on this template will show a light grey line at the value 50.

Adding the green, yellow, and red areas

You are now going to add your green, yellow, and red areas by making use of your newly created CDEF items.

Time for action – adding the color areas

Now you are going to add colors to the three areas of the graph.

1. Add another item.

2. Select the **Host-Resource-Mib: Running Processes** as the **Data Source**.

3. Select a red color.

4. Select **AREA** as the **Graph Item Type** and put **Over Threshold** into the **Text Format** field.

5. Click on **Create**.

6. For the yellow area, you need to add yet another item.

7. Select **AREA** as the **Graph Item Type**, choose a yellow color, and put **Near Threshold** into the **Text Format** field.

8. Select **isYellow_45-50** as the CDEF function to use.

9. Click on **Create**.

10. The last one will be the green area, so click on **Add** again.

11. Select **AREA** as the **Graph Item Type**, choose a green color, and put **Under Threshold** into the **Text Format** field.

12. Select **isGreen_0-44** as the CDEF function and check the **Insert Hard Return** box.

13. Click on **Create**. Your graph definition should now look like the following screenshot. Verify that you have defined all of the items in the same way.

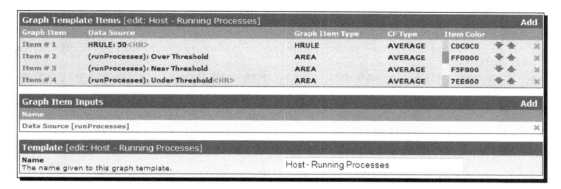

What just happened?

You have now added your three colored areas to the graph. Using the same principle as for the RRDtool graph command, you based the values of the single areas on a CDEF value. This will make sure that only the relevant area shows up on the graph, depending on the data value.

By selecting a data source you can also see that this data source is automatically added to the **Graph Item Inputs** list.

Adding a legend to the graph

Your graph is now nearly complete, but is missing the legend. So let's add this now to finish your graph template.

Time for action – adding a legend

1. The graph is still missing the Legend, so click on the **Add** link of the **Graph Template Items** again.

2. Select **Comment** as the **Graph Item Type**.

3. Enter **Running Processes** into the **Text Format** field.

4. Click on the **Create** button.

5. Let's add some more statistical information to your Legend. Click on the **Add** link.

6. Select **Legend** as the **Graph Item Type**.

7. Click on the **Create** button.

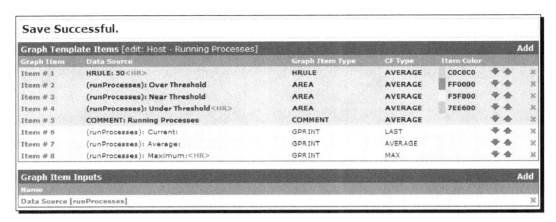

What just happened?

You have added a comment describing the statistical information relating to the graph. The **Legend** command adds three GPRINT statements to the graph. The first GPRINT statement prints the last polled value, the second statement prints the average value of the displayed graph and the last one prints the maximum value polled.

You can now assign this graph template to a device. After you have added the graph template to a device, you need to wait for three polls to pass. The first poll actually creates the necessary RRD file. The other two polls are needed for the RRDtool as it will start graphing values only when it has at least two data values within the RRD file. Once that time has passed, go to **Graph Management** within the **Management** section and look for the graph there:

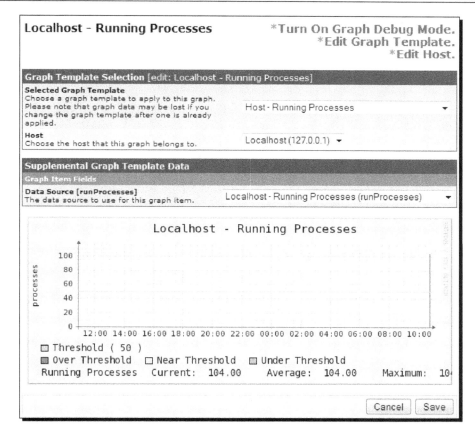

Turn on graph debugging mode

After turning on the graph debugging option, the graph management page will display the `rrdtool` graph command used to create the graph. Any errors, such as a missing RRD file, will be displayed here. This debugging information is useful for troubleshooting the graph generation.

Back to basics—rrdtool graph command

Let's look at the `rrdtool graph` command which Cacti uses to create the preceding graph.

```
/usr/bin/rrdtool graph -
--imgformat=PNG
--start=-86400
--end=-300
--title='Localhost - Running Processes'
--base=1000
--height=120
```

```
--width=500
--alt-autoscale-max
--lower-limit=0
--vertical-label='processes'
--slope-mode
--font TITLE:12:
--font AXIS:8:
--font LEGEND:10:
--font UNIT:8:
DEF:a="/var/www/html/cacti-0.8.7g/rra/localhost_runprocesses_11.rrd":
runProcesses:AVERAGE
CDEF:cdefc=a,45,50,LIMIT
CDEF:cdefd=a,0,44,LIMIT
HRULE:50#C0C0C0FF:"Threshold ( 50 )\n"
AREA:a#FF0000FF:"Over Threshold"
AREA:cdefc#F5F800FF:"Near Threshold"
AREA:cdefd#7EE600FF:"Under Threshold\n"
COMMENT:"Running Processes"
GPRINT:a:LAST:"Current\:%8.2lf %s"
GPRINT:a:AVERAGE:"Average\:%8.2lf %s"
GPRINT:a:MAX:"Maximum\:%8.2lf %s\n"
```

Doesn't this one look familiar? It's roughly the same command which you hopefully came up with in the "Have a go hero" challenge in *Chapter 2*. Here you can see the tight integration of the `rrdtool` with the Cacti web interface.

Defining a host template

As you have already learned, a host template is a collection of graph templates and data queries. Let's create a host template for an SNMP-enabled CentOS server now.

Time for action – defining a host template

1. Go to **Templates** | **Host Templates** and click on the **Add** link.

2. Enter **SNMP Enabled CentOS Server** as the name for this host template.

3. Click on **Create**.

4. Two additional sections will appear. At the **Associated Graph Templates** section, select your **Host - Running Processes** template and click on **Add**.

5. At the **Associated Data Queries** section, add **SNMP - Get Mounted Partitions**, **SNMP - Get Processor Information**, and the **SNMP - Interface Statistics** data query.

6. Click on the **Save** button.

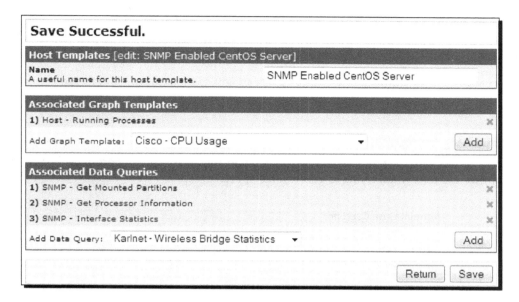

What just happened?

You created your first host template containing your newly created graph template and three SNMP-based data queries. Once you assign this host template to a device, all four items will be automatically added to that device.

Create host templates for standard devices in your network

Creating a host template will reduce the time needed for creating a device within Cacti, especially if there are many devices in a network that share the same graphs.

Assigning a host template to a device

You already assigned a host template to a device in Chapter 2, so now let's briefly talk about what is happening when a host template is assigned to a device.

As you know, host templates are a collection of graphs and data queries. Adding this collection to a host does not link the host back to the host template. The graphs and data queries are added to the host and the link back to the template is lost. Changes that later take place in the host template will not be reflected to the hosts where the specific template has already been added.

Importing/exporting templates

As graph, host, and data templates become very complex and are most of the time, crafted to fit a specific device type, Cacti offers the ability to export and share these templates with the community, as well as importing existing templates.

This really eases the administrative tasks for creating these templates! So let's see how you can import and export these templates.

Importing templates

As Cacti comes with a limited set of templates, importing templates will probably be the first action you will take when trying to graph some special data.

Templates on Cacti.net

A large number of Cacti templates can now be found at the documentation section of the Cacti website. You can find them on the following page:

`http://docs.cacti.net/templates`

As your Cacti installation is probably running on an Apache web server, you want to get and graph some additional information on it. So let's import such a template.

Time for action – importing a template

1. Start you web browser and go to `http://forums.cacti.net/about9861.html`. This is the topic on the forum containing all the links which we will be using later within this section. If the download links do not work, check back to this page and look for the new download links.

2. Download the XML file named `cacti087b_host_template_webserver_-_apache.xml` from the first post and save it to your desktop.

3. Logon to your Cacti server.

4. Go to your Cacti installation and navigate to the scripts directory. On CentOS the command is:

```
cd /var/www/html/cacti/scripts
```

5. Download the third file to that directory:

wget `http://forums.cacti.net/download/file.php?id=9907`

6. Rename the downloaded file to `ws_apachestats.pl.gz`:

mv download.php\?id\=9907 ws_apachestats.pl.gz

7. Unzip the file:

gunzip ws_apachestats.pl.gz

8. Now logon to your Cacti installation.

9. Go to **Import/Export | Import Templates**.

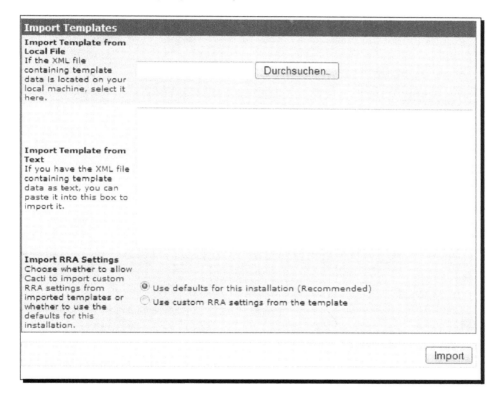

10. Select the XML file from your desktop and click on the **Import** button. You will see some status information as well as the templates, data input methods, and other items that have been imported to your Cacti system.

Import Results

Cacti has imported the following items:

CDEF

[success] Apache - Calculate Bytes / Request [update]
[success] Apache - Clean value for DEF a [update]
[success] Apache - Clean value for DEF b [update]
[success] Apache - Limit output to zero min and max [update]
[success] Turn Bytes into Bits [update]
[success] Total All Data Sources [update]
[success] Apache - A plus B [update]
[success] Apache - Calculate A as % of C [update]
[success] Apache - Calculate B as % of C [update]
[success] Trend [update]

GPRINT Preset

[success] Normal [update]
[success] Exact Numbers [update]

Data Input Method

[success] WebServer - Apache Statistics [update]

Data Template

[success] WebServer - Apache Statistics [update]

Graph Template

[success] WebServer - Apache Statistics - Bytes / Request [update]
[success] WebServer - Apache Statistics - Hits / s [update]
[success] WebServer - Apache Statistics - kBits / s [update]
[success] WebServer - Apache Statistics - Thread Details [update]
[success] WebServer - Apache Statistics - Thread Details (%) [update]
[success] WebServer - Apache Statistics - CPU Load [update]
[success] WebServer - Apache Statistics - Thread Scoreboard [update]

Host Template

[success] WebServer - Apache [update]

What just happened?

As in the preceding example, a template may not always consist of XML files, but may also have an associated script that needs to be added to the Cacti installation. The template you just imported contained such a script. You have downloaded, renamed, and extracted it into the scripts directory. This directory contains all the scripts being used within data input methods.

You then imported the XML file for the host template **WebServer - Apache**. The XML file contained all of the definitions for the necessary graph templates and input methods needed for Cacti to graph the data.

The imported host template can now be used and assigned to the devices. As with all external files, make sure you read and follow the corresponding `readme` files or installation instructions.

If you have done everything correctly, you should see the following graph after a few polling cycles:

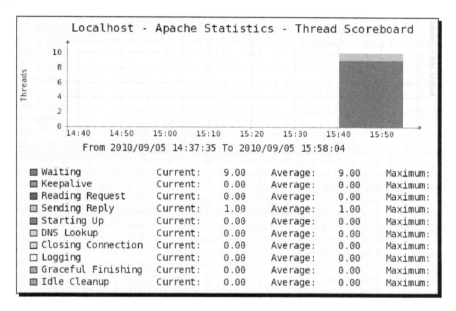

Exporting templates

Exporting a template allows users to share their hard work in creating these templates with the Cacti community. The export mechanism only exports the graph, host, or data template definitions, but not the scripts that are necessary for some of the data input methods. SNMP-based templates do not need scripts so these are exported complete.

Time for action – exporting a template

1. Go to **Import/Export** and click on the **Export Templates** link.

2. Select **Host Template** as the template type which you want to export.

3. Select your host template, **SNMP Enabled CentOS Server** as the **Host Template to Export**.

4. Leave the rest to their default values.

5. Click on **Export**. You can now store the XML file on your desktop.

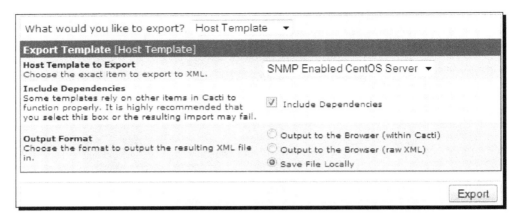

What just happened?

You have exported your first host template. The XML file contains all of the necessary information for the host template. This includes:

♦ The host template itself

♦ All graph templates

♦ All data templates

♦ All CDEFs needed (isYellow_45-50 and isGreen_0-45)

♦ Everything else needed for the host template to work

When re-importing this XML file, Cacti will only create items that do not already exist.

The template repository

As you have seen, you can export your templates and make them available to other users. A lot of Cacti administrators have used this feature to provide quite a number of templates to the community. In the past, finding these templates was a wearisome task as they were hidden in the **Scripts and Templates** section of the Cacti forum at forums.cacti.net.

More recently, however, the Cacti developers have created a page containing most of these templates. This template repository provides an overview of the existing templates, as well as some detailed information on how to add these to Cacti.

Go and have a look at http://docs.cacti.net/templates to see the template repository.

Before we continue

This chapter completes the basic administration of Cacti. You have installed Cacti, created a first host and also designed your own enhanced graph templates. The following chapters will dive into more advanced topics like Windows systems monitoring with WMI, enhancing Cacti with plugins, or enterprise reporting capabilities.

Pop quiz – a few questions about Chapter 3

1. Where can you change the width and height of graphs?
    a. At the general Cacti settings screen
    b. At the Data template
    c. At the Graph template

2. If an SNMP data template which you defined does not produce any data, what may be wrong?
    a. The **Maximum Value** field is set to 0
    b. The **Maximum Value** field is not set
    c. The **Minimum Value** field is not set

3. If you want to change the threshold of the processes graph, which items do you need to change?
    a. You need to define new CDEFs
    b. You need to add a new HRULE
    c. All of the above

Summary

You went through some of the more advanced topics of Cacti, including creating graphs, host and data templates. Specifically you have covered the following areas:

◆ Defining a data template—how to add a data template for retrieving SNMP-based data

◆ Defining a graph template—how to create a threshold-based graph template and use CDEF values to change the appearance of the graph depending on the data value

◆ Defining a host template—creating a selection of SNMP-based graphs and data queries

◆ Importing and exporting templates—how to import a template from the template repository and export our own host template

You have now learned the basic Cacti administration tasks for devices, graphs, and templates. In the next chapter, you are going to learn more about user management. You're going to learn how to automatically add new users and how to configure user permissions.

4
User Management

We now have a working Cacti installation which also has some nice graphs to show, so let's now add some users to our Cacti installation.

In this chapter we are going to:

- ◆ Add new users
- ◆ Set up Realms and Graph permissions for a user
- ◆ Create a template user
- ◆ Integrate LDAP/Active Directory authentication
- ◆ Manage users with the Cacti CLI

So let's get started....

An introduction to Cacti user management

Cacti integrates a granular user management approach, which lets administrators define access and permissions to trees, hosts, or single graphs. This section will provide you with some detailed information about user management.

Users

Generally speaking, users within Cacti can be divided into three different groups:

- ◆ Guest/anonymous users
- ◆ Normal users
- ◆ Administrators

The difference between these users is the way they authenticate against the system and the access rights that they have. There exist no special groups for these different types of users.

Guest accounts would be used for a public Cacti server, offering the viewing of graphs to any interested person. This can be an internal server or one which monitors your own home network.

Normal user accounts need to authenticate against the server and can then access different parts of the system. Normal users can be restricted to view just a single Cacti tree, therefore making them the first choice for sharing a Cacti installation between different customers (for example, within a hosting environment).

Administrator accounts can administer Cacti by using the Cacti console. They cannot be restricted to, for example, administer just a small group of users, but different tasks within Cacti can be allowed or denied to an administrator. These include permissions to access global settings as well as to update hosts or graph templates.

Groups

The concept of groups does not exist within Cacti, but to compensate for this, Cacti does offer the ability to copy "template users". Template users are normal users where all permissions and access rights have already been set up. Based on this concept you are going to learn about the `Batch Copy` function.

Permissions

As mentioned earlier, permissions in Cacti can be set as granular so that you can give access to one specific graph only. Permissions within Cacti are divided into **Realm Permissions** and **Graph Permissions**. **Realm Permissions** define the access rights of the **Console**, whereas the **Graph Permissions** define the access to the tree and graphs.

Creating a user

Let's get started with creating our first Cacti user!

Time for action – creating the first Cacti user

1. Logon to your Cacti system as the **admin user**.

2. Go to **Utilities | User Management**. You will be presented with a list of existing users. For a newly-installed Cacti system, there will only be **admin** and **guest** listed, as shown in the following screenshot:

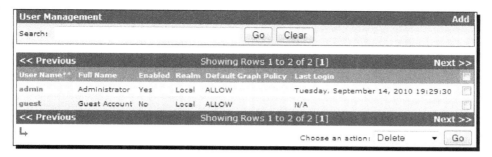

3. Click on the **Add** link. You will be redirected to the **User Management [new]** screen.

4. Fill in the fields **User Name**, **Full Name**, **Password** and check the **Enabled** box.

5. Within the **Realm Permissions** section, check the **View Graphs** checkbox and click on the **Create** button.

What just happened?

You just created your first Cacti user. If you try to log in to your Cacti system with this new user, you will see that this is working, but you will also see that there will be nothing displayed.

Why is that so? Although you added the **View Graphs** permission for your user, the user does not have any permission to actually view the tree or graphs defined. You are going to do this in the next step.

General user settings

There are a few general settings which can be checked for each user. These settings include the **Authentication Realm** or access to the different **Graph Options**.

Graph Options

The **Graph Options** are not related to any options to the actual graphs, but describe the type of view on the graphs which the user has access to. There are three different options available:

- ◆ User has rights to **Tree View**
- ◆ User has rights to **List View**
- ◆ User has rights to **Preview View**

These views relate to the small tabs on the upper right of the Cacti screen when you are using the **Graphs** tab:

Authentication Realm

The **Authentication Realm** defines the type of access authentication used when a user logs in to Cacti. There are three different options available:

- ◆ Local
- ◆ LDAP
- ◆ Web Basic

The Local realm uses the built-in authentication from Cacti. LDAP authentication can authenticate users against any LDAP server including Active Directory servers. Web Basic authentication is handled by the web server itself (for example, using `.htaccess` files)

Realm and graph permissions

By default, new Cacti users will not have any permission to view graphs or administer the system. The access rights for these functions are set in the realm and graph permissions.

Realm permissions

There are several realm permissions that can be set for a user. They are divided into the same groups as the console menu:

- Management
- Collection methods
- Templates
- Import/export
- Configuration
- Utilities

Management permissions

Management permissions include the ability to add graphs to a host or add a device to Cacti. The permission to add devices to Cacti is hidden under the **Update Data Sources** permission.

Collection methods permissions

The **Collection Methods Permission** can be given for the creation of data queries as well as data input methods.

Template permissions

Access to graph, data, and host template creation can be granted to users. In combination with the collection methods permissions, this will allow you to create administrator users who can create the data template together with the required data input method or data query and have other users create the graphs for these.

Import/export permissions

The import/export permissions allow users to export their templates or import external templates into Cacti. If you do not wish to have users export your templates then you can deny the permission.

Configuration permissions

Only users who know the Cacti internals should be allowed to change the global Cacti settings. Global settings include authentication settings as well as performance settings for the poller.

Utilities permissions

The user administration falls into this category. For a base Cacti installation this section does not contain any further items. You will see more items when you are going to install the Plugin Architecture addon for Cacti.

Time for action – setting realm permissions

It's time for you to add some permissions to your newly created user. So let's give them access to manage devices, collect methods, graphs, and templates.

1. Go to **Utilities | User Management** and select your previously created user.

2. Select all fields as shown in the following screenshot and click on the **Save** button.

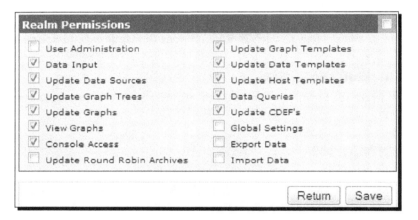

What just happened?

You just added all permissions to your user to manage devices and all that is required to create graphs. Your user will not be able to create new users or change their permissions and will also not be able to change the global settings for Cacti.

Graph permissions

Let's add some **Graph View Permissions** to the user, so you can actually go and view the graphs which you have created in the previous chapters.

Time for action – setting graph permissions

You will now add the permission to your user to view the default tree.

1. Got to **Utilities** | **User Management** and click on your user.

2. Click on the **Graph Permissions** tab. The bottom of the page will change and allow you to configure the graph permissions.

3. Add the **Default Tree** to the **Tree Permissions** section.

4. Leave the **Default Policy** for the tree permissions to **Deny** and change all other default policies to **Allow**.

5. Click on the **Save** button.

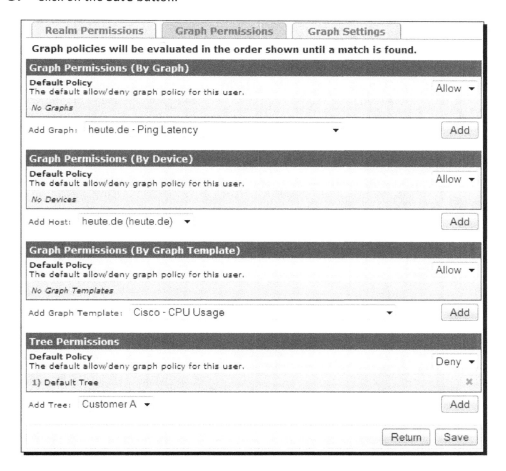

What just happened?

You just allowed your user to view all the graphs that have been added to the default tree. The default policy defines the default access granted for a user. By adding the **Default tree** to the list, access to it is allowed. This is also reflected by the blue characters in front of the tree. If you change the default policy to **Allow**, your user will have access to all trees except the default tree and the characters will change their color to red.

Denying or allowing access to a tree does not automatically deny or allow access to the graphs configured under the tree. Although you denied access to the **Customer A** tree, your user will still be able to access the graphs from **Customer A**, as the default policy for the graphs is set to **Allow**. To prevent this behavior, you will need to change the default policy for the **Graph Permissions (By Device)** to **Deny** and add all the devices belonging to **Customer A** to the list, so your user is only able to access the graphs for these devices.

Graph settings

Graph Settings are user-specific preferences for the graph presentation. Preferences can be set for nearly every aspect of the graph frontend. Settings such as the thumbnail dimensions or number of graphs displayed on the tree view panel can be set. Even the font type and size for the RRDtool (not shown in the screenshot) can be changed by the user. This allows users in need of large font letters to change the font size used for printing the legend, graph title, and other data in the graph.

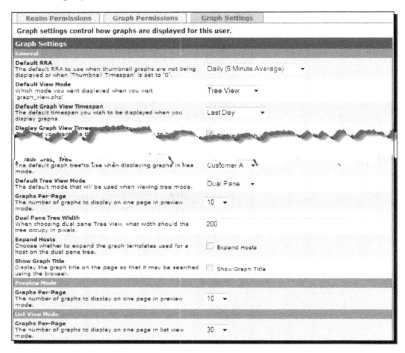

The template user

A template user can be any user and is not specifically marked as a template user. As Cacti does not include group management, template users should be created as templates for different users. As you have just learned, graph and realm permissions need to be set for a user to only view graphs for Customer A. If you are now going to have multiple customers, you do not want to start from scratch every time. This is where a template user becomes handy.

In a multi-customer environment the template user should follow an easy to understand naming standard and should always be disabled.

Use a naming standard for template users
An example for such a naming standard would be `_customername_user`.

Time for action – installing the missing packages

Let's create a template user for our Customer A.

1. Go to **Utilities | User Management** and add a new user.

2. Add **_CustomerA_user** as the **User Name**.

3. Add **Template User for Customer A** as the **Full Name**.

4. Make sure the **Enabled** checkbox is not checked, as shown in the following image:

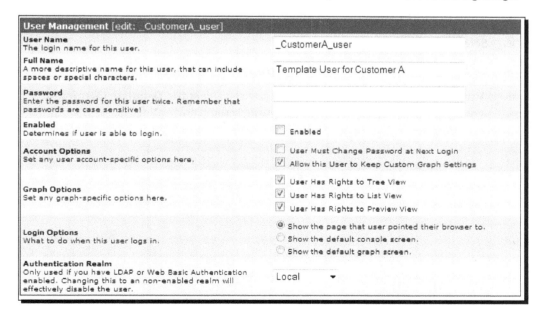

5. Click on the **Create** button.

6. Go back and edit the user.

7. Set the realm and graph permissions so the template user has access to the graphs of Customer A.

8. Save the user.

What just happened?

You just created your first template user. You can now use this template user to create new users or change the permissions of existing users.

Copying permissions – the Batch Copy mode

Within the user management section a function called **Batch Copy** exists. This function allows the copying of realm and user permissions from one user (for example, your template user) to one or more other users. It does not change any user-specific information such as username or passwords, but only transfers the permissions.

Time for action – the Batch Copy

As a preparation, you will need to create a new user. Just fill in the **User Name** and **Password** fields and click on **Save**. You do not need to worry about the permissions.

1. Go to **Utilities | User Management**.

2. Select the user you just created.

3. Choose **Batch Copy** from the drop-down box and click on **Go**.

4. A confirmation box will appear, where you can select the **Template User** from a drop-down box as shown in the following screenshot:

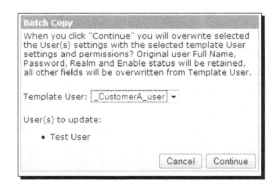

5. Select the **_CustomerA_user** as the **Template User** and click on the **Continue** button.

What just happened?

You just copied all realm and graph permissions, as well as some default user settings, to your newly created user. You can select more than one user for the `batch copy` function. Although this functionality does not replace real group management, it does greatly ease the administration of different user groups.

Integrate LDAP/Active Directory authentication

Cacti not only has its own built-in user authentication mechanism, but can also be configured to use an LDAP or even an Active Directory server for authentication. As the authorization (access rights, permissions) is not stored on the external server, the user still has to be created within Cacti. So, how does Cacti know if a user is going to authenticate against the external server, or is using the built-in method? Cacti uses the concept of "Realms" for this. A Realm is basically the authentication method an end user uses to logon to Cacti. A user can only belong to one realm. When using the LDAP authentication method, Local users can still logon by choosing the "Local" Realm from the login dialog:

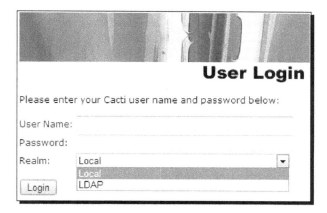

The Web Basic authentication does not allow this, however, as it always expects to get a user ID from the browser and displays an error message if it does not get a user ID.

External user management

You are now going to set up an LDAP/Active Directory authentication. Most companies either have an LDAP system running or else use the Active Directory equivalent. This section will deal with setting up an Active Directory authentication.

Time for action – setting up Active Directory authentication

Let's enable the LDAP/Active Directory integration.

1. Logon to your Cacti web interface as an admin user.

2. Click on the **Settings** link under the **Configuration** section.

3. On the new page which appears, click on the **Authentication** tab to bring up the settings for the authentication.

4. Select **LDAP Authentication** from the **Authentication Method** drop-down box.

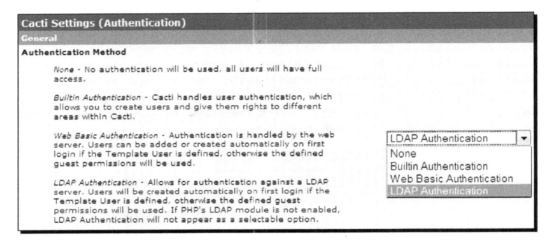

5. Select **No User** as the **Guest User.**

6. Select **_CustomerA_user** as the **User Template.**

7. Enter the IP address of your domain controller into the **Server** field.

8. As the **Distinguished Name (DN)** enter **<username>@MYDOMAIN.local** and replace **MYDOMAIN.local** with your domain name.

9. For the **Search Base** enter **dc=MYDOMAIN,dc=local** and replace **MYDOMAIN** and **local** accordingly.

10. Click on the **Save** button.

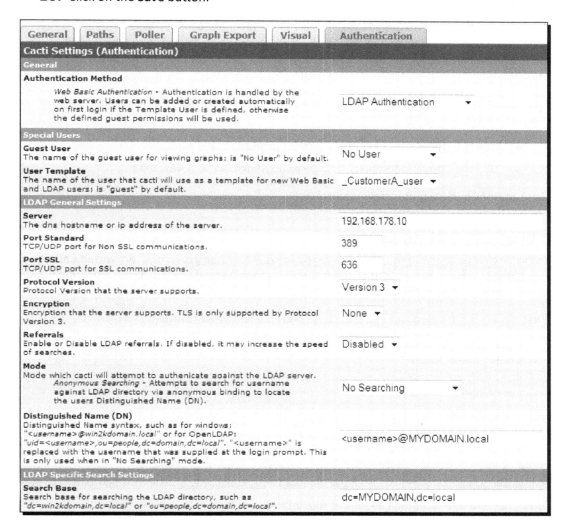

What just happened?

You just enabled your Cacti server to authenticate users against an LDAP/Active Directory server. Users can now logon to your Cacti system without you having to create them first. Once a user was created automatically, the permissions for this user will be based on the "User Template". In a multiple customer environment this may not be what you wanted, so you will still need to change the permission for this user.

Managing users with the Cacti CLI

Users can not only be managed using the web interface, but can also be created using the Cacti CLI scripts. In Cacti version 0.8.7g, the only script which exists is one which copies an existing user in order to create a new one out of it. An equivalent to the **Batch Copy** functionality is not available for the command line interface.

Let's assume that you need to add a large number of users to your Cacti system. You have two options for doing so:

- Use the web-based user management page to create each user
- Use the **Copy** functionality to copy an existing user as a new user

Both options involve quite a few manual steps.

Importing a list of users

In order to reduce the manual work needed to create a large group of users within Cacti, you are going to create a small PHP-based script that takes a list of users as input and creates the users based on a **Template User** within Cacti.

First, create a file called `user_list.txt` with the following content:

```
user1;User Name1
user2;User Name2
user3;User Name3
user4;User Name4
```

This will be the basis for the import. The first part is the actual username of the new user, the last part in the file is going to be the full name for that user.

Time for action – importing users from the CLI

Now that you have created the import file, let's import it.

1. Logon to the command line of your Cacti server.

2. Go to the `cli` subdirectory under the Cacti directory:

   ```
   cd /Var/www/html/cact/cli
   ```

3. Place the `import_user.php` script in this directory.

4. Put the `user_list.txt` file in the `/tmp` directory.

5. Run the following command to add the users to the **Local Realm** with the `_CustomerA_user` as the template user:

```
php import_user.php /tmp/users_list.txt _CustomerA_user 0
```

```
[root@localhost cli]# php import_user.php /tmp/users_list.txt _CustomerA_user 0

It is highly recommended that you use the web interface to copy users as this sc
cal Cacti users.

Cacti User Copy Utility
Template User: _CustomerA_user
Realm: Local

Copying/Creating User...
New User: user1
New User: user2
New User: user3
New User: user4
User copied...
[root@localhost cli]#
```

What just happened?

You just imported all users from the import file to your Cacti installation. The users now also have the same permissions as the **Template User**. Go to the **User Management** section of Cacti and you will see the users listed there:

user1	User Name1	No	Local	ALLOW
user2	User Name2	No	Local	ALLOW
user3	User Name3	No	Local	ALLOW
user4	User Name4	No	Local	ALLOW
_CustomerA_user	Template User for Customer A	No	Local	ALLOW

Let's take a closer look at the CLI script `import_user.php`. Besides reading the command line options and several print statements, it consists of three major parts. The first part deals with some input validation for the **Realm ID**, the second part reads the import file, and the last part actually copies the user and changes the **Full Name** and **Realm ID** for the user.

Input validation

As a quick run of the script without any parameters reveals, the CLI takes three input parameters:

```
Syntax:
 php import_user.php <import file> <template user> <realm id>
```

The import file is the text file with the userids which you created earlier. The **Template User** will be your _CustomerA_user. The **Realm ID** references the ID of the authentication realm and can be a number between 0 and 2:

- **Realm ID** 0—Local authentication
- **Realm ID** 1—LDAP authentication
- **Realm ID** 2—Web authentication

The following code checks the entered **Realm ID** for its valid range and sets it to Local Authentication (0) if it has not been set correctly.

```
// Realm Id can be: 0 - Local, 1 - LDAP, 2 - Web Auth
if ( ( $realm_id < 0 ) || ( $realm_id > 2 ) ) {
    // The realm id will be local unless a valid id was given
    $realm_id = 0;
}
```

Check the existence of the template user

The following code section checks the Cacti database to see if the template user does exist. If it does not exist, the program immediately stops with an error message.

```
/* Check that user exists */
$user_auth = db_fetch_row("SELECT * FROM user_auth WHERE username = '"
. $template_user . "' AND realm = 0");
if (! isset($user_auth)) {
        die("Error: Template user does not exist!\n\n");
}
```

Reading the import file

Now that the script has checked the **Template User** and the **Realm ID**, it starts reading the actual import file. The file command reads the file and provides the content of it as an array of the lines. The script then cycles through each single line, stripping off the newline character with the rtrim command. The remaining lines will be split at the semicolon resulting in an array holding the **Username** and **Full Name**.

```
if ( file_exists( $import_file ) ) {
    // read in the import file
    $lines = file( $import_file );
    foreach ($lines as $line)
    {
        // cycle through the file

        // remove the new line  character from the line
        $line = rtrim ($line);

        // split the line data at the ";"
        $data = preg_split("/;/",$line);

        $new_user_username = $data[0];
        $new_user_fullname = $data[1];
```

Now the script has all of the necessary information to create the **New User** by copying the **Template User**. The following code does this part of the job:

```
user_copy($template_user, $new_user_username)
```

Copying the template users would leave you with a list of users created with all of them having the same **Full Name** and authentication set to `Local`. Therefore the script then goes on and changes the **Full Name** and Realm ID of the newly created user by executing two database SQL Update statements:

```
db_execute("UPDATE user_auth SET full_name = '".$new_user_fullname."'
WHERE username='".$new_user_username."'");

db_execute("UPDATE user_auth SET realm=".$realm_id." WHERE
username='".$new_user_username."'");
```

The first SQL statement updates the `full_name` field of the new user, the second statement updates the `realm` field to match your selection from the command line parameter.

This import script is useful for environments where you do not automatically want to create all users based on a template user, but have different users be assigned different user profiles.

Before we continue

As you have learned quite some new information about the user management and the provided CLI interface, let's take a few questions to check your knowledge.

Pop quiz – a few questions about Chapter 4

1. What would you use the guest account for?
   a. To allow guest users to logon to the system
   b. To view the number of guest users within the company
   c. To allow the guests to use the internal network
   d. To allow public viewing of graphs

2. What realm permissions do you need to give a user to add new devices to Cacti?
   a. Console Access and Update Data Sources permissions
   b. Device Management permission
   c. Console Access and Graph Management permissions

3. What permissions do you need to use the CLI command line scripts from Cacti?
   a. Console Access permissions
   b. CLI Management permissions
   c. Update Data Sources Permissions
   d. No special permissions are required

Summary

You learned a lot in this chapter about user management with in Cacti.

We covered:

- Creating a user—how to apply some basic settings to a user
- Groups—there are no user groups in Cacti
- Realm Permissions—how to give access to different parts of Cacti to a user
- Graph Permissions—how to give access to trees and graphs to a user and limit access to a single customer
- Template User—how to create a template user holding all realm and graph permissions for a specific set of users and how to use the batch copy method to apply permissions from a template user to other users
- LDAP Authentication—how to make Cacti use an external LDAP system for user authentication
- Managing users through the CLI – how to import a list of users through the CLI

Now that you have users on your system, it's time to give them more than just the standard Cacti graphs. In the next chapter, you are going to learn how to gather data from other systems. You will create your own scripts and retrieve remote data using ssh.

5

Data Management

*Retrieving data for graphing with Cacti is more than just pulling SNMP data. Cacti allows several different methods for data retrieval. Besides SNMP, Cacti is able to retrieve data using remotely executed scripts, pulling data from databases, or building data by utilizing the **Windows Management Interface (WMI)**.*

In this chapter we are going to:

◆   Provide a short overview of Cacti's data management

◆   Explain how to build a data input method

◆   Build a data query

◆   Develop a complete remote SSH data input method

Let's get started!

An introduction to Cacti data management

Cacti provides different methods for remote data query. You have already learned about the data input methods for retrieving a single SNMP value, but this method is not limited to SNMP. You can use several other methods such as scripts or the WMI for retrieving and graphing data.

Data input methods

Data input methods are commonly used when it comes to basic data retrieval. They can be external scripts, simple SNMP queries, or anything that does not involve indexed data.

Data queries

Data queries are used for indexed data. A good example data is retrieving interface statistics for switches where each data entry (for example, for interface inOctets) is linked to the interface using an index. So, for complex data, you will need to create a data query.

Creating data input methods

We have already seen how to create a data input method for simple SNMP queries. Let's look into creating a script-based data input method for retrieving some information out of the `secure` log file. The `secure` log file contains information about failed and successful logins. Please note that the following example will only work on a Linux system.

Preparation—creating the script

For a script/command data input method, you obviously need a script for gathering the required data and providing it to Cacti. Look at the `unix_secure_log.pl` file. This Perl script will collect the necessary data for you.

Let's have a look at the commands used in the script. Within the first line of interest, you configure the path and filename to look for the data:

```
# Where do we find the secure log file ?
my $secure_log = '/var/log/secure';
```

Gathering the data

The following important lines within the script retrieve the relevant Cacti data by executing a sequence of operating system commands:

```
# Retrieve the number of lines containing a "Invalid user" string
$data{'invalid_users'} = `grep "Invalid user" $secure_log | wc -l`;

# Retrieve the number of lines containing a "Accepted password" string
$data{'valid_logons'} = `grep "Accepted password" $secure_log | wc -l`;
```

The first line looks for the string Invalid user within the `secure` log file by using the `grep` command. This command will print all lines containing this string. By using the special pipe character |, we redirect the output from this command to the `wc` (abbreviation for word count) command. By using the -l switch, the `wc` command will count the number of lines. The output of this command is then stored within the `$data{'invalid_users'}`.

Preparing the data for output

The variables $data{'invalid_users'} and $data{'valid_logons'} now contain the number of lines containing the Invalid user and Accepted password strings, but they also have a line ending character. In order for Cacti to use this data, you will need to remove this line ending character. This can be achieved by using the chomp function:

```
# Remove the line ending character from the string:
chomp( $data{'invalid_users'} );
chomp( $data{'valid_logons'} );
```

You can now use these variables to print the data as a Cacti compliant string:

```
# Print the data as "Name1:Var1 Name2:Var2". Do not put a line ending
to the string !
print "InvalidUsers:".$data{'invalid_users'}." ValidLogons:".$data{'v
alid_logons'};
```

As the comment already describes, the data needs to be printed as a Name:Variable pair separated by a space. This is the last step of the script. An example output of this script can be seen here:

```
# perl unix_secure_log.pl
InvalidUsers:0 ValidLogons:3#
#
```

Installation of the script

All scripts need to be placed into the scripts subdirectory of your Cacti installation. After you have copied the script to this location you can use it to create the data input method within Cacti.

Time for action – creating a data input method – Step 1

Logon to your Cacti installation as an admin user and change to the **Console** tab.

1. Go to **Collection Methods | Data Input Methods**.
2. Click on the **Add** link at the top right.
3. Enter **Unix - Secure Log Input** as the **Name**.
4. Select **Script/Command** as the **Input Type**.

5. Enter `perl <path_cacti>/scripts/unix_secure_log.pl` as the **Input String**.

6. Click on the **Save** button.

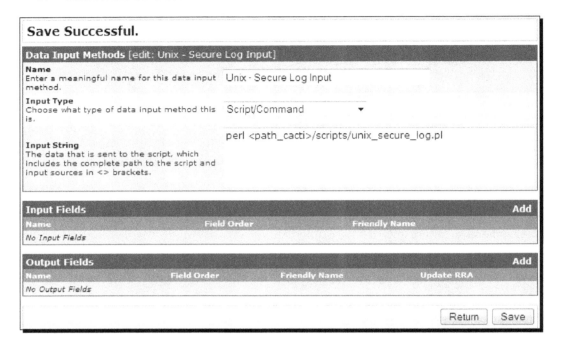

What just happened?

You just created a basic script/command-based data input method. You also told Cacti how to execute the script by defining the **Input String**. Selecting the **Script/Command** as **Input Type** made Cacti automatically add fields for data input and data output after clicking on the **Save** button.

Time for action – creating a data input method – Step 2

1. Click on the **Add** link at the **Output Fields** table. This will open a new form.

2. Enter **InvalidUsers** as the **Field [Output]**.

3. Enter **InvalidUsers** as the **Friendly Name**.

4. Click on the **Create** button.

5. Click on the **Add** link at the **Output Fields** table again.

6. Enter **ValidLogons** as the **Field [Output]**.

7. Enter **ValidLogons** as the **Friendly Name**.

8. Click on the **Create** button.

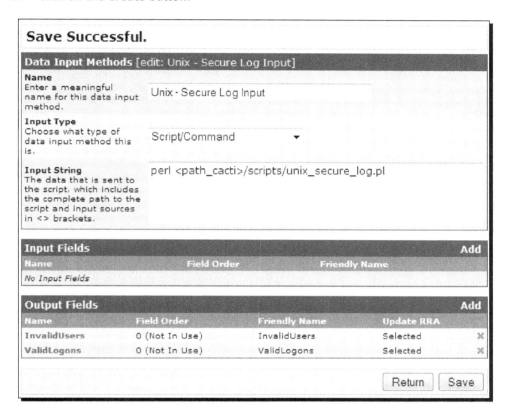

What just happened?

You just added the two output fields from the script to this data input method. Cacti is now able to use this information and fill the RRD files with the data retrieved from the script.

The data template

As you've already learned in *Chapter 3, Creating and Using Templates*, you will need to create a data template for this data input method to be used within a graph. You can now either import the template that comes with this book, or better still, try to create the data template yourself. The following picture shows the final data template:

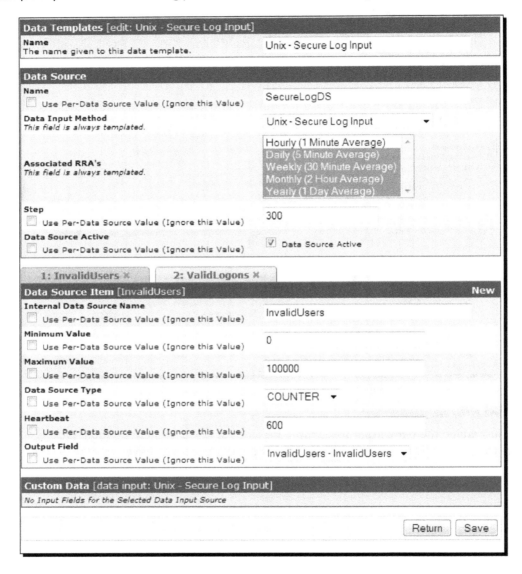

Creating data queries

Data queries are more complex than simple data input methods. As already mentioned, they involve indexes. In order for you to get off to an easy start with data queries, you will now rebuild the SNMP-based data query for network interfaces.

Building the XML data file

Building a script or SNMP query always starts with an XML file providing the relationship between input, output, and the index. Look at the `interface_book.xml` file that comes with this book for an example of such an XML file.

XML header

The XML header sets some generic information for Cacti. A generic description as well as the SNMP OID index can be set here:

```
<name>Get SNMP Interfaces</name>
<description>Queries a host for a list of monitorable interfaces</
description>
<oid_index>.1.3.6.1.2.1.2.2.1.1</oid_index>
<oid_num_indexes>.1.3.6.1.2.1.2.1.0</oid_num_indexes>
<index_order>ifDescr:ifName:ifHwAddr:ifIndex</index_order>
<index_order_type>numeric</index_order_type>
<index_title_format>|chosen_order_field|</index_title_format>
```

Let's look at the SNMP output of the `oid_index` and `oid_num_index` for the CentOS box:

```
# snmpwalk -c public -v 2c localhost .1.3.6.1.2.1.2.2.1.1
IF-MIB::ifIndex.1 = INTEGER: 1
IF-MIB::ifIndex.2 = INTEGER: 2
IF-MIB::ifIndex.3 = INTEGER: 3
# snmpwalk -c public -v 2c localhost .1.3.6.1.2.1.2.1.0
IF-MIB::ifNumber.0 = INTEGER: 3
```

This CentOS system has three interfaces, a loopback (127.0.0.1), one Ethernet interface (eth0), and something called sit, which is only used in mixed IPv6/IPv4 environments. The `oid_num_indexes` provides us with the number of interfaces available in the system, which is three. The `oid_index` provides a table of indexes available. The index is important to match an interface with its corresponding data value (for example, inOctets).

The `index_order` list defines a unique index on which Cacti can order and index the data. The `index_order_type` defines the default sort order of the `index_order`.

XML input

Input fields describe the fields taken as input for the data query. Basically the fields will be shown on the data query table when creating new graphs for a host. All input fields will be shown there.

Let's look at the very first input field, the `ifIndex` definition:

```
<ifIndex>
    <name>Index</name>
    <method>walk</method>
    <source>value</source>
    <direction>input</direction>
    <oid>.1.3.6.1.2.1.2.2.1.1</oid>
</ifIndex>
```

Input as well as output fields always contain at least the following five fields:

- `name`: A name that is being displayed on the data query table.
- `method`: The SNMP method to retrieve the data. It can be `get` or `walk`.
- `source`: The source for the field `VALUE` returns the plain data. There is also `OID/REGEXP` and `VALUE/REGEXP`. They both use regular expression to either get part of the `OID` as the value, or part of the retrieved plain data as the value.
- `direction`: Can be input or output, depending on the field type.
- `oid`: The `oid` to use for the `get` or `walk` method.

The example will walk the `ifIndex` oid and simply return the values (1,2, and 3) as input data. If you later look at the data query table, you will see those values again.

XML output

The `output` fields are used by Cacti to actually gather the data for the RRD files. Let's look at the interface `inOctets` definition:

```
<ifInOctets>
    <name>Bytes In</name>
    <method>walk</method>
    <source>value</source>
    <direction>output</direction>
    <oid>.1.3.6.1.2.1.2.2.1.10</oid>
</ifInOctets>
```

As you can see, it is defined similarly to the `input` fields, except that the direction is now output. If you take the `oid` and use the `snmpwalk` command to retrieve the data from the CentOS system, you can see the importance of the index:

```
# snmpwalk -On -c public -v 2c localhost .1.3.6.1.2.1.2.2.1.10
.1.3.6.1.2.1.2.2.1.10.1 = Counter32: 10155126
.1.3.6.1.2.1.2.2.1.10.2 = Counter32: 63092946
.1.3.6.1.2.1.2.2.1.10.3 = Counter32: 0
```

Each interface has its own `inOctets` number. The `oid` for it can be defined as `oid + index`. In order to retrieve the `inOctets` for the interface with index 1 (eth0), you will need to retrieve the `oid .1.3.6.1.2.1.2.2.1.10.1`

Installing the XML file

The final XML file needs to be put to the `resource/snmp_queries` subdirectory of Cacti. For script queries the directory will be `resource/script_queries`.

Creating the data query within Cacti

Now that you have created the base XML file for the data query, let's move on and finally create it within Cacti.

Time for action – creating a data query – Step 1

1. Go to **Collection Methods | Data Queries** and click on the **Add** link which is to the top right.

2. Enter **SNMP - Interface Statistics Simple** as the **Name**.

3. Enter **Simple (In/OutOctets) Interface Statistics** as the **Description**.

4. Enter `<path_cacti>/resource/snmp_queries/interface_book.xml` as the **XML Path**.

5. Select **Get SNMP Data (Indexed)** as **Data Input Method**.

6. Click on the **Save** button.

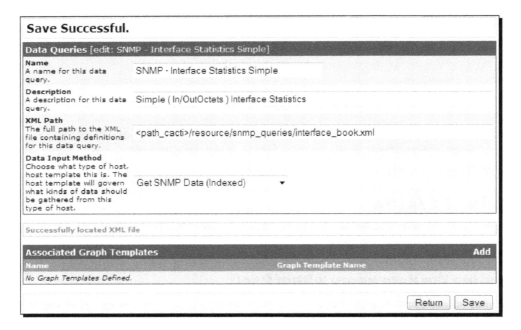

What just happened?

You just told Cacti where to find the XML file which you created earlier and what data input method to use for retrieving the data. You can now add one or more graph templates to this query.

During the next step you're going to add a graph and a data template to this data query. This step is needed as a data query can provide different "views" on the data. Interface traffic, for example, can consist of 32bit or 64bit values, or you may want to have the total bandwidth usage displayed, as calculated on some graphs. As all of this data, as well as the graphs, are based on the same data query for interface traffic, you need to add the **Associated Graph Templates** for these during the next step.

Time for action – creating a data query – Step 2

Now you're going to add one **Associated Graph Template** to this data query.

1. Click on the **Add** link on the **Associated Graph Templates** table

2. Enter **In/Out Bits** as the **Name**.

3. Select **Interface – Traffic (bits/sec)** as the **Graph Template**. If you do not find the graph template you need, you will need to create one first.

4. Click on the **Create** button. Several new tables will appear now:

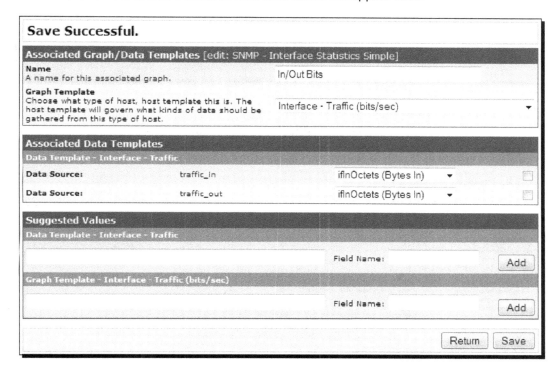

5. Select **ifOutOctets (Bytes Out)** for the **traffic_out** data source.

6. Check both checkboxes from the **Associated Data Templates** table.

7. Enter **|host_description|- Traffic - |query_ifName|** in the first field of the **Data Template – Interface –Traffic** section.

8. Enter **name** as the **Field Name** and click the **Add** button next to it.

9. Enter `|query_ifSpeed|` in the first field of the **Data Template – Interface –Traffic** section.

10. Enter **rrd_maximum** as the **Field Name** and click on the **Add** button again. You will now have two entries in the first table:

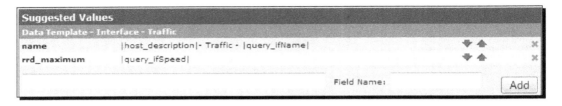

11. Now enter **|host_description|- Traffic - |query_ifName|** in the first field of the **Graph Template – Interface – Traffic (bits/sec)** section.

12. Enter **title** as the **Field Name** and click on the **Add** button.

13. Click on the **Save** button.

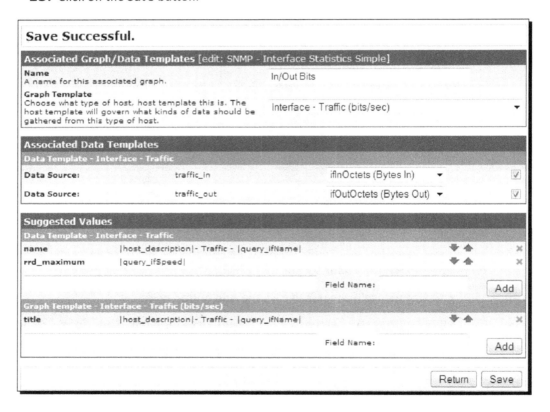

What just happened?

You have finished creating your first data query. You have defined the default names for the automatically created data templates and the maximum value which the RRD file for this data template can store by setting the **rrd_maximum** variable to the interface speed. You have also defined the default title for the graphs by defining the **title** variable. You can now add this data query to your device.

Create a remote SSH data input method

Besides SNMP queries, remote data retrieval is an important part of creating Cacti performance graphs. You may get into a situation where SNMP data retrieval is not possible and you only have SSH access to a device. Let's assume you want to graph the I/O performance of some server drives using the `iostat` utility. You will now learn the different steps it takes to create such a remote SSH data input method.

Preparation

As a preparation for the data input method, you will need to create two different scripts and set up public key authentication.

The remote script

The remote script will execute local commands and preparse/prepare the data on the remote system. The data will be returned to the local script. If you have not already installed the `iostat` utility on the remote system, you can call the following command to do so on a CentOS system:

```
yum install sysstat
```

This will install the `iostat` utility on the system.

Let's call this utility and look at the output:

```
# iostat
Linux 2.6.18-194.11.1.el5 (localhost.localdomain)        09/25/2010


avg-cpu:  %user   %nice %system %iowait  %steal   %idle
           0.14    0.09    1.15    0.03    0.00   98.59


Device:           tps    Blk_read/s   Blk_wrtn/s   Blk_read   Blk_wrtn
sda              1.31          2.62        22.84     844943    7369586
```

sda1	0.00	0.01	0.01	2490	2762
sda2	1.31	2.61	22.83	842149	7366824
dm-0	2.98	2.61	22.83	840962	7366824
dm-1	0.00	0.00	0.00	896	0
hdc	0.00	0.02	0.00	5736	0

In this example, we can see that this utility provides statistics for all partitions in the system. We are going to look at the `sda2` partition which, in this case, holds the root partition. The following command for retrieving extended status data just for the `sda2` device will be used:

```
iostat -dxk sda2
Linux 2.6.18-194.11.1.el5 (localhost.localdomain)        09/25/2010
```

Device:	r/s	w/s	rkB/s	wkB/s	await	%util
sda2	0.10	1.21	1.30	11.42	17.26	0.12

The `-dk` option will make sure that only the `sda2` device is shown and that we see the KB read and writes to the disk. The `-x` option will provide extended status information such as the IO utilization `%util`. One important notice about `iostat` utility is the fact that the very first status report will always be the combined data since system start. In order to get a more accurate snapshot of the actual data, the command needs to be told how often and how long it should gather IO status data.

The remote script looks like the following:

```
#!/bin/bash
iostat -dxk $1 10 6 | grep $1
```

The parameters tell `iostat` to poll IO data every 10 seconds for a total of 6 polls. The `$1` will be provided by the local calling script and is the first parameter to the remote script. The `grep $1` command will make sure that only the line with the device information will be returned. Of course, the drawback of this is that it will definitely increase the poller runtime as it needs to wait for the remote script to finish, but it will still finish before the default 5-minute polling interval ends.

The local script

The local script is dealing with connectivity to the remote system using SSH and executing the remote script. It also provides the returned data to Cacti. We will look at the different sections of the local script next:

Input variables

The local script takes several input variables:

```
# Get the command line arguments (input fields from Cacti)
my $host = $ARGV[0];
my $user = $ARGV[1];
my $sshKey = $ARGV[2];
my $diskDevice = $ARGV[3]; # e.g. sda2

# take care for tcp:hostname or TCP:ip@
$host =~ s/tcp:/$1/gis;
my $sshHost = $user.'@'.$host;
```

The $host variable takes the Cacti host information. The $user defines the remote userID under which the iostat command will run. The $sshKey defines the local SSH key used for the public key authentication. You will come back to this method later. Finally, the $diskDevice variable takes the partition to check. From these input values we also define the $sshHost variables which you will need for the SSH command.

The SSH command execution

Using the input values you can now create the SSH command for the remote command execution:

```
my $returnValue = `/usr/bin/ssh -i $sshKey $sshHost '/root/getIoStats.
sh $diskDevice'`;
```

This command assumes that the remote script getIoStats.sh is stored in the root directory. It connects to the remote system ($sshHost) using the locally stored private key (-i $sshKey) and calls the remote command with the $diskDevice as parameter. The data being returned by the remote script is stored in the variable $returnValue.

Preparing the data

The returned data is made out of a bunch of lines containing the relevant data. You first need to separate each line into a separate data item. This can be achieved using the split function, splitting the returned data at the line ending character \n:

```
# Separate the returned data at the line ending character
# and store each line as an element of the returnData array
my @returnData = split/\n/,$returnValue;
```

Now that you have each line stored as an item of the `returnData` array, you can move on and initialize the Cacti data to be returned. You are going to use a Perl hash variable to store the data. Hashes in Perl have the advantage that the key for the hash can be a string value. Therefore, it is more readable than using arrays, which only accept numbers as keys:

```
# Initialize the Cacti return data
my %cactiData;
$cactiData{'device'} = $diskDevice;
$cactiData{'Reads'} = 0;
$cactiData{'Writes'} = 0;
$cactiData{'kbReads'} = 0;
$cactiData{'kbWrites'} = 0;
$cactiData{'ioUtil'} = 0;
```

You also need to know how many lines you actually got back from the remote script. This can be achieved with the following command, returning the number of items within the `returnData` array:

```
my $allDataChecks = $#returnData;
```

Now that you have initialized the data, it is time to actually retrieve the data and to store the retrieved values into the corresponding hash value. As you have previously learned, you need to skip the first line, so the `for` loop starts from the second line. Please note that the very first item of a Perl array starts at 0:

```
# Cycle through each line and skip the very first one ( line = 0 )
for ( my $line = 1; $line < $allDataChecks; $line++ ) {
        my @lineData = split/\s+/,$returnData[$line];
        $cactiData{'Reads'} = $cactiData{'Reads'} + $lineData[3];
        $cactiData{'Writes'} = $cactiData{'Writes'} + $lineData[4];
        $cactiData{'kbReads'} = $cactiData{'kbReads'} + $lineData[5];
        $cactiData{'kbWrites'} = $cactiData{'kbWrites'} +
$lineData[6];
        $cactiData{'ioUtil'} = $cactiData{'ioUtil'} + $lineData[11];
}
```

Within the above `for` loop, each line is split at the space character `\s` treating several adjacent spaces as one by using the special + character. If you take the sentence you are reading now as an example, `$lineData[0]` would store `If,$ lineData[1]` you, `$lineData[2] take,` and so on.

As the remote script returned several lines with data, the `for` loop will sum up each line data. Therefore, your next step will be dividing the data by the number lines being returned. Again you will need to reduce the number by 1:

```
# Average the data
$cactiData{'Reads'} = $cactiData{'Reads'}  / ($allDataChecks - 1);
$cactiData{'Writes'} = $cactiData{'Writes'} / ($allDataChecks - 1);
$cactiData{'kbReads'} = $cactiData{'kbReads'} / ($allDataChecks - 1);
$cactiData{'kbWrites'} = $cactiData{'kbWrites'} / ($allDataChecks - 1);
$cactiData{'ioUtil'} = $cactiData{'ioUtil'} / ($allDataChecks - 1);
```

The final step will be to print out the retrieved, averaged data in a Cacti compliant way:

```
print "Reads:".$cactiData{'Reads'}." ".
      "Writes:".$cactiData{'Writes'}." ".
      "ReadsKb:".$cactiData{'kbReads'}." ".
      "WritesKb:".$cactiData{'kbWrites'}." ".
      "ioUtil:".$cactiData{'ioUtil'};
```

Now you're ready for the next step.

SSH public key authentication

SSH public key authentication is the recommended way of executing commands on a remote system. You'll need to create a public key for the remote system and a private key for the local system. For simplicity, let's assume that you will connect to the remote system using the root user account.

Let's start by creating the keys using the Putty Key Generator.

Time for action – create SSH keys with PuTTY Key Generator

1. Start the **PuTTY Key Generator**.

2. Click on the **Generate** button and follow the instructions provided.

3. Click on the **Conversions** menu, and then click on the **Export OpenSSH key** entry.

4. Store the key without a passphrase somewhere on your local disk.

5. Open the file using Notepad.

6. Copy the whole content of the file.

7. Connect to your Cacti system using PuTTY.

8. Issue the following command:

```
vi /home/cactiuser/ioStats_keyfile
```

9. Press the *i* key to get into the **Insert mode**.

10. Right click on the putty screen to insert the content of your clipboard to the file. This should still be the content of the **PuTTY Key Generator**.

11. Save the file and exit by pressing *ESC* and then entering :*x*.

12. Execute the following command to make the file only readable by your Cacti user:
```
chown cactiuser /home/cactiuser/ioStats_keyfile
chmod 600 /home/cactiuser/ioStats_keyfile
```

13. Go back to your **PuTTY Key Generator** window and copy the text from the upper part (Public key).

14. Connect to your remote system as the root user using PuTTY.

15. Open the `authorized_keys` file by executing the following command:
```
vi /root/.ssh/authorized_keys
```

16. Press the *i* key to get into the Insert mode.

17. Right-click on the PuTTY screen to insert the content of your clipboard to the file. This should still be the content of the **PuTTY Key Generator.**

18. Save and exit the file by pressing *ESC* and then entering :*x*.

19. Execute the following command to make the file only readable by your root user:
```
chmod 600 /root/.ssh/authorized_keys
```

20. Now on your Cacti server, try using the private key to execute the remote script. First become the Cacti user:
```
su - cactiuser
```

21. Execute the following `ssh` command:
```
ssh -i /home/cactiuser/ioStats_keyfile root@remotesystem '/root/getIoStats.sh sda2'
```

22. If the command asks whether it should store the remote host key, accept it by entering `yes`. You should then see the data from the remote script after some time.

What just happened?

You just created a public and private SSH key which can be used to automatically login to a remote system without any user interaction. You've allowed the Cacti system (`cactiuser`) to use this SSH key to execute the `getIoStats.sh` script on the remote system.

Creating the data input method

The data input method for this script involves some advanced steps as it contains input variables.

Time for action – creating the data input method

1. Create a data input method.

2. Enter **Unix - Remote IOStats Command** as the **Name**.

3. Select **Script/Command** as **Input Type**.

4. Enter `perl <path_cacti>/scripts/diskIo.pl <host> <user> <sshKey> <diskDevice>` as the **Input String**.

5. Click on the **Create** button.

6. Click on the **Add** link at the **Input Fields** section.

7. Select **host** as the **Field [input]**.

8. Enter **Hostname** as the **Friendly Name**.

9. Enter **hostname** as the **Special Type Code**.

10. Click on the **Create** button.

11. Add the other input fields by only adding a **Friendly Name**.

12. Add the output fields for `Reads,Writes,ReadsKb,WritesKb,` and `ioUtil`.

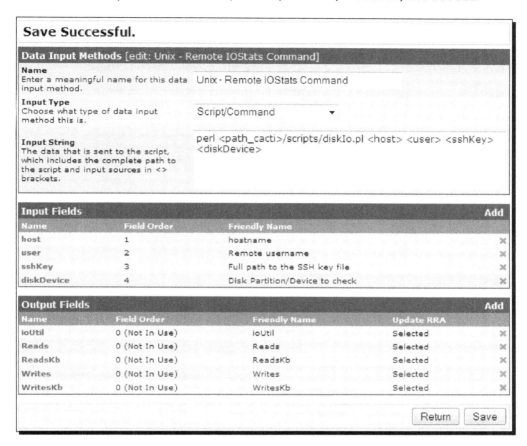

What just happened?

You've just created the data input method for retrieving the output from the `iostats` command of a remote system. You've defined the input fields such as the remote username to use for logging in to the system, as well as the location of the SSH key which you defined earlier. The data retrieved from this command will be stored in the output fields which you have defined.

Creating the data template

The data template can be built as outlined in the secure log input example described right at the beginning of this chapter. There will be a slight difference to it, however, as the data template will have a table called **Custom Data**. This table defines the input data. The following screenshot shows this table and the entries you'll need to make:

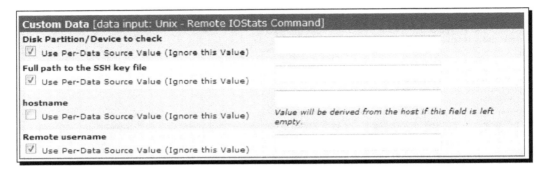

Creating the graph template

The data input method contains three different types of data: number of average reads, average KB reads, and a percentage value for the IO utilization. For each of these you'll need to create a graph template. As you've already learned how to create graph templates, this is a perfect opportunity for you to check your knowledge and create these.

Adding the graph to the device

Once you've created the graph templates you can go on adding the graph template to the device for which you want to gather the data. You're asked to enter the custom data for the disk partition/device to check the full path to the SSH key file and the remote username during the process, as seen in the following screenshot:

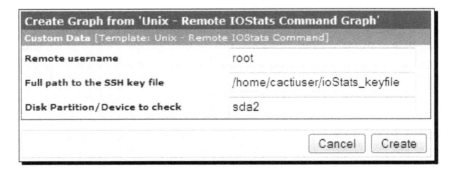

Alternative methods

If the system which you want to retrieve data from is able to provide data using SNMP, you can also use the special `exec` command within the remote SNMP server configuration to provide the data via the SNMP interface. There are many ways for retrieving data, from parsing command line output to retrieving web pages to be parsed, as well as using web services.

Have a go hero – remote command execution using SNMP

Let's assume that your remote system already runs an SNMP daemon. What do you need to do in order to retrieve the secure log data from a remote system utilizing the SNMP interface?

Solution: You need to create a script called `/root/getSecureLogonsData.sh` with the following lines of code:

```
#!/bin/bash
grep "Invalid user" /var/log/secure | wc -l
grep "Accepted password" /var/log/secure | wc -l
```

You also need to add the following line to the `/etc/snmp/snmpd.conf` file:

```
exec .1.3.6.1.4.1.2021.54 invalidLogons /bin/bash /root/
getSecureLogonsData.sh
```

After restarting the `snmpd` daemon, you can check the output of the oid:

```
# snmpwalk -c askdhaksd123 -v 2c localhost .1.3.6.1.4.1.2021.54

UCD-SNMP-MIB::ucdavis.54.1.1 = INTEGER: 1

UCD-SNMP-MIB::ucdavis.54.2.1 = STRING: "invalidLogons"

UCD-SNMP-MIB::ucdavis.54.3.1 = STRING: "/bin/bash /root/getInvalidLogons.
sh"

UCD-SNMP-MIB::ucdavis.54.100.1 = INTEGER: 0

UCD-SNMP-MIB::ucdavis.54.101.1 = STRING: "4557"

UCD-SNMP-MIB::ucdavis.54.101.2 = STRING: "9"

UCD-SNMP-MIB::ucdavis.54.102.1 = INTEGER: 0

UCD-SNMP-MIB::ucdavis.54.103.1 = ""
```

The values for `oids` ending with `101.1` and `101.2` are the numbers returned by the `Invalid user` and `Accepted password` lines of the script. You can then create a data input method using these **oids**.

Before we continue

Creating data input methods using scripts or queries involves quite some programming and network knowledge. This chapter built up the complexity by going from a simple local data input method to a more complex data query and building a remote executed input method. If you feel lost in any of these exercises you should try to focus on one of them before moving on to the next step. If you want to learn more about data queries, you should visit the **HowTo** sections on the Cacti website, as well as the relevant section in the Cacti online manual.

- ◆ HowTo: `http://docs.cacti.net/howto:data_query_templates`.
- ◆ Manual: `http://docs.cacti.net/manual:088:3a_advanced_topics.3d_script_data_query_walkthrough`.

Pop quiz – a few questions about Chapter 5

1. Where will you define the path to the SSH key file?
   a. In the `config.php` file of Cacti
   b. In the Cacti settings page
   c. When adding the special graph template to a device
   d. When adding or editing a device

2. What do you need an indexed SNMP query for?
   a. In order to easily retrieve special values from an SNMP tree
   b. In order to link SNMP data to the relevant device
   c. Indexed queries are required for data which is provided as a table with indexes
   d. In order to retrieve multiple SNMP values at once

3. Which user account will need to have the `authorized_keys` file configured?
   a. The **root** user
   b. The **cronjob** user
   c. The user on the remote system
   d. Your personal system account

Summary

You should now be able to create your own data input methods and create custom scripts to gather remote data.

This chapter covered:

◆ Creating data input methods—how to gather data from the local Cacti system using a local script

◆ Creating data queries—creating the underlying XML file and gathering indexed data for displaying in Cacti

◆ The remote SSH data input method—how to retrieve and display data from a remote system using the SSH public key authentication method

Having covered the data management chapter, you should now be able to comfortably manage a Cacti system. In the next chapter, you're going to take a closer look into maintaining Cacti by scheduling backup jobs, maintaining log files, and more.

6

Cacti Maintenance

So far, we have looked into installing and running a Cacti instance, but what about its maintenance and upkeep? This chapter will show you how to create backups and restores of your Cacti installation, as well as provide you with information on how to keep your Cacti instance clean of dead hosts and unnecessary files.

In this chapter we are going to:

◆ Provide a short overview of maintaining Cacti

◆ Explain the directory structure of Cacti

◆ Describe backup and restore procedures

◆ Look into log file management with logrotate

◆ Clean up unused RRD files

◆ Provide a short overview of the Cacti CLI functionality

Let's begin!

An introduction to Cacti maintenance

Cacti maintenance defines the standard procedures needed for backing up the database and managing the RRD files. As you've learned, the RRD files contain the polled performance data, whereas the database only holds configuration data. Let's take a look at both from a data management point of view.

Database

As you've seen in previous chapters, the MySQL is the main configuration repository for any Cacti installation and all your defined hosts, templates, and graph definitions are stored there.

RRD files

The RRD files contain all your performance data, but without the database you will be unable to link these files to their original devices and data sources. Cacti offers two different ways of storing these files. One method stores all RRD files within a single directory. The other method creates subdirectories based on the host and local graph ID.

The Cacti directory structure

Let's look at the default directory structure of Cacti and some of the important subdirectories:

```
# tree -d
.
|-- cli
|-- docs
|   |-- html
|   |   `-- images
|   |-- pdf
|   `-- txt
|-- images
|-- include
|   |-- jscalendar
|   |   `-- lang
|   `-- treeview
|-- install
|-- lib
|   `-- adodb
|       |-- datadict
|       |-- drivers
|       `-- lang
|-- log
|-- resource
|   |-- script_queries
|   |-- script_server
|   `-- snmp_queries
|-- rra
`-- scripts

24 directories
```

docs

The docs directory contains the full Cacti manual in different formats. The manual can be used as a quick reference for the various Cacti topics and also provides information on how to debug some of the more common issues you'll face.

The Cacti manual can be viewed within your browser by going to the following URL (replacing `<server>` with your Cacti Server):

```
http://<server>/<cacti dir>/docs/html/index.html.
```

include

The `include` directory contains files such as `config.php` and `global.php`. As you know, the `config.php` file contains the database and Cacti URL settings.

install

The `install` directory contains the installation files as well those needed in order to upgrade a Cacti installation. Once you have set up Cacti, you can safely delete this directory.

log

The `log` directory contains all of the Cacti log files. This is where the `cacti.log` file resides. In a default Cacti installation, there will be no log file management on these files.

resource

The `resource` directory holds all the XML files for Cacti's data queries. There are also some files used by the PHP script server stored in this directory.

rra

This is probably the most important directory. The `rra` directory contains all the RRD files that hold your performance data.

scripts

The `scripts` directory contains the scripts which are referenced in your data input methods.

Backup and restore procedures

As with any other application or data, you should always have well planned out and properly documented backup and restore procedures in place in order to keep your data secure. Backing up the Cacti data assures you that you're not going to lose weeks or even years of valuable performance data. Although the following steps show you how to backup Cacti to the local system, you should save the backup files to a remote system. Off-site backups are also a good idea.

The MySQL database

MySQL comes with a basic backup application called `mysqldump` which dumps the content of one or more databases out to a plain text file. You will be using this program to create your database backup file, but we'll further enhance its functionality by wrapping it in a shell script to automate the filename and compressions tasks.

Time for action – backup your Cacti database

1. Logon to your Cacti system.

2. Execute the following command to create a backup directory:

   ```
   mkdir /backup
   ```

3. Execute the following command and replace **<password>** with your MySQL database password (all in one line):

   ```
   mysqldump --user=root --password=<password> --add-drop-table --databases cacti > /backup/cacti_database_backup.sql
   ```

4. Verify that the backup file was created by issuing the following command:

   ```
   ls -l /backup
   ```

5. Look at the file with the `more` command:

   ```
   more /backup/cacti_database_backup.sql
   ```

```
root@cacti:~
-- MySQL dump 10.13  Distrib 5.1.49, for redhat-linux-gnu (i686)
--
-- Host: localhost    Database: cacti
-- ------------------------------------------------------
-- Server version       5.1.49

/*!40101 SET @OLD_CHARACTER_SET_CLIENT=@@CHARACTER_SET_CLIENT */;
/*!40101 SET @OLD_CHARACTER_SET_RESULTS=@@CHARACTER_SET_RESULTS */;
/*!40101 SET @OLD_COLLATION_CONNECTION=@@COLLATION_CONNECTION */;
/*!40101 SET NAMES utf8 */;
/*!40103 SET @OLD_TIME_ZONE=@@TIME_ZONE */;
/*!40103 SET TIME_ZONE='+00:00' */;
/*!40014 SET @OLD_UNIQUE_CHECKS=@@UNIQUE_CHECKS, UNIQUE_CHECKS=0 */;
/*!40014 SET @OLD_FOREIGN_KEY_CHECKS=@@FOREIGN_KEY_CHECKS, FOREIGN_KEY_CHECKS=0
*/;
/*!40101 SET @OLD_SQL_MODE=@@SQL_MODE, SQL_MODE='NO_AUTO_VALUE_ON_ZERO' */;
/*!40111 SET @OLD_SQL_NOTES=@@SQL_NOTES, SQL_NOTES=0 */;


--
-- Current Database: `cacti`
--

CREATE DATABASE /*!32312 IF NOT EXISTS*/ `cacti` /*!40100 DEFAULT CHARACTER SET
--More--(0%)
```

What just happened?

You just created a backup of your Cacti database which includes everything that is stored in your Cacti database, from user IDs to graph templates, and all the hosts added to your instance.

Although you now have a backup of your database, you don't have a backup of the actual database user. You will need to remember to create a database user for Cacti when restoring it to a freshly installed system.

Enhancing the database backup

Now that you've created a database backup, you should think about a way to automate this procedure. You definitely do not want to execute that command manually every night, so the first step is to create a script that takes care of your database backup. Later in this chapter, you will learn how to schedule this script to backup your database regularly.

Let's think about some basic requirements for a script:

- ◆ Automatically adding a date/time stamp to the filename
- ◆ Compressing the backup to save space
- ◆ Removing backup files which are more than 3 days old

Automatic file naming

The date command can be used to create a date string in the format: yyyymmdd, for example, 20100425. This can be used to create a filename which contains the current date. The following command will create such a string:

```
date +%Y%m%d
20101004
```

In a bash script file, this can be used to create the filename of the backup file:

```
# Set the backup filename and directory
DATE=`date +%Y%m%d` # e.g 20101025
FILENAME="cacti_database_$DATE.sql";
```

Removing old backup files

When using dynamic filenames like the one's created with the backup script, removing old backup files is essential to avoid filling the drive with backups. The following command will look for all Cacti database backup files older than 3 days in the backup directory and delete them:

```
find /backup/cacti_database*.sql.gz -mtime +3 -exec rm {} \;
```

The database backup

The actual database backup is performed by the `mysqldump` command, as mentioned earlier. This command is called with all the parameters defined so far:

```
# execute the database dump
mysqldump --user=$DBUSER --password=$DBPWD --add-drop-table --databases
$DBNAME > $BACKUPDIR$FILENAME
```

The `$DBUSER` and `$DBPWD` variables are the database user credentials to access your Cacti database. You should set `$DBNAME` to the name of your Cacti database.

Compressing the backup

On most Linux distributions, the `gzip` utility should be pre-installed, allowing us to compress the database dump. Calling `gzip` with the `-f` parameter will make sure that any already existing files (for example, from a test run) will be overwritten. The following command will compress the file `cacti_database_20101004.sql` and rename it to `cacti_database_20101004.sql.gz`:

```
gzip -f cacti_database_20101004.sql
```

The whole script

The finished database backup Bash script `backupCacti.sh` then consists of the following lines of code:

```bash
#!/bin/bash

# Set the backup filename and directory
DATE=`date +%Y%m%d` # e.g 20101025
FILENAME="cacti_database_$DATE.sql";
BACKUPDIR="/backup/";

# Database Credentials
DBUSER="cactiuser";
DBPWD="myPassw0rd";
DBNAME="cacti";

# Change to the root directory
cd /

# Where is our gzip tool for compression?
# The -f parameter will make sure that gzip will
# overwrite existing files
GZIP="/bin/gzip -f";
```

```
# Delete old backups older than 3 days
find /backup/cacti_ *gz -mtime +3 -exec rm {} \;

# execute the database dump
mysqldump --user=$DBUSER --password=$DBPWD --add-drop-table --
databases $DBNAME > $BACKUPDIR$FILENAME

# compress the database backup
$GZIP $BACKUPDIR$FILENAME
```

The backup could use the Cacti database user to create the dump, as this user does in fact have sufficient access rights to the database to do so. You do not need to use the root MySQL user for the database backup process.

The Cacti files

The Cacti files that you need to backup do not only consist of the files within the Cacti directory. Examples of other files that you will need to take care of are:

- The Cacti cron job file
- The MySQL database backup file
- System files like php.ini

Let's take a look at all the files we need to backup.

Building the backup file list

Depending on the setup of your Cacti installation, there are several files you will need to consider for a backup. Assuming you've followed this book closely and are using a CentOS-based Cacti installation with spine, you'll need to keep a backup of the following files and directories:

File/Directory	Description
/etc/cron.d/cacti	Cacti cron job
/etc/php.ini	PHP main configuration file
/etc/php.d	PHP modules configuration files
/etc/httpd/conf	Apache main configuration files
/etc/httpd/conf.d	Apache modules configuration files
/etc/spine.conf	Spine configuration
/usr/local/spine	Spine directory
/var/www/html/cacti	Symbolic link to the Cacti main directory
/var/www/html/cacti-0.8.7g	The Cacti main directory

Now that you have a list of which files need to be included in the backup, you can use the `tar` command to create a first backup file.

Time for action – backup your Cacti files

1. Logon to your Cacti system.

2. Go to the root directory:

```
cd /
```

3. Execute the following command to create a backup of all the files defined earlier:

```
tar -czvpf /backup/cacti_files_20101004.tgz ./etc/cron.d/cacti ./
etc/php.ini ./etc/php.d ./etc/httpd/conf ./etc/httpd/conf.d ./etc/
spine.conf ./usr/local/spine ./var/www/html/cacti ./var/www/html/
cacti-0.8.7g
```

4. Verify that the backup file exists by issuing the following command:

```
ls -l /backup
```

5. A listing similar to the following will be displayed:

```
# ls -l
-rw-r--r-- 1 root root    48888 Oct  5 20:29 cacti_database_20101004.sql.gz
-rw-r--r-- 1 root root 2468292 Oct  5 20:29 cacti_files_20101004.tgz
#
```

What just happened?

You just created your first complete backup that contains all the files and directories you defined and is also already compressed. Together with the database backup, you are now able to restore your Cacti installation.

Enhancing the database backup script

Now that you know how to backup the database and the Cacti-related files, you can add the `tar` command to the backup script which you created earlier.

Time for action – enhancing the backup script

1. Open the `backupCacti.sh` script and add the following line between the `FILENAME` and `BACKUPDIR` line:

```
TGZFILENAME="cacti_files_$DATE.tgz";
```

2. Add the following two lines at the end of the script:

```
# Create the Cacti files backup
tar -czpf $BACKUPDIR$TGZFILENAME ./etc/cron.d/cacti ./etc/php.ini
./etc/php.d ./etc/httpd/conf ./etc/httpd/conf.d ./etc/spine.conf
./usr/local/spine ./var/www/html/cacti ./var/www/html/cacti-0.8.7g
```

3. Remove any earlier backups from the backup directory:

```
rm /backup/cacti_*
```

4. Start the backup script:

```
/bin/bash /backup/backupCacti.sh
```

5. Verify whether the database and the files backup have been created:

```
ls -l /backup
```

What just happened?

You have enhanced the script to also create a backup of the Cacti files. Now you can issue this single command to create a complete backup. The extra dot you have added to the paths of the `tar` command will allow you to extract that tar file in a subdirectory without accidently overwriting an existing Cacti installation. This is especially useful if you only want to restore a specific file instead of all files.

Creating the cronjob—automating the backup

Now that you have created a single script that performs both the database and Cacti backups, you can use this script to schedule the backup on a regular basis. In Linux a scheduled task is called a cronjob, so this is what you are now going to create.

Time for action – creating a cronjob

1. Logon to your Cacti system.

2. Create a crontab file:

```
vi /etc/cron.d/cactiBackup
```

3. Enter the following lines to this file:

```
# Cacti Backup Schedule

0 2 * * * root /bin/bash /backup/backupCacti.sh > /dev/null 2>&1
```

4. Save the file and exit the editor.

What just happened?

You created a backup job which will start at 02:00 in the morning every day of the week. You now have a daily backup of your Cacti database and files.

Restoring from a backup

Now that you have a daily backup of your Cacti instance, what steps do you need to take to actually restore your backup? Let's have a look at the different tasks needed.

Restoring the Cacti database

Restoring the Cacti database involves using the standard `mysql` command.

Time for action – restoring the Cacti database

1. Logon to your Cacti server.

2. Change to the backup directory:

   ```
   cd /backup
   ```

3. Extract the latest backup file:

   ```
   gunzip cacti_database_20101004.sql.gz
   ```

4. Restore the database. Make sure to change the username and Cacti database name to fit your installation. Please note that this command is going to overwrite your existing database:

   ```
   mysql -u cactiuser -p cacti < cacti_database_20101004.sql
   ```

What just happened?

You restored your Cacti database from a backup. Please note that any changes you have made since the backup has been created, such as adding new devices to the server, will be lost.

Restoring the Cacti files

Restoring files from a backup will involve two methods:

- Restoring all of the Cacti files
- Restoring a single file

Restoring all Cacti files

Restoring all files is only necessary in case of a full disaster recovery like a hard disk failure. Thankfully, your backup should contain all necessary files to restore a Cacti installation from the ground up.

Time for action – restoring all Cacti files

1. Logon to your Cacti server.

2. For this example, let's assume you have it copied into the /backup directory.

3. Change to the root directory:

    ```
    cd /
    ```

4. Extract the contents of the backup:

    ```
    tar -xzvpf /backup/cacti_files_20101004.tgz
    ```

5. You will see the contents of the archive being displayed on the screen during the extraction process, as shown in the following screenshot:

```
root@localhost

./var/www/html/cacti-0.8.7g/scripts/diskfree.pl
./var/www/html/cacti-0.8.7g/scripts/ss_host_cpu.php
./var/www/html/cacti-0.8.7g/scripts/3com_cable_modem.pl
./var/www/html/cacti-0.8.7g/scripts/query_host_cpu.php
./var/www/html/cacti-0.8.7g/scripts/unix_processes.pl
./var/www/html/cacti-0.8.7g/scripts/ws_apachestats.pl
./var/www/html/cacti-0.8.7g/scripts/diskIo.pl
./var/www/html/cacti-0.8.7g/scripts/sql.php
./var/www/html/cacti-0.8.7g/scripts/loadavg_multi.pl
./var/www/html/cacti-0.8.7g/scripts/weatherbug.pl
./var/www/html/cacti-0.8.7g/scripts/unix_secure_log.pl
./var/www/html/cacti-0.8.7g/scripts/diskfree.sh
./var/www/html/cacti-0.8.7g/scripts/ss_host_disk.php
./var/www/html/cacti-0.8.7g/scripts/query_unix_partitions.pl
./var/www/html/cacti-0.8.7g/scripts/linux_memory.pl
./var/www/html/cacti-0.8.7g/scripts/ping.pl
./var/www/html/cacti-0.8.7g/graphs.php
./var/www/html/cacti-0.8.7g/rra.php
./var/www/html/cacti-0.8.7g/graph_templates.php
./var/www/html/cacti-0.8.7g/index.php
./var/www/html/cacti-0.8.7g/poller_export.php
./var/www/html/cacti-0.8.7g/README
./var/www/html/cacti-0.8.7g/graph_xport.php
#
```

What just happened?

You extracted the files from your backup. The -p option tells tar to maintain the permissions as they were at the time of the backup. By using the -v (verbose) option, the name of each file currently being extracted is displayed on the screen, allowing you to monitor its progress. You will need to restart all relevant services afterwards, or reboot the system to make all the changes to the configuration files active.

Restore the Cacti files to a separate system

If you intend to restore the backup archive to another Linux distribution, or just want to restore a single file, simply change to a subdirectory of your choice and run the restore tar command. All files within the archive will then be restored to the subdirectory without overwriting any existing files.

Restoring a single file from the backup

Sometimes it so happens that just a single file gets corrupted and needs to be restored. By using the dot character at the beginning of each file and directory during the backup creation, you can actually extract the backup file to any directory you want. Let's have a look at this.

Time for action – restoring the Cacti config.php file

1. Logon to your system.

2. Change to the /tmp directory:

   ```
   cd /tmp
   ```

3. Create a directory named cactirestore and change to that directory:

   ```
   mkdir cactirestore
   cd cactirestore
   ```

4. Extract the backup file to the cactirestore directory:

   ```
   tar -xzvpf /backup/cacti_files_20101004.tgz
   ```

5. Check the `tmp` directory for the existence of the `etc`, `var`, and `usr` directories:

`ls -l`

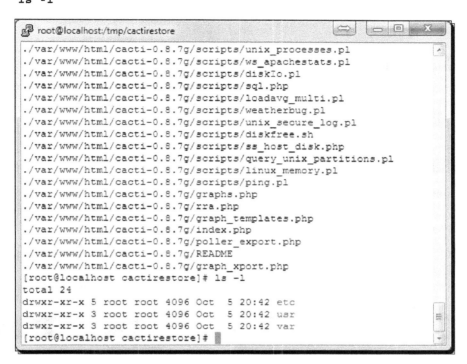

```
root@localhost:/tmp/cactirestore
./var/www/html/cacti-0.8.7g/scripts/unix_processes.pl
./var/www/html/cacti-0.8.7g/scripts/ws_apachestats.pl
./var/www/html/cacti-0.8.7g/scripts/diskIo.pl
./var/www/html/cacti-0.8.7g/scripts/sql.php
./var/www/html/cacti-0.8.7g/scripts/loadavg_multi.pl
./var/www/html/cacti-0.8.7g/scripts/weatherbug.pl
./var/www/html/cacti-0.8.7g/scripts/unix_secure_log.pl
./var/www/html/cacti-0.8.7g/scripts/diskfree.sh
./var/www/html/cacti-0.8.7g/scripts/ss_host_disk.php
./var/www/html/cacti-0.8.7g/scripts/query_unix_partitions.pl
./var/www/html/cacti-0.8.7g/scripts/linux_memory.pl
./var/www/html/cacti-0.8.7g/scripts/ping.pl
./var/www/html/cacti-0.8.7g/graphs.php
./var/www/html/cacti-0.8.7g/rra.php
./var/www/html/cacti-0.8.7g/graph_templates.php
./var/www/html/cacti-0.8.7g/index.php
./var/www/html/cacti-0.8.7g/poller_export.php
./var/www/html/cacti-0.8.7g/README
./var/www/html/cacti-0.8.7g/graph_xport.php
[root@localhost cactirestore]# ls -l
total 24
drwxr-xr-x 5 root root 4096 Oct  5 20:42 etc
drwxr-xr-x 3 root root 4096 Oct  5 20:42 usr
drwxr-xr-x 3 root root 4096 Oct  5 20:42 var
[root@localhost cactirestore]#
```

6. Change to the Cacti directory under `var`:

`cd var/www/html/cacti/`

7. Use the `pwd` command to check if you are in the correct directory:

[root@localhost cacti]# pwd

/tmp/cactirestore/var/www/html/cacti

8. Copy the `config.php` file from the `include` directory to your existing Cacti installation:

cp include/config.php /var/www/html/cacti/include

```
root@localhost:/tmp/cactirestore
[root@localhost cactirestore]# cd var/www/html/cacti
[root@localhost cacti]# pwd
/tmp/cactirestore/var/www/html/cacti
[root@localhost cacti]# cp include/config.php /var/www/html/cacti/include
cp: overwrite `/var/www/html/cacti/include/config.php'? y
[root@localhost cacti]#
```

9. Change to the root directory and delete the temporary restore location:

```
cd /
rm -rf /tmp/cactirestore
```

What just happened?

You just restored your `config.php` file from a backup. You can use this method to restore any file from your backup archive, such as corrupted RRD files or data queries which you may have accidentally deleted.

Log file management

Cacti is able to create a log file with information on what it is doing, but depending on the log settings, this log file can become huge and can stop Cacti from working properly. Therefore you will need to introduce some log file management.

Fortunately, Linux comes with a tool for this called `logrotate`. This tool is able to manage any log file on the system and is already configured to do so for most of the files in `/var/log`. Let's look at how you can configure it to also manage your Cacti logs.

Time for action – configuring Logrotate

1. Logon as root to your Cacti system.

2. Create a new file in the `/etc/logrotate.d` directory using vi:

```
vi /etc/logrotate.d/cactilog
```

3. Insert the following code:

```
/var/www/html/cacti/log/cacti.log {
    daily
    rotate 7
    copytruncate
    compress
    notifempty
    missingok
}
```

4. Save the file and quit.

5. Check if the configuration file is correct:

```
logrotate /etc/logrotate.conf -v
```

6. You should see text similar to the following somewhere in the output:

```
root@localhost:/tmp/cactirestore
rotating pattern: /var/www/html/cacti/log/cacti.log  after 1 days (7 rotations)
empty log files are not rotated, old logs are removed
considering log /var/www/html/cacti/log/cacti.log
  log does not need rotating
```

What just happened?

You just created a configuration file for logrotate to manage the `Cacti` log. The settings you entered will make sure that logrotate will rotate the file on a daily basis, keeping 7 days worth of logs and compressing the old files at the same time. Logrotate will not rotate the file if it is empty and will also not throw an error if the file is missing.

Cacti maintenance

You have now learned how to perform some general maintenance tasks for making backups and managing the `Cacti` log file. Let's look into some more specific Cacti maintenance tasks.

List RRD files with no associated host

After running a Cacti installation for some time, data items and files may get orphaned as you delete and recreate graphs. Let's check for the common issue of left-over RRD files.

Time for action – finding orphaned RRD files

1. Logon to your Cacti system.

2. Change to the `rra` directory of your Cacti installation:

```
cd /var/www/html/cacti/rra
```

3. List the directory content:

```
ls -l
```

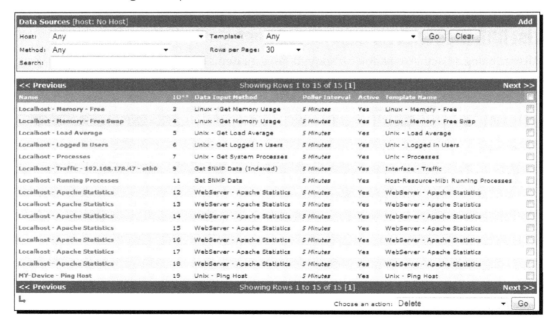

```
root@localhost:/var/www/html/cacti/rra

[root@localhost rra]# ls -l
total 6772
-rw-r--r-- 1 cactiuser cactiuser  47844 Sep 20 00:00 heute_de_ping_8.rrd
-rw-r--r-- 1 cactiuser cactiuser 880988 Oct  5 21:35 localhost_apache_cpuload_12.rrd
-rw-r--r-- 1 cactiuser cactiuser 880988 Oct  5 21:35 localhost_apache_cpuload_13.rrd
-rw-r--r-- 1 cactiuser cactiuser 880988 Oct  5 21:35 localhost_apache_cpuload_14.rrd
-rw-r--r-- 1 cactiuser cactiuser 880988 Oct  5 21:35 localhost_apache_cpuload_15.rrd
-rw-r--r-- 1 cactiuser cactiuser 880988 Oct  5 21:35 localhost_apache_cpuload_16.rrd
-rw-r--r-- 1 cactiuser cactiuser 880988 Oct  5 21:35 localhost_apache_cpuload_17.rrd
-rw-r--r-- 1 cactiuser cactiuser 880988 Oct  5 21:35 localhost_apache_cpuload_18.rrd
-rw-rw-r-- 1 cactiuser cactiuser 141492 Oct  5 21:35 localhost_load_1min_5.rrd
-rw-rw-r-- 1 cactiuser cactiuser  47844 Oct  5 21:35 localhost_mem_buffers_3.rrd
-rw-rw-r-- 1 cactiuser cactiuser  47844 Oct  5 21:35 localhost_mem_swap_4.rrd
-rw-rw-r-- 1 cactiuser cactiuser  47844 Oct  5 21:35 localhost_proc_7.rrd
-rw-r--r-- 1 cactiuser cactiuser  47844 Sep  5 10:35 localhost_runprocesses_10.rrd
-rw-r--r-- 1 cactiuser cactiuser  47844 Oct  5 21:35 localhost_runprocesses_11.rrd
-rw-r--r-- 1 cactiuser cactiuser  94668 Oct  5 21:35 localhost_traffic_in_9.rrd
-rw-rw-r-- 1 cactiuser cactiuser  47844 Oct  5 21:35 localhost_users_6.rrd
-rw-r--r-- 1 cactiuser cactiuser  47844 Oct  5 21:35 my-device_ping_19.rrd
[root@localhost rra]#
```

4. Keep a note of the RRDs listed as shown in the preceding screenshot.

5. Login to your Cacti web interface as an admin user.

6. Go to **Management | Data Sources** to list all the data sources:

Name	ID**	Data Input Method	Poller Interval	Active	Template Name	
Localhost - Memory - Free	3	Linux - Get Memory Usage	5 Minutes	Yes	Linux - Memory - Free	
Localhost - Memory - Free Swap	4	Linux - Get Memory Usage	5 Minutes	Yes	Linux - Memory - Free Swap	
Localhost - Load Average	5	Unix - Get Load Average	5 Minutes	Yes	Unix - Load Average	
Localhost - Logged In Users	6	Unix - Get Logged In Users	5 Minutes	Yes	Unix - Logged In Users	
Localhost - Processes	7	Unix - Get System Processes	5 Minutes	Yes	Unix - Processes	
Localhost - Traffic - 192.168.178.47 - eth0	9	Get SNMP Data (Indexed)	5 Minutes	Yes	Interface - Traffic	
Localhost - Running Processes	11	Get SNMP Data	5 Minutes	Yes	Host-Resource-Mib: Running Processes	
Localhost - Apache Statistics	12	WebServer - Apache Statistics	5 Minutes	Yes	WebServer - Apache Statistics	
Localhost - Apache Statistics	13	WebServer - Apache Statistics	5 Minutes	Yes	WebServer - Apache Statistics	
Localhost - Apache Statistics	14	WebServer - Apache Statistics	5 Minutes	Yes	WebServer - Apache Statistics	
Localhost - Apache Statistics	15	WebServer - Apache Statistics	5 Minutes	Yes	WebServer - Apache Statistics	
Localhost - Apache Statistics	16	WebServer - Apache Statistics	5 Minutes	Yes	WebServer - Apache Statistics	
Localhost - Apache Statistics	17	WebServer - Apache Statistics	5 Minutes	Yes	WebServer - Apache Statistics	
Localhost - Apache Statistics	18	WebServer - Apache Statistics	5 Minutes	Yes	WebServer - Apache Statistics	
MY-Device - Ping Host	19	Unix - Ping Host	5 Minutes	Yes	Unix - Ping Host	

7. You can now compare the list of data sources with the RRD files listed on the command line. In the example shown, the RRD file named `heute_de_ping_8.rrd` does not exist in the web interface and is therefore an orphaned file.

What just happened?

You have used the CLI and the Cacti GUI to find unused RRD files which can be removed from the file system. As you create more graphs and data sources, the manual process quickly becomes overwhelming, so you are going to build a short script to perform this task for you.

 The `RRDCleaner` plugin provides the same functionality but adds this to the Cacti GUI itself.

Automating the orphaned RRD file check

Automating the RRD file check involves some interaction with the Cacti database. The following script will read the data source IDs from the database and compare these with the RRD files from the file system:

```perl
#!/usr/bin/perl

# be strict with ourselves
use strict;

# Set some constants to make the code better readable
use constant FALSE => 0;
use constant TRUE => 1;

# where is the rra directory of Cacti ?
my $rraDir = '/var/www/html/cacti/rra';

# What are the database credentials ?
my $dbUser = 'cactiuser';
my $dbPwd = 'myPassw0rd';

# get all the data source ids from the database:
my $commandOutput = `echo "Select id from data_local;" |
 mysql -B -N -L -u $dbUser --password=$dbPwd cacti |
 awk '{ print $1}'`;

# create an array with he data source ids by
# splitting the output string at the newline char:
my @dataSourcesList = split/\n/,$commandOutput;
```

```
# open the rra directory for reading
opendir( DIR, $rraDir );

# while the directory contains files,
# read the filename one by one:
while ( my $file = readdir ( DIR ) ) {
    # skip all files that do not end with rrd:
    next if ( not( $file =~ m/\.rrd$/ig ) );

    # We do not know yet if the file exists:
    my $fileExists = FALSE;

    # Cycle through each of the data source ids and check
# if the file exists
    foreach my $dataSource ( @dataSourcesList ) {
            # The filename should end with e.g. '_8.rrd'
            if ( $file =~ m/_$dataSource\.rrd$/ ) {
                    # if it does, then we did find the file !
                    $fileExists = TRUE;
            }
    }
    # If we did not find the file, we can/should remove it:
    if ( $fileExists == FALSE ) {
            print "File [$file] does not exist`in the db. Removing\n";
            # unlink( $file );
    }
}
closedir( DIR );
```

Let's have a closer look at the different parts of this script. It first defines some variables and constants before connecting to the database, using the built-in `mysql` commands and executing a SQL statement:

```
echo "Select id from data_local;" | mysql -B -N -L -u $dbUser --
password=$dbPwd cacti
```

This command will list all datasource IDs from the Cacti database. Using these IDs the script then goes on and cycles through each of the RRD files found in the `rra` directory. If the filename matches the data ID, it marks it as valid; otherwise it is marked as orphaned. The line of the script that actually performs the deletion of the file is commented out. You can choose whatever you like to do with the file, for example, just rename it or move it to another directory.

When executing this script, you will see an output similar to the following:

```
[root@localhost cacti]# perl  /root/checkRRDfiles.pl
File [localhost_runprocesses_10.rrd] does not exist`in the database. Removing
File [heute_de_ping_8.rrd] does not exist`in the database. Removing
[root@localhost cacti]#
```

A short overview of the Cacti CLI functionality

As you've learned in previous chapters, Cacti comes with several CLI scripts suitable for some of Cacti's maintenance tasks. The CLI scripts can be found in the `cli` directory of the base Cacti installation.

The `cli` directory contains two repair scripts which you may want to use in case of database corruption or template errors, and if you do not want to lose all the configuration data since your last backup.

Repairing templates

It may happen that some of the data or graph templates have errors. You can then try to repair these templates by using the `repair_templates.php` script. Issue the following command to check for errors. Using the `-execute` parameter will help fix any errors shown:

`cd /var/www/html/cacti/cli`

`php repair_templates.php`

The following output will be shown on a working system:

```
[root@localhost cli]# php repair_templates.php
NOTE: Performing Check of Templates
NOTE: Performing Check of Data Templates
NOTE: No Damaged Data Templates Found
NOTE: Performing Check of Graph Templates
NOTE: No Damaged Graph Templates Found
[root@localhost cli]#
```

Repairing the database

Cacti also provides a repair utility for checking and repairing the database structure. Using the `repair_database.php` script may save you from restoring an older database backup. The following script should be run in order to check for any database issues:

```
cd /var/www/html/cacti/cli
php repair_database.php
```

The following output will be shown on a working system:

```
root@localhost:/tmp/cactirestore
[root@localhost cli]# php repair_database.php
Repairing All Cacti Database Tables
Repairing Table -> 'cdef' Successful
Repairing Table -> 'cdef_items' Successful
Repairing Table -> 'colors' Successful
Repairing Table -> 'data_input' Successful
Repairing Table -> 'data_input_data' Successful
Repairing Table -> 'data_input_fields' Successful
Repairing Table -> 'data_local' Successful
Repairing Table -> 'data_template' Successful
Repairing Table -> 'data_template_data' Successful
Repairing Table -> 'data_template_data_rra' Successful
```

Pop Quiz – a few questions about Chapter 6

1. Where do you add a new scheduled task?
   a. To the `config.php` file of Cacti
   b. To the `/etc/tasks` file
   c. To a new file in the `/etc/cron.d` directory

2. What MySQL command will you need to run after a full restoration on a newly installed system?
   a. `mysql -u cactiuser -p cacti import cacti_database_20101004.sql`
   b. `mysql -u cactiuser -p cacti` restore cacti_database_20101004.sql
   c. `mysql -u cactiuser -p cacti < cacti_database_20101004.sql`

3. What file do you need to change if you want to have the automated backup run at 22:00 each day?
   a. `/etc/tasks`
   b. `/etc/cron.d/cacti`
   c. `/etc/cron.d/cactiBackup`

Summary

You should now be able to create automated backups of your Cacti installation as well as do some basic maintenance work.

Specifically, you've covered:

◆ Creating an automated database and file backup—how to create a full Cacti database backup together with all-important Cacti data files

◆ Restoring from a backup—how to restore a database backup and restoring single or all Cacti files

◆ Managing the `Cacti` log file—how to include the `Cacti` log file in logrotate's configuration

◆ Basic Cacti file maintenance—how to check for orphaned RRD files

◆ Using Cacti repair utilities—how to use the Cacti CLI scripts for repairing templates and the database

You should now be able to perform some basic Cacti maintenance tasks. In the next chapter, you're going to learn how to retrieve performance data from network devices and servers using various methods. You're going to configure Windows servers and VMWare ESX systems so you can monitor the performance of these within your Cacti installation. You're also going to learn how to use the WMI interface for retrieving detailed performance statistics from Windows based operating systems.

7
Network and Server Monitoring

Let's now look at how you set up the different devices to be monitored by Cacti. In this chapter you'll learn how to set up some Cisco devices and prepare Windows systems to be monitored using WMI.

In this chapter we are going to:

- Provide a short overview of device monitoring
- Describe the setup of Cisco network devices
- Configure a VMware ESX server
- Prepare a Windows system for WMI monitoring

Let's start!

An introduction to network and server monitoring

The main task of Cacti is to measure the performance of network devices and SNMP capable servers. With some add-ons Cacti is also able to monitor WMI-enabled Windows hosts. So let's first look in more detail at the different options which you have.

Network devices

Most business class network devices are SNMP capable and therefore can be monitored by Cacti. For security reasons, SNMP access should be limited to the network management stations only using an access list. The most common performance values measured on a network device are inbound and outbound traffic of network ports and the CPU utilization of the device itself. There are many more performance items available depending on the specific capabilities of the network device.

VMware ESX

During the last few years more and more physical servers have been converted to virtual machines using one of the available virtualization platforms. VMware's main hypervisor offering is ESXi and it can be configured to allow SNMP-based performance measurement of the host and guest systems. In general, it is always better to do performance measurements of the guest systems directly because you get platform-specific numbers and features.

Linux server

By default most Linux servers come with an SNMP daemon for performance monitoring. This daemon can be configured to not only provide the basic network statistics, but also provide information by executing external programs. You have already seen this configuration earlier in this book. Therefore, the configuration of Linux systems will be skipped in this chapter.

Windows WMI monitoring

Performance measurement of Windows systems can be achieved by either enabling the SNMP service or by using WMI. WMI provides a common method for applications to provide performance statistics, so this is what you will use.

Monitoring a network device

Let's look at the configuration of a Cisco switch and PIX firewall device. You will learn how to secure the SNMP communication to the Cisco devices by using access lists and by specifically defining the Cacti server as a trusted communication partner. The configuration will only deal with SNMPv2.

Configuring SNMP access on a Cisco switch

In order to configure and secure SNMP communication between the network device and your Cacti server, you will need to know its IP address or network range. For the following examples, let's assume that your Cacti server has the IP address `10.40.0.161` and the network range of your network management systems is `10.40.0.0/255.255.255.0` Look at the following access list and SNMP commands:

```
access-list 80 remark /*****************************************
access-list 80 remark SNMP RO authorized servers
access-list 80 remark *****************************************/
access-list 80 permit 10.40.0.161
access-list 80 permit 10.40.0.0 0.0.0.255
access-list 80 deny    any
```

```
access-list 83 remark /*****************************************
access-list 83 remark SNMP RW authorized servers
access-list 83 remark *****************************************/
access-list 83 permit 10.40.0.161
access-list 83 permit 10.40.0.0 0.0.0.255
access-list 83 deny    any
!
snmp-server community public RO 80
snmp-server community private RW 83
snmp-server location EMEA/GERMANY/Kressbronn/BA/+1/
snmp-server contact +49 0123 456789/IT-Group
```

The commands define two access lists, one for accessing the read-only community and one for the read-write community of the device. The `remark` statements define some comments which will be displayed when looking at the device configuration.

The `snmp-server` commands assign the previously defined access lists to the different SNMP community strings. They also define some basic information such as the location string and contact information for the device. The location and contact information string will be shown in Cacti when adding the device.

Time for action – set up SNMP on Cisco devices

Let's now look at how to add the SNMP configuration of the preceding section to a Cisco device.

1. Logon to your network device.

2. Go into enable mode:

   enable

3. Go into configure mode:

   configure terminal

4. Copy and paste, or manually enter, the SNMP commands from the preceding section.

5. Press *CTRL+Z*.

6. Save the configuration:

   write mem

7. View the current configuration:

   sh run

What just happened?

You just configured a Cisco network device to allow SNMP polls from your Cacti server. You also set up access lists to limit the hosts that are allowed to poll the device using SNMP.

Adding Cisco switch to Cacti

Now that you have configured the SNMP agent of the device, you can add it to Cacti.

Time for action – adding a Cisco switch to Cacti

1. Go to **Management** and click on **Devices**.

2. Click on the **Add** link in the top right corner.

3. Enter the **hostname** and **description** of your Cisco device.

4. Select **Cisco Router** as the **Host Template**.

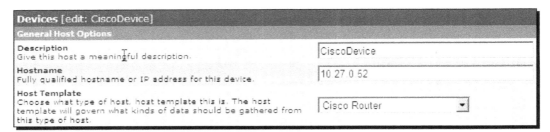

5. Select **Version 2** for the **SNMP Version** and enter the community name of your Cisco device.

6. Click on **Save** at the bottom.

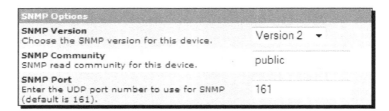

What just happened?

You just added your newly configured Cisco device to Cacti. You can now go on and monitor the different network interfaces and other statistics available on the device.

Configuring SNMP access on a Cisco PIX firewall

Cisco PIX firewalls have some useful information on network performance and the number of connections in use on the firewall. The following commands will enable a PIX firewall to be polled from a specific host. Each host needs to be entered separately, as there's no range command available on the PIX firewall:

```
snmp-server host inside 10.27.0.181
snmp-server location EMEA/Germany/Kressbronn/FW/+1/
snmp-server contact +49 0123 456789/IT-Group
snmp-server community public
```

Time for action – set up SNMP access on Cisco PIX

1. Logon to your network device.

2. Go into enable mode:

   `enable`

3. Go into configure mode:

   `configure terminal`

4. Copy and paste, or manually enter, the SNMP-server commands from the preceding section.

5. Press *CTRL+Z*.

6. Save the configuration:

   `write mem`

7. View the current configuration:

   `sh run`

What just happened?

You just configured a Cisco PIX firewall device to allow SNMP polls from your Cacti server.

Adding Cisco PIX Firewall to Cacti

As with most host types, Cisco PIX devices aren't included as a host template with the base install of Cacti. If you don't have a host template yet, either go to the template repository on the Cacti site or download the Cisco PIX template from this book. This template has been tested against a Cisco PIX Firewall Version 6.3(5). For the next few steps, let's assume you're using the version from this book.

Time for action – adding a Cisco PIX Firewall to Cacti

1. Download the `cacti_host_template_pix_firewall.xml` file.

2. Login to Cacti as an admin user.

3. Go to **Import/Export** and click on the **Import Templates** link.

4. Select the downloaded file in the **Import Template from Local File box**

5. Click on the **Import** button.

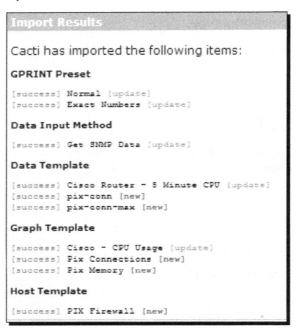

6. Go to **Management** and click on **Devices.**

7. Click on the **Add** link in the top right corner.

8. Enter the **hostname** and **description** of your Cisco PIX firewall.

9. Select **PIX Firewall** as the host template.

10. Select **Version 2** for **the SNMP Version** and enter the community name of your Windows system.

11. Click on the **Create** button.

What just happened?

You've just imported the Cisco PIX Firewall template and used it during device creation. You can now select the different graphs and poll performance data from your PIX firewall.

Monitoring VMware ESX servers

The monitoring of VMware or any other kind of virtualization server is as important as the guests running on it. Unlike normal systems, performance problems on the virtualization hosts will affect many more systems and applications. Therefore, knowing the current, past, and possible future state of the hosts' performance is of great importance.

Set up SNMP access for VMware ESXi 4

In order to set up SNMP access on a VMware ESXi server, you'll need to have the vSphere CLI client installed. The client can be obtained free of charge from www.vmware.com. Let's assume you've already downloaded and installed the CLI client on a Windows system.

Time for action – set up SNMP access on an ESXi 4 server

1. Go to **Start**, click on **Run ...** and enter:
   ```
   cmd
   ```

2. Click on **Ok.**

3. Go to the directory where you installed the vSphere CLI:
   ```
   cd C:\Program Files\VMware\ VMware vSphere Client\bin
   ```

4. Change the community of the ESXi host (change the IP and user credentials):
   ```
   vicfg-snmp.pl -server esxhost -username root -password rootpwd -c
   public
   ```

```
C:\Programme\VMware\VMware vSphere CLI\bin>vicfg-snmp.pl --server
public
Changing community list to: public...
Complete.
```

5. Enable the SNMP agent on the server:

```
vicfg-snmp.pl -server esxhost -username root -password rootpwd -E
```

6. The following message will confirm that the agent has been enabled:

```
C:\Programme\VMware\VMware vSphere CLI\bin>vicfg-snmp.pl

Enabling agent...
Complete.
```

What just happened?

You just configured and enabled the SNMP agent on a VMware ESXi 4 server using the vShpere CLI.

Set up SNMP access to VMware ESX 3.5

The SNMP access on a VMware ESX 3.5 system differs in that it comes with the NET-SNMP agent included with most Linux distributions. You will need to edit the SNMP configuration file and allow the SNMP traffic to go through the firewall. Let's look at how you can achieve this.

Time for action – set up SNMP access on an ESX 3.5 server

1. Login to your ESX system and become the root user.

2. Edit the SNMP configuration file.

```
vi /etc/snmp
```

3. Change the file to fit your settings:

```
192.168.178.47 - KiTTY
# Sample snmpd.conf containing VMware MIB module entries.

# This is a simple snmpd.conf that may help you test SNMP.
# It is not recommended for production use. Consult the
# snmpd.conf(5) man pages to set up a secure installation.

syscontact root@localhost (edit snmpd.conf)
syslocation room1 (edit snmpd.conf)
rocommunity public
trapcommunity trapCommunity
trapsink 10.40.0.200

# VMware MIB modules. To enable/disable VMware MIB items
# add/remove the following entries.
dlmod SNMPESX              /usr/lib/vmware/snmp/libSNMPESX.so

# Allow Systems Management Data Engine SNMP to connect to snmpd using SMUX
smuxpeer .1.3.6.1.4.1.674.10892.1

-- REPLACE --
```

4. Save the file.

5. Allow SNMP traffic to go through the firewall:

   ```
   esxcfg-firewall -e snmpd
   esxcfg-firewall -blockOutgoing
   ```

6. Enable the SNMP daemon on startup and restart the daemon:

   ```
   chkconfig snmpd on
   /etc/init.d/snmpd restart
   ```

What just happened?

You just enabled the SNMP daemon on your ESX 3.5 host and also opened the SNMP port in the ESX firewall. You can now add the ESX host to Cacti and perform SNMP-based polling.

Adding VMware ESX servers to Cacti

Now that you have enabled the SNMP agent on your ESX server, you can proceed with adding it to Cacti. There are some templates available on the Cacti website which work for version 3.5 of ESX, but they are only recommended if you are not using VMware's vMotion technology (as the virtual guest systems will move around without the SNMP agent realizing this).

Time for action – adding a VMware ESX host to Cacti

1. Go to **Management** and click on **Devices.**

2. Click on the **Add** link at the top right corner.

3. Enter the **hostname** and **description** of your ESX server.

4. Select **Version 2** for **the SNMP Version** and enter the community name of your VMware ESX system.

5. Click on the **Create** button.

6. You'll see the SNMP information on top showing the ESX version:

   esxhost (10.40.0.60)
   SNMP Information
   System:VMware ESX 4.1.0 build-260247 VMware, Inc. x86_64
   Uptime: 357388500 (41 days, 8 hours, 44 minutes)
   Hostname: esxhost
   Location: not set
   Contact: not set

Windows monitoring

There are several ways in which you can monitor a Windows host:

- By retrieving data using SNMP
- By retrieving data using WMI
- By collecting data with Windows PowerShell commands (for example, using the remote SSH command execution method)

Let's look into the SNMP and WMI methods in more detail using a Windows 2008 R2 server.

Windows SNMP setup

On a new Windows Server 2008 R2, by default the SNMP service is not installed. In order for Cacti to poll this server, you will need to enable this feature.

Time for action – enabling the SNMP server feature

1. Logon to your Windows system as an administrator.

2. Go to **Control Panel** then to **Administrative Tools.**

3. Start the **Server Manager** and click on the **Add Features** link:

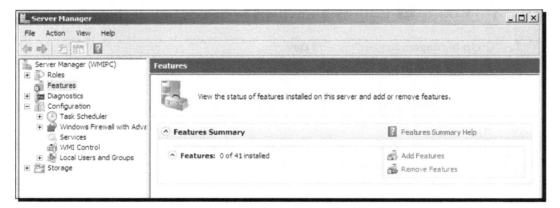

4. In the new window, select the **SNMP features** as shown in the following screenshot:

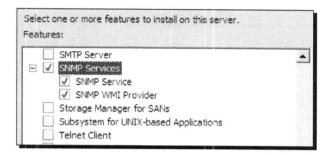

5. Click on **Next** , then on **Install.**

6. When the installation is finished, close the window and reboot the server.

What just happened?

You just installed and enabled the **SNMP Service** on Windows. After rebooting you'll be able to set security settings like community and allowed management stations. Changing these settings is your next step.

Configuration of the Windows SNMP service

After the installation of the SNMP feature, you'll not be able to poll the system for any performance data because the default settings only allow the localhost system to access the SNMP service. You'll now add your Cacti server to the list of allowed hosts and set a read-only community name for Cacti to use.

Time for action – configuring the Windows SNMP service

1. Logon to your Windows system as an administrator.

2. Go to **Start** then to **Administrative Tools** and click on **Services.**

3. Look for the **SNMP Service** and right-click on it.

4. Select **Properties** and make sure the **Startup type** is set to **Automatic.**

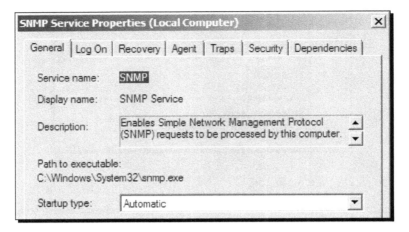

5. Select the **Agent** tab and enter the **Contact** and **Location** information.

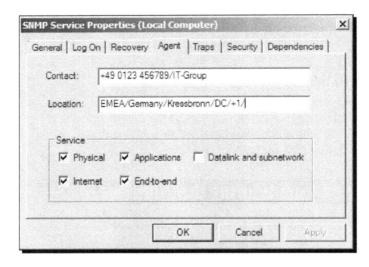

6. Select the **Security** tab and add some **Community names** and your Cacti server's IP address to the list at the bottom.

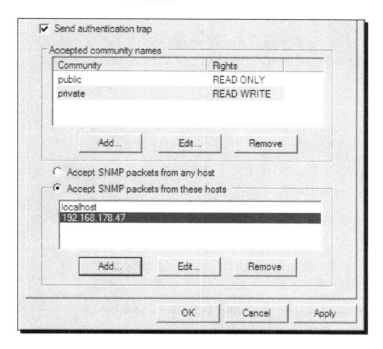

7. Click on **Apply** and then on **Ok.**

8. Restart the SNMP Service to activate the changes you made.

What just happened?

You just configured your Windows SNMP service. You can now add this Windows server to Cacti and start polling some of the basic SNMP information provided such as hard disk space and interface statistics.

WMI setup

WMI is secured by the normal Windows security methods, therefore you'll need to create a dedicated WMI user and assign it the appropriate access rights to WMI. In this case you're creating a local user account, but if the Windows server is part of an Active Directory domain it's possible to perform these steps (except 1-7) with a domain account.

Time for action – setting up a Windows WMI user

1. Logon to your Windows system as an administrator.

2. Go to **Control Panel** then to **Administrative Tools** and double-click on **Computer Management.**

3. Click on **Local Users and Groups** and then click on **Users.**

4. Click on the **Action** menu and select **New User**.

5. Enter **wmiuser** as the **User name** and enter a password.

6. Set everything as shown in the following screenshot:

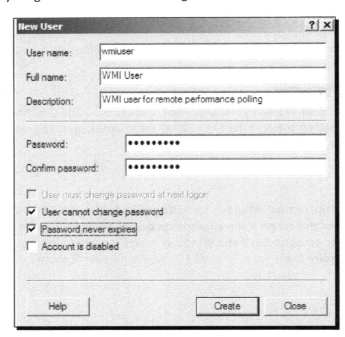

7. Click on the **Create** button.

8. Edit the user and go to the **Member Of** tab.

9. Add the **Performance Log Users** and **Performance Monitor Users** group to the list.

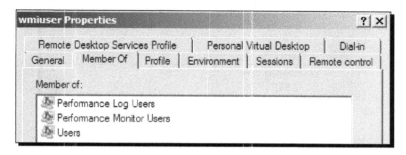

10. Click on **Apply**, then click on **Ok**.

11. In the left pane, expand the **Services and Applications** group and right-click on **WMI Control**.

12. Select the **Properties** entry.

13. In the new dialog box, click on the **Security** tab and select **CIMV2** from the list.

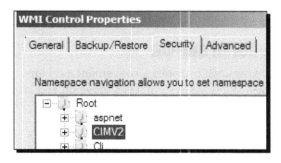

14. Click on the **Security** button.

15. Add the **wmiuser** you created earlier to the list and assign it **Enable Account** and **Remote Enable** permissions.

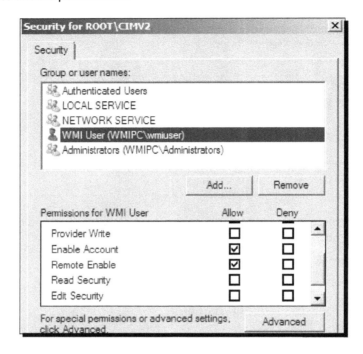

16. Click on **Apply** and then click on **Ok**.

17. Now restart the WMI service in order to apply these changes.

What just happened?

You just added a user capable of doing remote WMI calls. You will be using this user to remotely poll performance data with the CactiWMI add-on from a Linux system.

Installing the CactiWMI add-on

The WMI add-on available for Cacti provides a convenient data input method to access the WMI features provided by a Windows system. Let's move on and install it.

Installing the wmi.php Cacti interface

As already mentioned, the CactiWMI add-on comes with a script which is used by the different data input methods. The script needs to be placed in the appropriate directory and some minor configuration tasks need to be carried out.

The forum entry for the CactiWMI add-on can be found here:

`http://forums.cacti.net/viewtopic.php?f=12&t=30438`.

Time for action – installing the CactiWMI add-on – Part 1

1. Logon to your Cacti server.

2. Change to the `/tmp` directory:

   ```
   cd /tmp
   ```

3. Download the Cacti WMI add-on (`http://forums.cacti.net/download/file.php?id=16949`):

   ```
   wget -O CactiWMI.tgz
   ```

4. Extract the files from the archive:

   ```
   tar -xzvf CactiWMI.tgz
   ```

5. Change into the created directory:

   ```
   cd 0.0.6.r101/
   ```

6. Run the following commands. They will copy the `wmi` script to the correct Cacti path as well as create the necessary directories. The `chmod` commands change the permissions of the files so Cacti is able to perform WMI calls:

   ```
   cp wmi.php /var/www/html/cacti/scripts
   mkdir -p /etc/cacti
   mkdir -p /var/log/cacti/wmi
   chown cactiuser:cactiuser /etc/cacti -R
   chown cactiuser:cactiuser /var/log/cacti/wmi -R
   chmod 700 /etc/cacti -R
   chmod 700 /var/log/cacti/wmi -R
   ```

7. Now create the `auth.conf` file which will contain your WMI user credentials:

   `vi /etc/cacti/cactiwmi.pw`

8. The file should have the following format:

   ```
   username=<your username>
   password=<your password>
   domain=<your domain>
   ```

What just happened?

You set up the files needed for the CactiWMI add-on. The `wmi.php` file provides the interface between Cacti and the program that talks to the WMI service on Windows servers.

Installing the wmic command

The `wmic` command is responsible for communication with the WMI service and is utilized by the `wmi.php` script.

Time for action – installing the CactiWMI add-on – Part 2

1. Logon to your Linux Cacti server with root privileges.

2. Make sure you've got the subversion client installed:

   `yum install subversion`

3. Checkout the latest version of the source files containing the wmic command:

   `svn checkout http://dev.zenoss.org/svn/trunk/wmi/Samba/source`

4. Change into the source directory:

   `cd source`

5. Run the `autogen` script to generate the `configure` script:

   `./autogen.sh`

6. Run configure:

   `./configure`

7. After the command finishes you can run the `make all` command to compile all necessary binaries:

```
make all
```

8. This will create the `bin` directory. Change into it:

```
cd bin
```

9. Look for the `wmic` binary file and run it:

```
# ls -l wmic
-rwxr-xr-x 1 root root 6908608 Oct 17 18:28 wmic
# ./wmic --version
Version 4.0.0tp4-SVN-build-21646
```

10. Copy the `wmic` binary to `/usr/local/bin`:

```
cp wmic /usr/local/bin
```

What just happened?

You compiled the `wmic` binary which is needed to poll the WMI service on Windows systems. You've made sure that it compiled properly by running it with the version switch. You also copied the binary to a directory in your path.

Performance measurement with CactiWMI

Now that you have all the prerequisites for retrieving performance data using the WMI and SNMP interface, let's look into setting up a host with WMI.

Time for action – performance measurement with CactiWMI

1. Download the `cacti_host_template_wmi_-_all.xml` file from `http://svn.parkingdenied.com/CactiWMI/tags/0.0.6/templates/`.

2. Login to Cacti as an admin user.

3. Go to **Import/Export** and click on **Import Templates**.

4. Select the downloaded file for the **Import Template from Local File** box.

5. Click on **Import**.

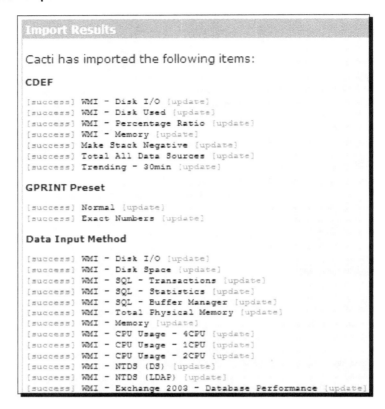

6. Go to **Management** and click on **Devices**.

7. Click on **Add** on the top right corner.

8. Enter the **Hostname** and **Description** of your Windows server.

9. Select **WMI – All** as the host template.

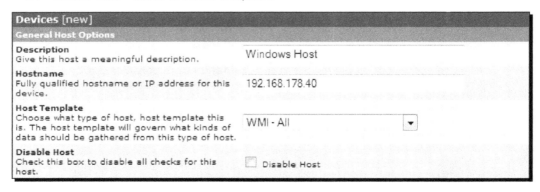

10. Select **Version 2** for **the SNMP Version** and enter the community name of your windows system.

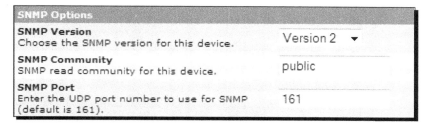

11. Click on **Create.**

12. You'll now see some of the SNMP information you entered during the SNMP service configuration.

Windows Host (192.168.178.40)
SNMP Information
System:Hardware: AMD64 Family 16 Model 2 Stepping 3 AT/AT COMPATIBLE –
Software: Windows Version 6.1 (Build 7600 Multiprocessor Free)
Uptime: 403070 (0 days, 1 hours, 7 minutes)
Hostname: WMIPC
Location: EMEA/Germany/Kressbronn/DC/+1/
Contact: +49 0123 456789/IT-Group

13. You will also see all of the WMI-based data input methods currently associated with the selected host template.

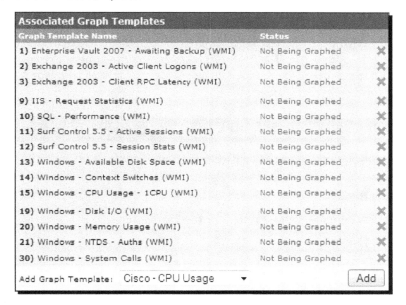

14. Click the **Create Graphs for this Host** link at the top.

15. Select some of the basic WMI graphs:

- ❑ Create: Windows - Available Disk Space (WMI)
- ❑ Create: Windows - CPU Usage - 1CPU (WMI)
- ❑ Create: Windows - Disk I/O (WMI)
- ❑ Create: Windows - Memory Usage (WMI)
- ❑ Create: Windows - Processes (WMI)

16. Click on the **Create** button. You will see the specific settings for each of the WMI graphs.

Create Graph from 'Windows - Available Disk Space (WMI)'	
Graph [Template: Windows - Available Disk Space (WMI)]	
Title (--title) The name that is printed on the graph.	|host_description| - Available Disk Space
Data Source [Template: Windows - Disk Space (WMI)]	
Name Choose a name for this data source.	|host_description| - Windows - Disk Space
Custom Data [Template: Windows - Disk Space (WMI)]	
Credential	/etc/cacti/cactiwmi.pw
Filter Value	C:

17. Confirm the settings on the following page and click on **Create**.

What just happened?

You just enabled WMI-based performance polling through Cacti. You can also configure some interface polling, by adding the **SNMP – Interface Statistics** data query to the **Associated Data Queries** list, as you've seen in earlier chapters. Don't forget to add your new host to one of your Cacti trees.

Pop quiz – a few questions about Chapter 7

1. What do you need to use to configure the SNMP daemon on an ESXi 4 vSphere host?

    a. An ssh client

    b. The system management tool for the ESXi system

    c. The vSphere CLI client

2. How do you create a new graph with WMI performance items?

   a. Add the imported WMI graph template to the device

   b. Add a WMI data query to the device

   c. Add an SNMP community to the device

3. What do you need to edit when you change the password of the WMI userID?

   a. `cactiwmi.pw in /etc/cacti`

   b. `config.php` in the include directory of the Cacti base directory

   c. `/etc/passwd`

Summary

You now have several guides at hand to configure your network devices, Windows servers, and VMware ESX servers. Each of the different systems requires different methods and configuration tasks in order to poll the performance data.

Specifically, you have covered:

◆ How to configure Cisco-based network and firewall devices to allow SNMP polling from Cacti

◆ Setting up and enabling the SNMP daemon on VMware ESX 3.5 and ESXi 4 servers

◆ How to create a WMI capable user on Windows and how to give this user enough permissions to poll WMI remotely

◆ How to install and configur the CactiWMI add-on to poll WMI of Windows systems from a Linux based Cacti system

You should now be able to extend your performance polling to a much broader range of systems including Windows servers and VMware ESX systems. In the next chapter, you're going to enhance Cacti by installing the Plugin Architecture. You are also going to install your first plugins.

8
Plugin Architecture

Now, that you have learned about the basic Cacti features, you are going to learn how to extend the capabilities of your Cacti instance with the available Plugin Architecture.

In this chapter we are going to:

- Provide a short overview of Plugin Architecture
- Install and configure Plugin Architecture
- Learn how to extend Cacti with plugins
- Allow users to use the extended features of plugins

Let's start!

Introduction to the Plugin Architecture

The Plugin Architecture is an optional set of files that extend the basic functionality of Cacti with the ability to call external functions and applications, also called "plugins".

Why plugins?

Plugins allow other external developers to implement open source as well as commercial features for Cacti without the need to change the core Cacti sources. Security patches for the core can also be safely applied without interfering with the functionality of the plugins.

Plugins allow end users to implement missing features or create specific enhancements needed for internal corporate usage.

Plugin features

As already mentioned, plugins can have different functionalities. The following is a list of features implemented by some of the available plugins:

- ◆ User interface enhancements—such as re-branding the login screen
- ◆ Accessing the Cacti database—interaction with external tools
- ◆ Manipulating RRD files—removing spikes from the graphs
- ◆ Implementing caching/performance enhancements—providing support for very large Cacti deployments
- ◆ Adding new functionality such as Reporting, Syslog, or Threshold monitoring

As you can see, plugins can extend the functionality of Cacti beyond performance monitoring to a powerful integrated network monitoring solution.

Common plugins

As there is quite a large list of plugins, not all of them are actively supported and some are still under development. Some of the plugins are quite old and are commonly known throughout the Cacti community. The following is a list and short description of three well-known plugins.

MAC Track plugin

The MAC Track plugin adds MAC address tracking functionality to Cacti. It is able to track end devices based on their IP and/or MAC address and can help tracking down the root cause of attacks, for example, virus attacks. If you have a large network and need to know the location of your devices, this plugin is worth a look.

Network WeatherMap

The Network WeatherMap plugin adds the ability to create your own network map to Cacti. Using this plugin allows you to create buildings/sites or just maps of your datacenter racks including graphical representation of link utilization and performance. The Network WeatherMap plugin can create stunning graphs which tell the story in a single easy-to-understand picture. Go and have a look at the "Show off your Weathermaps" thread in the forum at: http://forums.cacti.net/viewtopic.php?t=24433.

Thold

Thold adds threshold monitoring and alerting to Cacti. Thresholds can be set on any kind of data stored within the RRD files. Either fixed or dynamic thresholds based on an automatic baseline calculation can be set. E-mail alerts can also be configured to be sent out to one or more recipients.

You will be installing and configuring the Thold plugin in the next chapter.

Installing the Plugin Architecture

Let's start with installing the Plugin Architecture, also abbreviated as PIA.

1. Go to `http://www.cacti.net/downloads/pia/`.

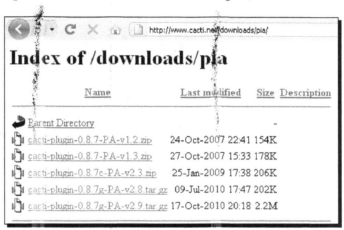

2. Right-click on the latest PIA version compatible with your installation.

3. Copy the link-target to the clipboard.

4. Logon to your Cacti installation as root.

5. Change to the Cacti base directory:

```
cd /var/www/html/cacti/
```

6. Download the PIA:

```
wget http://www.cacti.net/downloads/pia/cacti-plugin-0.8.7g-PA-
v2.9.tar.gz
```

7. Unpack the archive:

```
tar -xzvf cacti-plugin-0.8.7g-PA-v2.9.tar.gz
```

8. A new directory will be created named `cacti-plugin-arch`.

9. Run the patching process using the following command. Alternatively, you can also use the pre-patched files contained in the PIA archive:

```
patch -p1 -N < cacti-plugin-arch/cacti-plugin-0.8.7g-PA-v2.9.diff
```

10. Check for any error message as shown in the following screenshot:

11. In case of errors, you can copy the already patched files from the cacti-plugin-arch/files-0.8.7g/ directory:

```
cp cacti-plugin-arch/files-0.8.7g/poller.php .
cp cacti-plugin-arch/files-0.8.7g/data_sources.php .
```

12. Import the additional SQL statements:

```
mysql -u root -p cacti < cacti-plugin-arch/pa.sql
```

13. Check your config.php file for any settings that may have changed. The following line in particular should be checked:

```
$url_path = "/cacti/";
```

What just happened?

You just installed the latest Plugin Architecture. You are now able to add and enable plugins for your Cacti installation. However, before you do this, let's have a look at how to upgrade an existing PIA installation.

Upgrading the Plugin Architecture

When upgrading the Plugin Architecture, patching the files using the provided diff may create issues. If you have a standard Cacti installation, without any customized code within the Cacti source files, you can use the provided replacement files.

Time for action – upgrading the Plugin Architecture

1. Logon to your Cacti server as root.

2. Change to the Cacti installation directory:
   ```
   cd /var/www/html/cacti
   ```

3. Download the PIA:
   ```
   wget http://www.cacti.net/downloads/pia/cacti-plugin-0.8.7g-PA-
   v2.9.tar.gz
   ```

4. Unpack the archive:
   ```
   tar -xzvf cacti-plugin-0.8.7g-PA-v2.9.tar.gz
   ```

5. A new directory will be created named `cacti-plugin-arch`.

6. Create a backup of your `config.php` file:
   ```
   cp include/config.php include/config.php.bak
   ```

7. Copy the replacement files to your Cacti installation:
   ```
   'cp' -R cacti-plugin-arch/files-0.8.7g/* .
   ```

8. Restore your original `config` file:
   ```
   cp include/config.php.bak include/config.php
   ```

9. Import the additional SQL statements:
   ```
   mysql -u root -p cacti < cacti-plugin-arch/pa.sql
   ```

What just happened?

You just upgraded the Plugin Architecture on your Cacti instance by replacing the existing Cacti files with the provided patched versions.

Configuring the Plugin Architecture

Once you have installed the Plugin Architecture, you can assign one new realm permission to users who you want to allow the plugin administration.

Time for action – configuring the Plugin Architecture

1. Logon to your Cacti web interface as an admin user.

2. Go to **Utilities | User Management**.

3. Select the user to whom you want to allow the plugin administration.

4. Select the **Plugin Managment** box within the **Real Permissions** list.

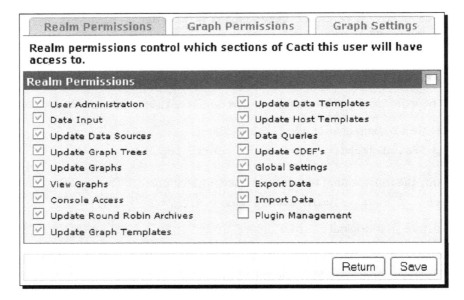

5. Click on the **Save** button.

6. You should notice a new menu called **Plugin Management** within the **Configuration** settings:

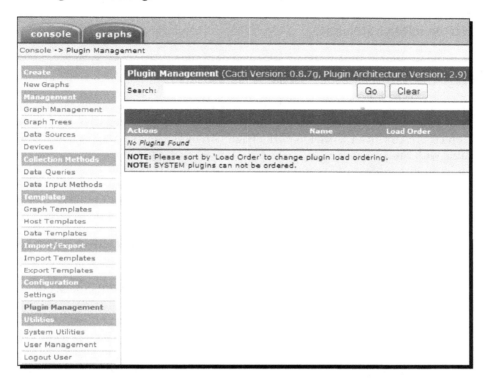

7. Click on the **Plugin Management** menu entry.

8. You will see a list of installed plugins. At the moment this list should be empty, as shown in the following screenshot:

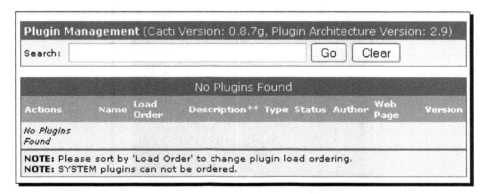

What just happened?

You just added permissions to install, enable, disable, and uninstall plugins to a user. By default, no user will have this permission, so you need to give it to at least one user in order to be able to use plugins.

Downloading and installing plugins

Now that you have successfully installed the Plugin Architecture, you can go on and install some basic plugins. The plugins available can be divided into two categories: plugins which have been created for the 1.x version of the Plugin Architecture and plugins which are compatible with the 2.x version.

The Plugin Architecture version 2.x supports pre-PIA 2.x plugins.

PIA directory structure

Besides the patching of some source files of Cacti, the Plugin Architecture also adds a new directory to the Cacti installation. The directory is named `plugins`.

Each plugin needs to be placed into this directory. The following files are needed as a minimum for each plugin to work properly:

- `setup.php`
- `index.php`

The `index.php` file only contains a redirection to the main Cacti site in order to disallow end users to browse the plugin directory freely. The `setup.php` file contains the setup and enablement code, as well as code for the different plugin hooks introduced with the patching of the Cacti source files. The following screenshot shows the directory structure of the plugins directory with one installed plugin:

Pre-PIA 2.x plugins

Up to PIA 2.8, pre-PIA 2.x plugins had to be configured manually by editing the `config.php` file and adding the plugin to a special array variable. Since 2.8, this is not needed any more and installation of PIA 1.x plugins is identical to PIA 2.x plugins.

PIA 2.x plugins

There are several basic plugins which deliver additional functionality to other plugins. These plugins include the settings plugin which, besides other functions, also provides mail support.

The plugin repository

Since the announcement and public availability of the Plugin Architecture, there has been a growing list of plugins in the Cacti forum. In order for users to get a better overview of these plugins, the Cacti team created a special plugin section within the documentation wiki. The following screenshot shows a limited list of the available plugins along with some information about each of them:

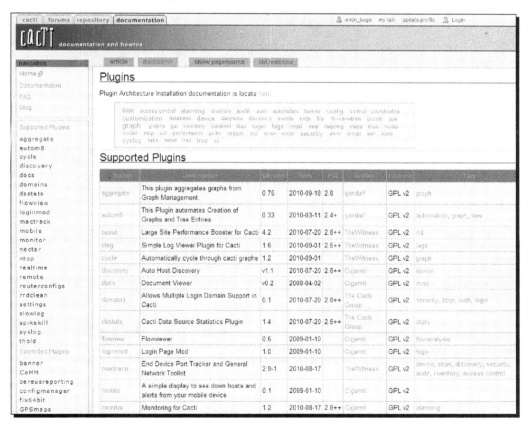

The plugin repository can be found at the following webpage:
`http://docs.cacti.net/plugins`.

The settings plugin

Besides the mail functionality which we have already mentioned, the settings plugin also provides DNS functionality. You are now going to install the settings plugin.

Time for action – installing the settings plugin

1. Go to the plugins web page at `http://docs.cacti.net/plugins`.

2. Click on the **Settings** plugin.

3. Right-click on the download link and copy the link target to the clipboard.

4. Logon to your Cacti installation as root using PuTTY.

5. Go to the new **plugins** directory:

    ```
    cd /var/www/html/cacti/plugins
    ```

6. Download the settings plugin using the following command:

    ```
    wget -O settings-v0.7-1.tgz http://docs.cacti.net/_media/plugin:
    settings-v0.7-1.tgz?id=plugin%3Asettings&cache=cache
    ```

7. Extract the archive:

    ```
    tar -xzvf settings-v0.7-1.tgz
    ```

8. Logon to your Cacti web interface using a user with **Plugin Management permissions**.

9. Go to **Configuration | Plugin Management**.

10. You should now be able to see the settings plugin in the list of available plugins:

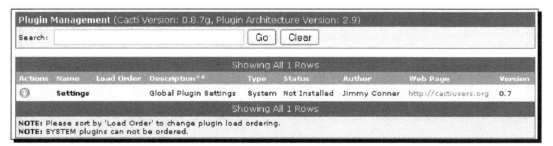

11. Click on the blue arrow icon in the **Actions** column to install the plugin. The list of icons on the **Actions** column should change as seen in the following screenshot:

12. Click on the green arrow icon on the **Actions** column to enable the plugin:

13. Now go to **Configuration | Settings**.

14. You should see a new tab called **Mail / DNS**. This tab is being provided by the settings plugin:

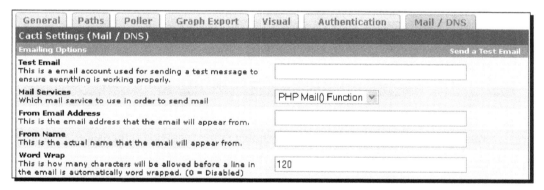

What just happened?

You just installed and enabled the settings plugin. By enabling and installing the plugin, the Plugin Architecture ran the setup function of the plugin. This special function makes sure that all required files and database tables are created and also adds the necessary links to the hooks provided by the Plugin Architecture.

Removing a plugin

Sometimes you may just want to test a new plugin and later decide to disable and remove it from your Cacti server. Let's look into the steps necessary to do so.

Time for action – removing the settings plugin

1. Logon to your Cacti web interface using a user with **Plugin Management permissions**.

2. Go to **Configuration | Plugin Management**.

3. You should now be able to see the settings plugin on the list of available plugins:

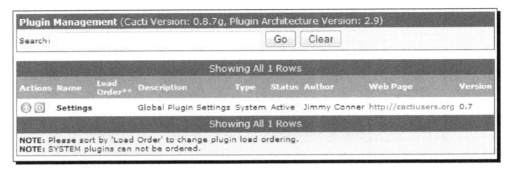

4. Click on the red icon with the circle in it in the **Actions** column to disable the plugin. The list of icons in the **Actions** column should change as seen in the following screenshot:

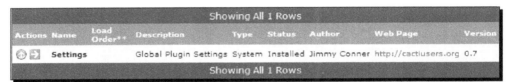

5. Click on the red arrow icon in the **Actions** column to uninstall the plugin. You will then see a blue arrow icon appear, as shown in the following screenshot:

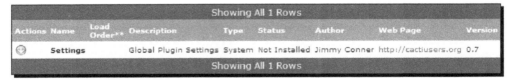

6. Now logon to your Cacti installation as root using PuTTY.

7. Go to the **plugins** directory:

    ```
    cd /var/www/html/cacti/plugins
    ```

8. Remove the settings plugin using the following command:

    ```
    rm -rf settings
    ```

What just happened?

You successfully uninstalled and removed the Settings plugin from your Cacti installation. This will also remove any database tables or columns created. If a plugin had used these tables to store some data in them, then this data will be lost after the plugin is removed. Therefore, be careful when removing or disabling a plugin.

Updating a plugin

Now that you have learned how to add and remove plugins to and from Cacti, what about updating plugins? The update of a plugin heavily depends on the plugin developer. In most cases, the update process simply involves the extraction of the new plugin and over-writing of the existing files from the old plugin installation.

The Plugin Architecture provides some functionality for the plugin developer to check for the existence of an older version and to update this accordingly.

The Settings plugin is a good example of a plugin where the update process only involves over-writing the existing files.

Before updating a plugin, make sure that you read the `readme` files or ask within the specific plugin forum topics for help on the update process.

Adding plugin permissions

Some plugins add new realm permissions in the user management page. This allows you to grant access to one user group, but deny access to another. The following screenshot shows the new user realm permission **Send Test Mail** for the settings plugin, which allows a specific user to send out a test mail in order to check the correct configuration of the settings plugin:

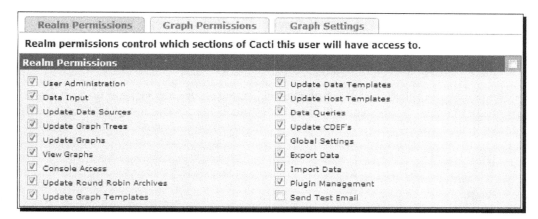

Pop Quiz – a few questions about Chapter 8

1. What do you need to check if you are unable to see the new **Plugin Management** link?

    a. The `config.php` file

    b. The `Cacti log` file

    c. The realm permissions of the user

2. How do you disable a plugin?

    a. By using the Plugin Management page

    b. By editing the `global.php` file

    c. By editing the `config.php` file

3. What plugin should you use to find out where a specific computer is located?

    a. The WeatherMap plugin

    b. The MacTrack plugin

    c. The Thold plugin

Summary

You have now successfully installed the Plugin Architecture (PIA) and are now able to add new features and functionality to your Cacti instance using external plugins.

In this chapter, you have covered:

◆ What features and functionalities plugins can provide

◆ How to install and configure the Plugin Architecture and how to provide plugin management access to a specific user

◆ Installation, update, and removal of a plugin

◆ How to set up specific plugin permissions for a user

You should now be able to add other plugins and extend your Cacti installation with new features. In the next chapter, you will learn how the plugins are structured and how to write your own plugin.

9
Plugins

Installing the Plugin Architecture enables you to extend your Cacti installation by adding new functionality through using a plugin.

In this chapter, we are going to:

◆ Provide an overview of the general plugin design based on the ntop plugin
◆ Describe commonly used plugins
◆ Create your first plugin

Let's move on!

Plugin design

Let's look at how plugins actually communicate with Cacti and the Plugin Architecture.

As mentioned earlier, the Plugin Architecture introduced several hooks into Cacti. Plugins can use these hooks to:

◆ Display additional information
◆ Add functionality to a core Cacti function
◆ Manipulate data and graphs

Let's look at some of these hooks now.

Plugin hooks

Each plugin needs to register for a hook to use. Let's have a look into the ntop plugin as it is one of the simplest plugins available.

Right at the top, the `setup.php` file contains the following function:

```
function plugin_ntop_install() {
    api_plugin_register_hook('ntop', 'top_header_tabs',          'ntop_
show_tab',              "setup.php");
    api_plugin_register_hook('ntop', 'top_graph_header_tabs', 'ntop_
show_tab',              "setup.php");
    api_plugin_register_hook('ntop', 'draw_navigation_text',    'ntop_
draw_navigation_text', "setup.php");
    api_plugin_register_hook('ntop', 'config_settings',          'ntop_
config_settings',      "setup.php");
    api_plugin_register_realm('ntop', 'ntop.php', 'View NTop', 36);
}
```

This is the install function. It is being called when you hit the install button in the plugin management screen. As you can see, it calls the special function `api_plugin_register_hook`. This function registers some of the plugin functions with the Plugin Architecture hooks. Let us look into the `ntop_config_settings` and the `ntop_show_tab` functions.

Plugin settings

Each plugin can have its own settings. Settings are normally used to let end users add special information needed for the plugin to work. In the case of the ntop plugin, this is the full URL to the ntop server.

The ntop_config_settings function

The `ntop_config_settings` function uses the special `config_settings` hook. This hook allows plugins to add fields, sections and even a new tab to the Cacti settings page (the **Configuration | Settings** menu on the Console). The following code provides this functionality:

```
function ntop_config_settings () {
    global $tabs, $settings;
    $tabs["misc"] = "Misc";

    $temp = array(
        "ntop_header" => array(
            "friendly_name" => "NTop",
            "method" => "spacer",
            ),
```

```
        "ntop_url" => array(
            "friendly_name" => "NTop URL",
            "description" => "some description",
            "method" => "textbox",
            "max_length" => 255,
            )
    );

    if (isset($settings["misc"]))
        $settings["misc"] = array_merge($settings["misc"], $temp);
    else
        $settings["misc"]=$temp;
}
```

The function is using two global variables, $tabs and $settings. The variable $tabs holds the different tabs available on the settings page. You can see these tabs in the following screenshot:

The $settings variable holds the current settings data. In order to append data to it, you will need to use these global variables.

The function starts with adding a **Misc** tab to the list of tabs using the following code:

```
$tabs["misc"] = "Misc";
```

The string to the right will be displayed on the screen. The string on the left is a unique identifier which will be used again later for the settings.

The function goes on with creating a temporary array $temp. This array holds the settings data to be displayed on the settings page. Cacti and the Plugin Architecture will take care of the database backend, so when you add fields here, they will automatically be stored in the database when you hit the save button on the settings page.

The ntop plugin adds two fields, ntop_header and ntop_url:

```
$temp = array(
    "ntop_header" => array(
        "friendly_name" => "NTop",
        "method" => "spacer",
        ),
    "ntop_url" => array(
        "friendly_name" => "NTop URL",
        "description" => "some description",
```

```
                    "method" => "textbox",
                    "max_length" => 255,
                    )
        );
```

The type of the field is defined in the special **method** variable. The `ntop_header` field is defined as a `spacer`, which will create a new section on the **Misc** tab. The `ntop_url` field is defined as a `textbox` taking a string with a maximum length of 255 characters.

The last part of the function is checking for any already existing misc settings and merging the new ntop settings with these. If it does not exist, then it simply adds the new misc settings to the global settings array.

When installing the ntop plugin, you will see the new **Misc** tab and the new fields which have been added to this tab:

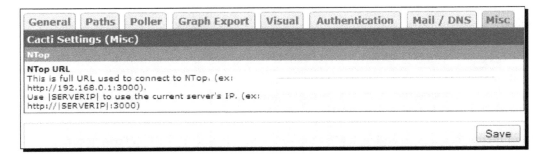

Display plugin data within Cacti

You have now seen how to add plugin-specific settings, but how can you actually use these settings and display some data within Cacti? Let's start with displaying an additional tab on the default Cacti interface next to the **graphs** tab:

The ntop_show_tab function

The `ntop_show_tab` function is registered to the two hooks `top_header_tabs` and `top_graph_header_tabs`. The `top_graph_header_tabs` will be called when you click on the **graphs** tab and view the Cacti graphs. The `top_header_tabs` will be shown when you are in the Cacti **console**.

Look at the following code segment:

```
function ntop_show_tab () {
    global $config, $user_auth_realms, $user_auth_realm_filenames;

    if (api_user_realm_auth('ntop.php')) {
        $cp = false;
        if (basename($_SERVER["PHP_SELF"]) == "ntop.php") {
        {
            $cp = true;
        }
        print '<a href="' . $config['url_path'] . 'plugins/ntop/ntop.
php"><img src="' . $config['url_path'] . 'plugins/ntop/images/tab_
ntop' . ($cp ? '_down': '') . '.gif" alt="View NTop" align="absmiddle"
border="0"></a>';
    }
}
```

This function first checks for the correct realm permissions of the user. If the user has access, it checks whether the current select page is the ntop.php page or not and sets a special variable accordingly. In the last step, the function prints the special html link including the graphical tab. Depending on the special variable set earlier, it either displays a blue tab image, or a red one, indicating that the current page is the ntop.php page. The final result on the screen can be seen on the following image:

You can now go back to the console and configure the plugin at the new **Misc** tab. Try to add the following URL as the **Ntop url: http://www.google.com**, and then click on the **ntop** tab again. You should see the Google homepage showing up within the Cacti page, as shown in the following screenshot:

Commonly used plugins

Since the introduction of the Plugin Architecture a lot of plugins for different functions have been created. There are specialized plugins that only provide one function and other more common plugins that act as a sort of container for several functions.

When creating new plugins, you should first check for already existing functionalities. Let's look at some of these plugins.

The settings plugin

You have already downloaded and installed the settings plugin in the previous chapter, but what is this settings plugin actually being used for?

Functionality

The settings plugin is a container for commonly used functions. These functions include:

- E-mail sending
- DNS lookup

The e-mail sending functionality takes care of the different options available. PHP provides an internal function, but in some situations, it makes sense to either use the tools provided by the operating system (for example, sendmail) or connect to an external mail system via SMTP. The different options and methods that need to be taken care of are handled by the settings plugin.

Therefore, many other plugins use the mail sending functionality of the settings plugin.

The superlinks plugin

The superlinks plugin provides an interface for integrating external tools or websites into Cacti. You can see it as a very advanced version of the ntop plugin described earlier.

Functionality

The superlinks plugin is great for integrating network documentation or other network management tools such as ntop within the Cacti interface. This plugin offers the following functions:

- Automated tab creation
- Creating links to other sites like an internal knowledge base or helpdesk system

Installation

For the automated tab creation feature to work properly, you will need to install and load the GD module for PHP. To do this, simply type in the following command as the root user on the command line interface of your Cacti server. Other distributions may require a different command:

```
yum install php-gd
```

Follow the on-screen guidelines and accept the installation. You will need to restart your web server for the module to become active:

```
/etc/init.d/httpd restart
```

You will also need to make the `tab_images` directory writeable by the web server:

```
chown apache /var/www/html/cacti/plugins/superlinks/tab_images/
```

You can now install the plugin using the plugin management frontend within Cacti.

The version that comes with this book has been rewritten to work with version 0.8.7g of Cacti.

Configuration and usage

If you are the admin user within Cacti, you will notice a new menu entry in the console menu. Let's see how we can use the superlinks plugin to add our Google page here.

Time for action – adding an external page to Cacti

1. Logon to your Cacti web interface as the admin user.

2. Go to **Management | SuperLinks Pages**.

3. Click on the **Add** link at the top right of the table that appears.

4. As can be seen in the following screenshot, you will be presented with a list of available options. Click on the **Add** link next to the **Generic Hypertext Document URL** option.

5. Add **Google** as the **Tab/Menu Name**.

6. Add **http://www.google.com** as the **Content File/URL** as seen in the following screenshot:

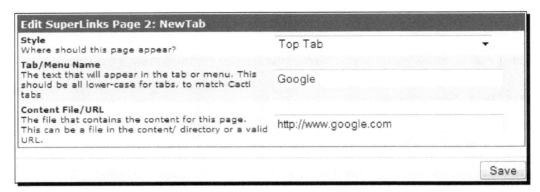

7. Click on the **Save** button. You can now click on the new Google tab and should be able to see the Google home page.

What just happened?

You just installed the superlinks plugin and added an external web page to your Cacti installation. You are now able to integrate intranet and Internet resources into Cacti, as well as create HTML-based websites to be displayed. Have a look at the examples that come with the superlinks plugin for some further information.

Creating a new plugin

Now it is time for you to create your very first plugin. You will go through the different steps from the concept of the plugin to its installation within Cacti.

The plugin will be quite simple but will show you most of the common features and hooks of the Plugin Architecture.

File structure

All plugins should at least consist of an `index.php` and `setup.php` file. These two files are required for any plugin to work properly, but of course, you should consider adding a `readme` file, as well as further documentation to your plugin. You can find a more complete file structure for plugins on the Cacti website here:

`http://docs.cacti.net/plugins:development.reference_plugin.`

Concept and design

Let's assume that you want to display additional data such as a table at the end of each host graph. The data to be displayed will have the following requirements:

- Display the hostname and IP address
- Show location information (country, site, room)
- Display a contact address (e-mail)
- Have a longitude and latitude field
- Free text/HTML can be added

Based on this information you will need to decide where you want to add this information. The following options are possible:

- Add fields to the host form offered by Cacti
- Add a separate form where this information can be entered

In order to show you the different types, you are going to use both options. You will add some of the fields to the host form, and you will also create a new form for adding those fields.

You will also need to think about the permissions of this plugin:

- User permissions: Decides which users will be able to see the information
- Admin permissions: Admin users will be able to add the information

As you can already see here, there are many ways to interact with Cacti using the Plugin Architecture.

The name of the plugin will be `cbEnhancedInfo`, where `cb` is an abbreviation for "Cacti Book".

Now that you have a basic concept, let's look at the hooks which we will need.

PIA hooks

The Plugin Architecture hooks allow a plugin to interact with Cacti. There are a lot of hooks available. Let's look at the hooks which we are going to use.

The tree_after hook

This special hook allows additional information to be displayed at the end of the graph display on the tree view page. Using this hook allows you to include all of the information defined earlier.

The draw_navigation_text hook

This special hook adds the breadcrumb information when adding additional form and web pages to the console. It's always a good idea to use this hook to fill the special $nav variable with data.

The config_arrays hook

This hook can be used to add new menu entries to the console menu. In general, this hook provides access to the generic Cacti `config` arrays. You will add a new entry for your special form in here.

The config_settings hook

As you have learned earlier, this hook can be used to create plugin-specific settings tabs. You are going to add an option to the Misc tab to enable or disable the display of this information.

The config_form hook

This hook allows the manipulation of the core Cacti forms. You will add some of the fields to the host form using this hook.

The api_device_save hook

As you have manipulated the host form, this hook allows you to actually store the data you have entered in your new host field.

No other plugin hooks are needed.

The plugin setup

Based on the concept and the hooks you are going to use, let's start building the `setup.php` file. For better readability, the `setup.php` file will be split into the different functions used.

The plugin_cbEnhancedInfo_install function

This function is needed in order for the Plugin Architecture to register the hooks used and setup the realm permissions. Let's look at the function for the `cbEnhancedInfo` plugin:

```
function plugin_cbEnhancedInfo_install () {
    api_plugin_register_hook('cbEnhancedInfo',
            'draw_navigation_text',
            'cbEnhancedInfo_draw_navigation_text',
            'setup.php');
    api_plugin_register_hook('cbEnhancedInfo',
            'config_arrays', '
            cbEnhancedInfo_config_arrays',
            'setup.php');
    api_plugin_register_hook('cbEnhancedInfo',
            'config_settings',
            'cbEnhancedInfo_config_settings',
            'setup.php');
    api_plugin_register_hook('cbEnhancedInfo',
            'config_form',
            'cbEnhancedInfo_config_form',
            'setup.php');
    api_plugin_register_hook('cbEnhancedInfo',
            'console_after',
            'cbEnhancedInfo_console_after',
            'setup.php');
    api_plugin_register_hook('cbEnhancedInfo',
            'tree_after',
            'cbEnhancedInfo_tree_after',
            'setup.php');
    api_plugin_register_hook('cbEnhancedInfo',
            'api_device_save',
            'cbEnhancedInfo_api_device_save',
            'setup.php');
    cbEnhancedInfo_setup_table_new ();

}
```

This function registers all of the hooks mentioned earlier. As you can see, the hooks are matched to the plugin function which you still need to create.

Unfortunately, this function is still missing the permission setup. Let's look at how to add this next.

Time for action – adding the realm permission functions

You're going to register two realms, one realm allows the viewing of the enhanced information, the other one allows the creation of this information. You're going to use the files from Example 1 for this part.

1. Open the `setup.php` from the `cbEnhancedInfo` directory.

2. Go to the end of the first function named `plugin_cbEnhancedInfo_install`.

3. There's a comment displayed:
   ```
   /* The realm permissions are missing here --->*/
   /* <--- */
   ```

4. Between these two errors, enter the following line:
   ```
   api_plugin_register_realm('cbEnhancedInfo',
               '',
               'Plugin - cbEnhancedInfo - View Information',
               2701);
   ```

5. This line will register the permission realm which allows a user to view the enhanced information on the tree-view page.

6. After the code you just entered, add the following lines:
   ```
   api_plugin_register_realm('cbEnhancedInfo',
   'cbEnhancedInfo_listInformation.php,cbEnhancedInfo_addInformation.
   php',
   'Plugin - cbEnhancedInfo - Add Information',
   2702);
   ```

7. This code allows a user to add the enhanced information on a separate management page described later in this chapter.

8. Now save the file.

9. Upload the `cbEnhancedInfo` directory to your `plugins` directory, install, and enable the plugin. You will be able to see the realms in the user management screen.

What just happened?

You just added the realm permissions needed to allow users to add and view the enhanced information. Realm permissions are automatically checked when a user calls one of the PHP files.

The cbEnhancedInfo_draw_navigation_text function

This function adds some navigational text to the PHP files you are about to create. Let's have a look at it:

```
function cbEnhancedInfo_draw_navigation_text ( $nav ) {
    // Report Scheduler
    $nav["cbEnhancedInfo_listInformation.php:"] = array(
     "title" => "Enhanced Information List",
     "mapping" => "index.php:",
     "url" => "cbEnhancedInfo_listInformation.php",
     "level" => "1"
    );
    $nav["cbEnhancedInfo_addInformation.php:add"] = array(
     "title" => "(Add)",
     "mapping" => "index.php:,?",
     "url" => "cbEnhancedInfo_addInformation",
     "level" => "2"
    );
    $nav["cbEnhancedInfo_addInformation.php:update"] = array(
     "title" => "(Edit)",
     "mapping" => "index.php:,?",
     "url" => "cbEnhancedInfo_addInformation.php",
     "level" => "2"
    );
    return $nav;
}
```

As you can see, there are three entries for the special $nav variable. The first one adds a navigation entry for the listInformation view. The other two add some navigation entries for adding and updating information.

Each entry contains several fields. Only the title and level fields are actually important. The title is the text being displayed on the navigational bar. The level item tells Cacti where to put the text.

Example: Home | Level 1 | Level 2

The cbEnhancedInfo_config_form function

This function adds three fields to the host screen: Country, Site, and Room. In order to add fields to a host, you will need to manipulate the special variable $fields_host_edit by adding more elements to it.

```
function cbEnhancedInfo_config_form() {
    global $fields_host_edit;

    $fields_host_edit2 = $fields_host_edit;
    $fields_host_edit3 = array();
    foreach ($fields_host_edit2 as $f => $a) {
      $fields_host_edit3[$f] = $a;
     if ($f == 'disabled') {
        $fields_host_edit3["ebEnhancedInfo_country"] = array(
        "method" => "textbox",
        "friendly_name" => "Host Country",
        "description" => "The country where this host is.",
        "value" => "|arg1:ebEnhancedInfo_country|",
        "max_length" => "255",
        "form_id" => false
        );
        $fields_host_edit3["ebEnhancedInfo_site"] = array(
         "method" => "textbox",
         "friendly_name" => "Host Site",
         "description" => "The site where this host is.",
         "value" => "|arg1:ebEnhancedInfo_site|",
         "max_length" => "255",
         "form_id" => false
        );
        $fields_host_edit3["ebEnhancedInfo_room"] = array(
        "method" => "textbox",
        "friendly_name" => "Host Room",
        "description" => "The room where this host is.",
        "value" => "|arg1:ebEnhancedInfo_room|",
        "max_length" => "255",
        "form_id" => false
        );
      } // end $f == disabled
    } // end foreach
    $fields_host_edit = $fields_host_edit3;
}
```

The new fields are added right after the **Disable Host** field as shown in the following image:

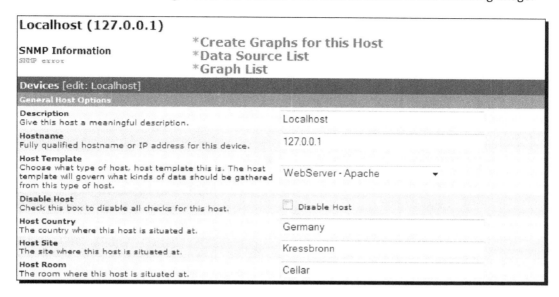

The cbEnhancedInfo_api_device_save function

This function is responsible for storing the new host fields in the Cacti database. In order to do so, it is populating the special $save variables with the new information. The following code shows this functionality using the ebEnhancedInfo_country field as an example:

```
function cbEnhancedInfo_api_device_save ($save) {
    if (isset($_POST['ebEnhancedInfo_country'])) {
    $save["ebEnhancedInfo_country"] =
      form_input_validate($_POST['ebEnhancedInfo_country'],
        "ebEnhancedInfo_country",
        "",
        true,
        255
      );
    } else {
    $save['ebEnhancedInfo_country'] =
      form_input_validate('',
        "ebEnhancedInfo_country",
        "",
        true,
        255
      );
    }
}
```

Depending on the information provided by you when saving the device, the `$save` variable is populated differently. If you did not provide any input, the variable would hold an empty string for the `ebEnhancedInfo_country` field. Otherwise the field would be filled with the data you provided.

The cbEnhancedInfo_setup_table_new function

This is a special function called when installing the plugin. It takes care of modifying the existing Cacti tables as well as adding new tables. Let's look into this function in a little more detail:

```
function cbEnhancedInfo_setup_table_new () {
    global $config, $database_default;
    include_once($config["library_path"] . "/database.php");

    // Check if the cbEnhancedInfo tables are present
    $s_sql  = 'show tables from `' . $database_default . '`';
    $result = db_fetch_assoc( $s_sql ) or die ( mysql_error() );
    $a_tables = array();

    foreach($result as $index => $array) {
        foreach($array as $table) {
            $a_tables[] = $table;
        }
    }
}
```

This first part is preparing some variables which are needed later on to check for the existence of the plugin table. It uses the standard MySQL database access to connect to the MySQL database and executes the `show tables` SQL statement on the Cacti database.

Time for action – adding additional fields to the host table

Besides the country information, the plugin is also going to store the site and room information. You're not going to store this information in a new table, but will instead add new columns to the existing host table. Let's look at how you can do this. You're going to use Example 2 for this. As a preparation, you should now disable and uninstall the plugin from Example 1.

1. Open the `setup.php` file from Example 2.

2. Go to the `cbEnhancedInfo_setup_table_new` function.

3. Search for the following code:

```
/* The additional columns are missing here --->*/
/* <--- */
```

4. Between these two lines, enter the following code:

```
api_plugin_db_add_column ('cbEnhancedInfo',
                'host',
                array('name' => 'ebEnhancedInfo_country',
                'type' => 'varchar(1024)',
                'NULL' => true,
                'default' => ''
                )
                );
    api_plugin_db_add_column ('cbEnhancedInfo',
                'host',
                array('name' => 'ebEnhancedInfo_site',
                'type' => 'varchar(1024)',
                'NULL' => true,
                'default' => ''
                )
                );
    api_plugin_db_add_column ('cbEnhancedInfo',
                'host',
                array('name' => 'ebEnhancedInfo_room',
                'type' => 'varchar(1024)',
                'NULL' => true,
                'default' => ''
                )
                );
```

5. This code will append three columns to the host table which is going to be used once you add some enhanced information on the host page and click on the **Save** button.

What just happened?

Each of the three statements adds a new column to the default Cacti host table. They are given an empty string as default values and can also be NULL values. These fields can now be used to store and retrieve the enhanced information which you provide when adding or updating a host. When you uninstall the plugin, the Plugin Architecture will make sure that it also removes these additional fields from the host table.

Now let's look at the actual table creation:

```
if (!in_array('plugin_cbEnhancedInfo_dataTable', $a_tables)) {
// Create Report Schedule Table
$data = array();
$data['columns'][] = array('name' => 'Id',
            'type' => 'mediumint(25)',
            'unsigned' => 'unsigned',
            'NULL' => false,
            'auto_increment' => true);
$data['columns'][] = array('name' => 'hostId',
            'type' => 'mediumint(25)',
            'unsigned' => 'unsigned',
            'NULL' => false,
            'default' => '0');
$data['columns'][] = array('name' => 'longitude',
            'type' => 'varchar(1024)',
            'NULL' => false);
$data['columns'][] = array('name' => 'latitude',
            'type' => 'varchar(1024)',
            'NULL' => false);
$data['columns'][] = array('name' => 'contactAddress',
            'type' => 'varchar(1024)',
            'NULL' => false);
$data['columns'][] = array('name' => 'additionalInformation',
            'type' => 'text',
            'NULL' => true);
$data['primary'] = 'Id';
$data['keys'][] = array('name' => 'hostId', 'columns' =>
'hostId');
$data['type'] = 'MyISAM';
$data['comment'] = 'cbEnhancedInfo Data Table';
api_plugin_db_table_create ('cbEnhancedInfo', 'plugin_
cbEnhancedInfo_dataTable', $data);
    }
```

As you can see, this part first checks if the table already exists, and only creates the table if it does not. The table creation consists of creating a special `table` array and adding the different columns, also as arrays, to it. If you have some experience with database table creation, this should be self-explanatory for you.

The cbEnhancedInfo_config_settings function

As we have already seen earlier, this function will add some plugin-specific settings to the **Misc** tab:

```
function cbEnhancedInfo_config_settings () {
    global $tabs, $settings;
    $tabs["misc"] = "Misc";

    $temp = array(
            "cbEnhancedInfo_header" => array(
        "friendly_name" => "cbEnhancedInfo Plugin",
        "method" => "spacer",
        ),
         "cbEnhancedInfo_showInfo" => array(
                "friendly_name" => "Display enhanced information a the
tree view",
                "description" => "This will display enhanced
information after the tree view graph.",
                "method" => "checkbox",
                "max_length" => "255"
            ),
    );

        if (isset($settings["misc"]))
                $settings["misc"] = array_merge($settings["misc"],
$temp);
        else
                $settings["misc"] = $temp;
}
```

The function will add two entries to the **Misc** tab, one is only a separator, the other entry adds a checkbox where you can turn on and off the enhanced information display on the tree view page. Look at the following screenshot to see the result of this code:

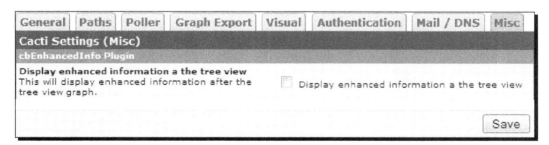

The cbEnhancedInfo_config_arrays function

This function enables you to create special menu entries on the console menu:

```
function cbEnhancedInfo_config_arrays () {
    global $menu;
    $temp = array(
        "plugins/cbEnhancedInfo/cbEnhancedInfo_listInformation.php" =>
    "Enhanced Info"
    );

        if (isset($menu["cbPlugins"]))
          $menu["cbPlugins"] = array_merge($temp,
                $menu["cbPlugins"]
            );
    else
        $menu["cbPlugins"] = $temp;
}
```

As you can see, this function adds an array of links title pairs. It then checks the special
$menu variable for the existence of the cbPlugins menu. You can add the links to existing
Cacti core menus, but for demonstration purposes, let's create a new menu section. If the
menu exists, the $temp array is merged with the existing menu, otherwise the $temp array
will be assigned to the new menu item. The result on the console menu can be seen in the
following screenshot:

Data presentation

There's one large function left now, the cbEnhancedInfo_tree_after function. This
function creates the HTML data to be presented after the last graph on the tree view page.

Retrieve data from the database

One of the main tasks for data presentation is the retrieval of this data. Your function will retrieve the data from the Cacti database, so let's have a look at the relevant section. This is going to use the files from Example 3. As a preparation, you should remove Example 2 from Cacti and install and enable the plugin contained in Example 3. You should also add some sample data to the localhost device.

Time for action – retrieve data from the database

1. Open the `setup.php` file from Example 3.

2. Go to the `cbEnhancedInfo_tree_after` function.

3. Search for the following code:

    ```
    /* Example 3 - Data retrieval is missing here ---> */
    /* <--- */
    ```

4. Between these two lines, enter the following code:

    ```
    // Retrieve the enhanced information for that host from the table
    $host_longitude = db_fetch_cell("
    SELECT longitude
    FROM plugin_cbEnhancedInfo_dataTable
    WHERE hostId=$host_leaf_id");
    $host_latitude = db_fetch_cell("
    SELECT latitude
    FROM plugin_cbEnhancedInfo_dataTable
    WHERE hostId=$host_leaf_id");
    $host_contactAddress = db_fetch_cell("
    SELECT contactAddress
    FROM plugin_cbEnhancedInfo_dataTable
    WHERE hostId=$host_leaf_id");
    $host_additionalInformation = db_fetch_cell("
    SELECT additionalInformation
    FROM plugin_cbEnhancedInfo_dataTable
    WHERE hostId=$host_leaf_id");

    // Retrieve the host specific information from the host table
    $host_country = db_fetch_cell("
    SELECT ebEnhancedInfo_country
    FROM host
    WHERE id=$host_id");
    $host_site = db_fetch_cell("
    ```

```
SELECT ebEnhancedInfo_site
FROM host
WHERE id=$host_id");
$host_room = db_fetch_cell("
SELECT ebEnhancedInfo_room
FROM host
WHERE id=$host_id");
```

5. Save the file.

6. These lines are going to fetch the enhanced information from the database. Let's see how these values actually look.

7. Logon to your Cacti system and start the MySQL client using the following command:

   ```
   mysql -u root -p
   ```

8. If you followed the book closely, the above command will ask for a password. Enter it and you will be presented with the MySQL client prompt.

9. Enter the following code to change to the Cacti database:

   ```
   use cacti;
   ```

10. The following line will retrieve the country information from the localhost device. By default, the localhost device should have the ID 1, as it's automatically added as the first device by Cacti itself:

    ```
    mysql> SELECT ebEnhancedInfo_country FROM host WHERE id=1;
    +------------------------+
    | ebEnhancedInfo_country |
    +------------------------+
    | Country A              |
    +------------------------+
    1 row in set (0.00 sec)
    ```

11. As you can see in this example, the $host_country variable is going to have **Country A** as its value.

What just happened?

The code you've entered is using the default database function to retrieve the relevant host-specific data from the Cacti database. As the enhanced information data is distributed between the host table and the newly created plugin_cbEnhancedInfo_dataTable, the data needs to be retrieved from each of these tables accordingly.

With this information stored in the $host_ variables, you can now go on and look at the actual data presentation.

Presenting data on the tree view page

As a matter of fact, data that will be presented using the `tree_after` hook needs to be embedded within a table row element `<tr>`. Let's look into the `setup.php` file from Example 3 again, to see how this can be achieved.

Time for action – presenting data on the tree view page

You're going to present the enhanced information as a table embedded in a table row.

1. Go to the `cbEnhancedInfo_tree_after` function again and search for the following code:

```
/* Example 3 - Data presentation is missing here ---> */
/* <--- */
```

2. As you can see, there's already some data between these two lines. If you're now going to the tree view page for your localhost device, you should actually see some data being displayed.

3. Replace the lines between the two code lines with the following code:

```
?>
<tr bgcolor='#6d88ad'><td>
    <tr bgcolor='#a9b7cb'>
        <td colspan='3' class='textHeaderDark'>
                <strong>Enhanced Information</strong>
        </td>
    </tr>
    <tr align='center' style='background-color: #f9f9f9;'>
        <td align='center'>
<?php

print "<table border=1>\n";
print " <tr>\n";
print "   <td>Contact Address</td>\n";
print "   <td>".$host_contactAddress."</td>\n";
print " </tr>\n";
print " <tr>\n";
print "   <td>Country/Site/Room</td>\n";
print "   <td>".$host_country.'/'.$host_site.'/'.$host_room."</td>\
n";
print "   </tr>\n";
print "   <tr>\n";
print "   <td>Longitude/Latitude</td>\n";
print "   <td>".$host_longitude.'/'.$host_latitude."</td>\n";
```

```
print "    </tr>\n";
print "  <tr>\n";
print "    <td>Additional Information</td>\n";
print "    <td>".$host_additionalInformation."</td>\n";
print "    </tr>\n";
print "</table>\n";

print "</td></tr></td></tr>";
```

4. Save the file and refresh the localhost page.

5. You should now be able to see something similar to the following screenshot:

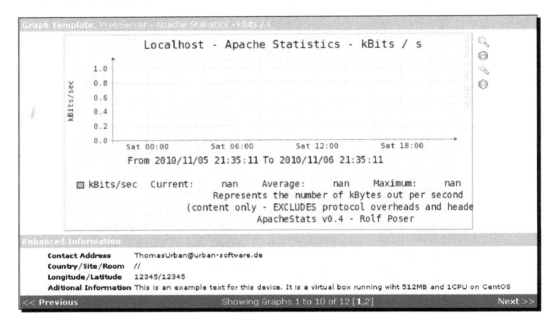

What just happened?

You just created an HTML table containing the previously defined variables. This table is embedded in a parent table row. As the `tree_after` hook is always executed at the end of the parent table presentation, the additional table you just created is going to be appended to the last shown graph, as seen in the preceding screenshot.

Creating the table list web page

In general, each Cacti web page that lists specific items comes with an action part (for example, for deleting items), a data retrieval part, and the data display part. Let's look into the action part.

The action section

This section deals with actions that are being executed on one or more selected items from the table list. The main action that all lists come with is the delete action.

Time for action – deleting data

Actions normally come with some data posted. In the case of the delete action, this data is a list of items that need to be deleted. Let's look at this action with regards to the enhanced information data:

```
function form_delete() {
    /* loop through each of the selected tasks and delete them */
    while (list($var,$val) = each($_POST)) {
        // Check $var for the number part and store the number in
        // the matches array
        if (ereg("^chk_([0-9]+)$", $var, $matches)) {
            /* ================= input validation =============== */
            input_validate_input_number($matches[1]);
            /* ================================================== */
                db_execute("
                    DELETE FROM
                        `plugin_cbEnhancedInfo_dataTable`
                    WHERE
                        `Id`='" . $matches[1] . "'"
                );
        }
    }
    // when done, redirect the end-user to the listing page
    header("Location: cbEnhancedInfo_listInformation.php");
}
```

This function analyzes all HTTP post variables and checks for any variable, the name of which starts with chk_ and ends with a number ([0-9]+). If you select one or more items on the web page, then this variable will hold the selected items. The number that is retrieved from the variable name is the actual database ID of the selected item.

After validating the number, it calls a database function to delete the item from the database.

Assuming you already added some items, let's look into the database and check what's happening here. The following command lists all current entries in the plugin_cbEnhancedInfo_dataTable:

```
mysql> SELECT * FROM plugin_cbEnhancedInfo_dataTable;
```

You should see an output similar to the following screenshot:

```
+----+--------+-----------------+-----------------+-----------------+------------------------------+
| Id | hostId | longitude       | latitude        | contactAddress  | additionalInformation        |
+----+--------+-----------------+-----------------+-----------------+------------------------------+
| 1  |      1 | Longitude Sample | Latitude Sample | Contact Sample | Some additional information   |
+----+--------+-----------------+-----------------+-----------------+------------------------------+
1 row in set (0.00 sec)
```

Let's now look at the code again:

```
db_execute("
            DELETE FROM
              `plugin_cbEnhancedInfo_dataTable`
            WHERE
              `Id`='" . $matches[1] . "'"
          );
```

As you can see this special line contains a SQL statement. Let's execute that one on the CLI:

```
mysql> DELETE FROM `plugin_cbEnhancedInfo_dataTable` WHERE `ID`='1';
Query OK, 1 row affected (0.00 sec)
```

If you now execute the previous statement again, based on this example, you will get a single line with the following text:

```
Empty set (0.00 sec)
```

This means that the entry has successfully been deleted.

What just happened?

Generally speaking, action functions are being used to work on data. This can be as simple as deleting an item, or more complex actions such as updating an existing set of data. The form_delete function described here is being used to delete one or more existing items.

The data retrieval section

This section deals with retrieving the data from the database. As you sort the HTML table from the web page, the data also needs to be sorted, too.

Time for action – sorting and retrieving data

Let's look at the following code. This code is made up of two parts; the first part is taking care of preparing the sorting statement by looking into the sort_column and sort_direction items. Using these, it builds an ORDER BY SQL statement.

The second part is then selecting different fields from two combined tables and returning the items in the requested sorting order by using the previously defined SQL statement:

```
// Take care of the sorting, did the user select any column
// to be sorted ?
if ( isset($_REQUEST["sort_column"]))
{
    // Did the user select a column that is actually sortable ?
    if (
        ( $_REQUEST["sort_column"] == 'Id' )
        || ( $_REQUEST["sort_column"] == 'hostId' )
        || ( $_REQUEST["sort_column"] == 'contactAddress' )
        || ( $_REQUEST["sort_column"] == 'longitude' )
        || ( $_REQUEST["sort_column"] == 'latitude' )
       )
    {
        // What direction should the table be sorted, ascending or
        // descending ?
        if (
            ( $_REQUEST["sort_direction"] == 'ASC' )
            || ( $_REQUEST["sort_direction"] == 'DESC' )
           )
        {
            // Finally, we can build the sort order sql statement
            $where_clause   .= ' ORDER BY ' .
                $_REQUEST["sort_column"] .
                ' ' .$_REQUEST["sort_direction"];
        }
    }
}

// Select all data items from the table. The data will be stored
// in an array. Note the $where_clause being used
$a_enhancedInfos = db_fetch_assoc("
    SELECT
        `plugin_cbEnhancedInfo_dataTable`.`Id`,
        `host`.`description` as hostDescription,
        `plugin_cbEnhancedInfo_dataTable`.`longitude`,
        `plugin_cbEnhancedInfo_dataTable`.`latitude`,
        `plugin_cbEnhancedInfo_dataTable`.`contactAddress`,
        `plugin_cbEnhancedInfo_dataTable`.`additionalInformation`
```

```
        FROM
            `plugin_cbEnhancedInfo_dataTable` INNER JOIN
            `host` ON `plugin_cbEnhancedInfo_dataTable`.`hostId` =
    `host`.`Id`
            $where_clause
    ");
```

However, why use such a complicated SQL statement when you could just do a `SELECT *` as previously seen? Let's compare these statements:

Run the following SQL statement on the MySQL CLI, assuming you've entered the data already:

```
mysql> SELECT * FROM plugin_cbEnhancedInfo_dataTable;
```

You will see a similar image as previously shown:

```
+----+--------+------------------+------------------+-----------------+--------------------------------+
| Id | hostId | longitude        | latitude         | contactAddress  | additionalInformation          |
+----+--------+------------------+------------------+-----------------+--------------------------------+
| 1  |      1 | Longitude Sample | Latitude Sample  | Contact Sample  | Some additional information     |
+----+--------+------------------+------------------+-----------------+--------------------------------+
1 row in set (0.00 sec)
```

Look at the `hostId` column. There's only a number being displayed. Now execute the following:

```
mysql> SELECT
  `plugin_cbEnhancedInfo_dataTable`.`Id`,
  `host`.`description` as hostDescription,
  `plugin_cbEnhancedInfo_dataTable`.`longitude`,
  `plugin_cbEnhancedInfo_dataTable`.`latitude`,
  `plugin_cbEnhancedInfo_dataTable`.`contactAddress`,
  `plugin_cbEnhancedInfo_dataTable`.`additionalInformation`
FROM
  `plugin_cbEnhancedInfo_dataTable`
INNER JOIN
  `host`
ON
  `plugin_cbEnhancedInfo_dataTable`.`hostId` = `host`.`id`
ORDER BY
   `hostId` DESC;
```

This time you will see the following:

```
+----+------------------+-------------------+------------------+
| Id | hostDescription  | longitude         | latitude         |
+----+------------------+-------------------+------------------+
|  1 | Localhost        | Longitude Sample  | Latitude Sample  |
+----+------------------+-------------------+------------------+
1 row in set (0.00 sec)
```

As you can see, the `hostId` column has been replaced with the `hostDescription` column which provides more useful information than a `hostId` number. As you have joined together two databases, a `SELECT *` statement would return all fields from both databases which, in this case, would amount to more than 30 fields.

You will see how to actually get down to the column data in the next section, where we will look at data presentation.

What just happened?

In this section, you have seen how to retrieve data from the database and how to order the data using the `ORDER BY` SQL statement. You have seen that you can join tables to retrieve more useful information and to replace database IDs with more descriptive values such as a hostname. Now that you have the data prepared, let's move on with the actual data presentation.

The data presentation section

This section is displaying the data using some Cacti integrated functions and some HTML-based code.

Time for action – presenting the data

If you look into the code section, you will see that the code segment begins with creating the form that is needed for the action items to work. It then goes on and checks the size of the array which has been created earlier. If the array contains items, it continues with creating the table header (`$menu_text`).

Let's look into the relevant part for actually displaying the data you retrieved in the previous step. This part can be found in the `cbEnhancedInfo_listInformation.php` file of Example 4:

```
// The html header will contain a checkbox, so the end-user can
// select all items on the table at once.
html_header_sort_checkbox(
    $menu_text,
```

```
        $_REQUEST["sort_column"],
        $_REQUEST["sort_direction"]
    );

    // This variable will be used to create te alternate colored
    // rows on the table
    $i = 0;

    // Let's cycle through the items !
    foreach ($a_enhancedInfos as $a_enhancedInfo)
    {
        // Data presentation is missing here
    }
    html_end_box(false);
```

You can see that this code is made up of three sections. The first one is creating the table header using the `html_header_sort_checkbox` function, the second section cycles through the data, and the last part is closing the table.

Let's look into the second section. As you can see, this is missing the data presentation part, so let's look into what needs to be in there.

Open the `missing_data_presentation_part.txt` file. You will see several function calls. For better readability the following call does not display all of the items contained in the file:

```
    form_alternate_row_color($colors["alternate"],
        $colors["light"],
        $i,
        'line' . $a_enhancedInfo['Id']);
    $i++;
    ...
    form_selectable_cell($a_enhancedInfo['Id'],$a_enhancedInfo["Id"]);
    form_checkbox_cell('selected_items', $a_enhancedInfo["Id"]);
    form_end_row();
```

Copy all of the lines and paste them into the `cbEnhancedInfo_listInformation.php` file. The code is starting off by creating a table row using alternate row colors by using the `form_alternate_row_color` function. It then goes on with adding each of the data items previously retrieved using the `form_selectable_cell` function. The `form_checkbox_cell` function adds a special cell to the table, allowing the user to mark the row, in order to choose an action for it. The `form_end_row` makes sure the table row is ended properly.

The following screenshot shows the resulting table, along with an item, the action drop-down box, and the page header:

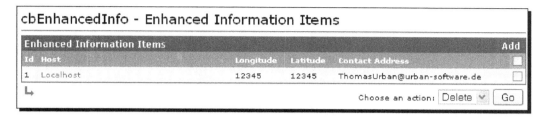

What just happened?

Using the functions provided by Cacti and the data retrieved previously, you created a table containing all the data. As you have seen, the Cacti functions take care of the actual HTML code generation and also provide the functionality for creating alternate colored table rows.

Creating the add items form

The Add Items Form will be displayed when you click on the Add link or select an existing item from the list page. A form page where you can add or update items always uses at least two functions, one of which displays the form and the other that handles the saving and updating of the Cacti database. Let's look in more detail at the functions used on your form.

The form_display function

The `form_display` function handles the data retrieval, in the case of updating an item, and the display of the Add/Update Form.

The data retrieval section

The data retrieval is nearly the same as for the list page you created earlier. This time you need to check if the `form_display` function is called in update mode or a new item will be added. When in update mode, you will need to retrieve the existing data from the database to be displayed in the form fields, so that you can see and change the data on the web page later:

```
// Initiate the default variables
$i_defaultHostId = 0;
$s_defaultLongitude = '';
$s_defaultLatitude = '';
$s_defaultContactAddress = '';
$s_defaultAdditionalInformation = '';
```

```
// Are we in the update mode?
if ( $dataId > 0 )
{
   // Yes we are, so retrieve the existing data
   // from the database:
    $a_items = db_fetch_assoc("
     SELECT
       `plugin_cbEnhancedInfo_dataTable`.`Id`,
       `plugin_cbEnhancedInfo_dataTable`.`hostId`,
       `plugin_cbEnhancedInfo_dataTable`.`longitude`,
       `plugin_cbEnhancedInfo_dataTable`.`latitude`,
       `plugin_cbEnhancedInfo_dataTable`.`contactAddress`,
       `plugin_cbEnhancedInfo_dataTable`.`additionalInformation`
     FROM
       `plugin_cbEnhancedInfo_dataTable`
     WHERE Id='$dataId'
    ");
   // Let's populate the default variables with the data
   // we retrieved from the database:
   foreach ($a_items as $a_item)
   {
     $i_defaultHostId =   $a_item['hostId'];
     $s_defaultLongitude = $a_item['longitude'];
     $s_defaultLatitude = $a_item['latitude'];
     $s_defaultContactAddress = $a_item['contactAddress'];
     $s_defaultAdditionalInformation =
        $a_item['additionalInformation'];
   }
}
```

When calling this function without a `dataId`, the first `if` function is skipped and the initial variables are used to populate the form fields.

The data presentation section

This section handles the display of the different form fields. Cacti provides several types of form fields that can be used. Some of the common ones that you'll need often are:

◆ `form_text_box`
◆ `form_hidden_box`
◆ `form_dropdown`
◆ `form_checkbox`
◆ `form_radio_button`
◆ `form_text_area`
◆ `form_save_button`

Let's look at how to use the `form_text_box`, `form_text_area`, and `form_dropdown` functions and how to start the Add/Update Form:

```
// Let's start with displaying the form
?>
<form method="post" action="cbEnhancedInfo_addInformation.php"
enctype="multipart/form-data">
<?php

// What mode are we in ?
$s_mode = '[new]';
if ( $dataId > 0 ) {
  $s_mode = '[update]';
}


// Display the html start box
html_start_box("<strong>Enhanced Information Data</strong> ".$s_mode,
"100%", $colors["header"], "3", "center", "");
```

This part should be straightforward. It's starting the HTML form and displaying the mode in the HTML start box as shown in the following screenshot:

Now let's look at the actual form elements. The first entry is using the `form_dropdown` function to display a list of all available Cacti hosts. The list of hosts is retrieved directly from the database as an `id => name` array. This array is provided to the `form_dropdown` function, which creates the actual drop-down box on the web frontend. The form field data is going to be stored in the `hostId` variable and contains the select database ID for that host:

```
form_alternate_row_color($colors["form_alternate1"],$colors["form_
alternate2"],0); ?>
    <td width="50%">
        <font class="textEditTitle">Device Name</font><br>
        The device this data set is for.
    </td>
    <td>
        <?php
        $a_hosts = db_fetch_assoc("
            SELECT
                id,
                CONCAT(description,' [',hostname,'] ') as name
            FROM
                host
        ;");
```

```
        form_dropdown("hostId",$a_hosts, "name", "id", $i_
defaultHostId, "" ,$i_defaultHostId ,"",");
        ?>
    </td>
</tr>
```

Now a `form_text_box` element is added to the frontend:

```
<?php form_alternate_row_color($colors["form_alternate1"],$colors["for
m_alternate2"],0); ?>
    <td width="50%">
        <font class="textEditTitle">Contact Address</font><br>
        A name, email or any other contact information.
    </td>
    <td>
        <?php  form_text_box("contactAddress","",$s_
defaultContactAddress,255); ?>
    </td>
</tr>
```

As you can see the `form_text_box` function takes the initial variable for the contact address as an argument and limits the input to 255 characters. The data is going to be stored in the `contactAddress` variable.

Finally, let's have a look at a text area element:

```
<?php form_alternate_row_color($colors["form_alternate1"],$colors["for
m_alternate2"],1); ?>
    <td width="50%">
        <font class="textEditTitle">Additional Information</font><br>
        Some additional information for this device.
    </td>
    <td>
        <?php form_text_area("additionalInformation",$s_
defaultAdditionalInformation,5,50,""); ?>
    </td>
</tr>
```

The `form_text_area` element provides enough space to enter larger information. This function displays an area box of 5 lines which can hold 50 characters each. The text entered is going to be stored in the `additionalInformation` variable once you click on the **Save** button.

The last part of the form is to present the save button to the end users. Depending on the mode of this form, some additional hidden fields need to be created, too:

```
if ( $dataId > 0) {
    form_hidden_box("update_component_import","1","");
    form_hidden_box("dataId",$dataId,"");
} else {
    form_hidden_box("save_component_import","1","");
}
html_end_box();
form_save_button("cbEnhancedInfo_listInformation.php", "save");
```

The existence of the different hidden fields will make sure that the form_save function knows if the data provided is going to be used for updating an existing entry, or creating a new one.

The final form page can be seen in the following screenshot:

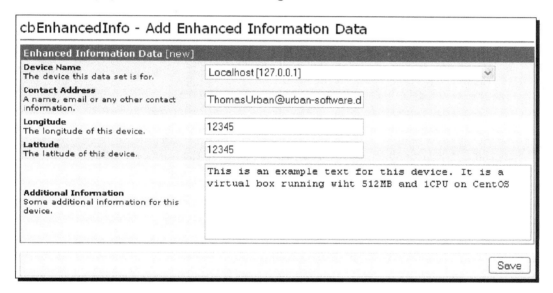

The form_save function

The form_save function takes care of creating new items or updating existing ones, depending on the hidden fields created earlier.

Time for action – retrieving data from the form post

When pressing the save button, the form values are posted to the server. The `form_save` function needs to retrieve these values and store them into the database. Let's look at how the different parts of this function work.

As the data is going to be used for updating the Cacti database, it's always a good idea to make it more secure by using the available `mysql_escape_string` function:

```
// Retrieve the data from the form post
/* Add hostId statement here */
if (isset ($_POST['longitude'])) {
    $s_dataLongitude = mysql_escape_string($_POST['longitude']);
}
if (isset ($_POST['latitude'])) {
    $s_dataLatitude = mysql_escape_string($_POST['latitude']);
}
if (isset ($_POST['contactAddress'])) {
    $s_dataContactAddress =
        mysql_escape_string($_POST['contactAddress']);
}
if (isset ($_POST['additionalInformation'])) {
    $s_dataAdditionalInformation =
        mysql_escape_string($_POST['additionalInformation']);
}
```

The special `$_POST` variable is checked for the existence of the form data and the corresponding variable is set accordingly.

As you can see, there's a comment telling you that the `hostId` statement is missing. Open the `cbEnhancedInfo_addInformation.php` file from Example 5 and add the following statement right after this comment:

```
if (isset ($_REQUEST['hostId'])) {
    $s_dataHostId= mysql_escape_string($_REQUEST['hostId']);
}
```

So why did you add a `$_REQUEST['hostId']` here instead of the `$_POST['hostId']` one? In fact, both statements are valid. The `$_REQUEST` variable holds values transmitted via a POST or GET request, while the `$_POST` variable will only have values when a form is transmitted using the POST method.

What just happened?

You just created the necessary statements for retrieving the posted data from the form described earlier. Using the special `mysql_escape_string` function you prepared the data for being stored in the database. This function will take care of converting the user-provided text strings into SQL values.

The variables can now be used to update an existing item or to add a new item to the database. Let's look into how to create new items.

Time for action – creating a new database item

Creating a new item is done by using an `INSERT` SQL statement. The following code adds a new item to the Cacti database:

```
db_execute("
  INSERT INTO `plugin_cbEnhancedInfo_dataTable`
    (`hostId`, `longitude`, `latitude`,`contactAddress`,
    `additionalInformation`)
  VALUES
    ($s_dataHostId, '$s_dataLongitude','$s_dataLatitude',
    '$s_dataContactAddress','$s_dataAdditionalInformation')
");
```

If you look into the `cbEnhancedInfo_addInformation.php` file from Example 5, you will see that this code is actually missing. You can add it right after the comment in the following section:

```
if ( (isset ($_POST['contactAddress'])) &&
     (isset ($_POST['save_component_import']) ) ) {
  /* Add Save statements here */
}
```

As you can see, the code checks for the existence of the form fields `save_component_import` and `contactAddress` before creating the new item. This will make sure that the function is only creating a new item (save) if data has been entered for the `contactAddress` field.

Let's find out what this command will look like with real data. Open a MySQL CLI and execute the following statement:

```
mysql> INSERT INTO
  `plugin_cbEnhancedInfo_dataTable`
  (`hostId`, `longitude`, `latitude`,`contactAddress`,
  `additionalInformation`)
VALUES
  (1, 'Sample Longitude','Sample Latitude',
  'My Sample Contact Address','This is a test');
```

You will see the following text:

```
Query OK, 1 row affected (0.00 sec)
```

Let's look at the database table:

```
mysql> SELECT * FROM plugin_cbEnhancedInfo_dataTable;
```

An output similar to the following will be displayed:

```
+----+--------+------------------+-----------------+--------------------------+
| Id | hostId | longitude        | latitude        | contactAddress           |
+----+--------+------------------+-----------------+--------------------------+
|  3 |      1 | Sample Longitude | Sample Latitude | My Sample Contact Address|
|  1 |      1 | Longitude Sample | Latitude Sample | Contact Sample           |
+----+--------+------------------+-----------------+--------------------------+
2 rows in set (0.00 sec)
```

What just happened?

As you can see, the function is using the SQL INSERT statement to add data to the Cacti database. The function will only use this statement if the save_component_import field has been set and the user has entered some text in the contactAddress field.

Let's look at how an update to an existing dataset is done.

Time for action – updating an existing item

When updating a new item, the special UPDATE SQL keyword can be used. The following code updates an existing item:

```
db_execute("
 UPDATE `plugin_cbEnhancedInfo_dataTable`
 Set
   hostId=$s_dataHostId,
   longitude='$s_dataLongitude',
   latitude='$s_dataLatitude',
   contactAddress='$s_dataContactAddress',
   additionalInformation='$s_dataAdditionalInformation'
 WHERE
   Id='$dataId'
");
```

As with the creation of a new item, this code is also missing from the file. You can enter it after the comment in the following section:

```
if ( (isset ($_POST['contactAddress'])) &&
    (isset ($_POST['update_component_import']) ) ) {
  /* Add Update statements here */
}
```

Let's look how the db_execute command will look with real data. Open a MySQL CLI and execute the following statement. You may have to change the Id to match your database data from the SELECT * statement in the previous section:

```
mysql> UPDATE `plugin_cbEnhancedInfo_dataTable`
  Set
    hostId=1,
    longitude='New Longitude',
    latitude='New Latitude',
    contactAddress='New Contact Address',
    additionalInformation='not available'
  WHERE
    Id=3;
```

You will see the following output:

```
Query OK, 1 row affected (0.01 sec)
Rows matched: 1  Changed: 1  Warnings: 0
```

Let's look at the database table again to see the changes:

```
mysql> SELECT * FROM plugin_cbEnhancedInfo_dataTable;
```

An output similar to the following will be displayed:

```
+----+--------+-----------------+-----------------+---------------------
| Id | hostId | longitude       | latitude        | contactAddress
+----+--------+-----------------+-----------------+---------------------
| 3  |      1 | New Longitude   | New Latitude    | New Contact Address
| 1  |      1 | Longitude Sample| Latitude Sample | Contact Sample
+----+--------+-----------------+-----------------+---------------------
2 rows in set (0.00 sec)
```

As you can see, the item has been updated accordingly.

What just happened?

You just created the update section which takes care of updating existing items. As you can see, there's only a small difference between the two preceding sections. The only difference between them are the SQL statements used.

You have now created all of the relevant parts of the plugin.

Installing the plugin

You can install this plugin using the default methods. You have created all relevant parts which are needed for the plugin management to install and enable the plugin within Cacti.

Publishing

If you created a cool new plugin which you wanted everyone to know about, you could publish it on the `cacti.net` website.

Simply go to `http://docs.cacti.net/plugins.guidelines` and follow the guidelines published there or ask in the Cacti forums for help.

Pop Quiz – a few questions about Chapter 9

1. When adding new fields to a host, which plugin hook do you need to register?
   a. The `api_device_save` hook
   b. The `config_arrays` hook
   c. The `config_settings` hook

2. How do you add new tables to the database using the Plugin Architecture?
   a. Using `api_plugin_db_table_create`
   b. Using `api_plugin_db_table_modify`
   c. Using `api_plugin_db_table_add`

3. What can you use the `tree_after` hook for?
   a. You can execute some functions after you create a new Cacti tree
   b. You can display additional information at the end of the graph tree view page
   c. You can display additional fields on the Cacti tree creation page

Summary

During this chapter you have learned quite a lot about creating your own plugin.

Specifically, you have covered:

- Installing and using the superlinks plugin
- Creating a concept for a plugin
- How to create the main `setup.php` file
- How to present data
- Adding a new web page for viewing a list of enhanced information items
- Creating a web page for adding new enhanced information items

You should now be able to create your own personal Cacti plugins. In the next chapter, you're going to install and configure a threshold monitoring plugin to further enhance Cacti.

10
Threshold Monitoring with Thold

Now that you've installed several plugins and know how to create your own, let's look at how one of the more complex plugins can help you monitor your devices and send out alerts based on thresholds.

In this chapter, we are going to:

- Provide an overview of the Thold plugin
- Describe the different threshold types available
- Create a threshold
- Create a threshold template and assign it to a data source

Let's start with some basics!

Threshold monitoring

With the addition of a threshold monitoring plugin, Cacti becomes more and more of a performance management tool. Setting thresholds on the gathered performance data for alerting allows you to:

- Repair hardware problems before users are impacted
- Identify performance issues before there are real problems
- Identify virus outbreaks

With thresholds set, you do not have to look at all your graphs every day to identify these items.

Thold

Thold is a threshold monitoring and alerting plugin for Cacti which dates back as far as December 2004, but has since been replaced by the currently available plugin. Thresholds can be created per host and data source but Thold also supports threshold template creation.

Installing Thold

Let's start with installing the Thold plugin.

Downloading and installing Thold

Thold is not published on the `cacti.net` website, but is, however, freely available from the `cactiusers.org` website.

Time for action – installing Thold

1. Go to `http://cactiusers.org/`, right-click on the Thold link, and save the target location.

2. Logon to the shell of your Cacti server.

3. Change to the Cacti plugins directory:

   cd /var/www/html/cacti/plugins

4. Download the Thold plugin:

   wget http://cactiusers.org/downloads/thold.tar.gz

5. Extract the file:

   tar -xzvf thold-0.4.3.tar.gz

6. Login to Cacti, install, and enable the plugin which appears in the Plugins page.

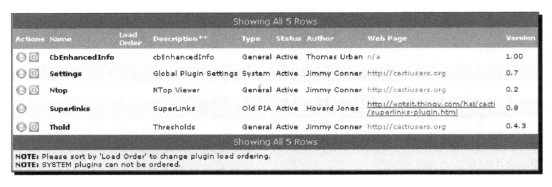

				Showing All 5 Rows				
Actions	Name	Load Order	Description**	Type	Status	Author	Web Page	Version
◉ ◎	CbEnhancedInfo		cbEnhancedInfo	General	Active	Thomas Urban	n/a	1.00
◉ ◎	Settings		Global Plugin Settings	System	Active	Jimmy Conner	http://cactiusers.org	0.7
◉ ◎	Ntop		NTop Viewer	General	Active	Jimmy Conner	http://cactiusers.org	0.2
◉	Superlinks		SuperLinks	Old PIA	Active	Howard Jones	http://wotsit.thingy.com/hai/cacti/superlinks-plugin.html	0.8
◉ ◎	Thold		Thresholds	General	Active	Jimmy Conner	http://cactiusers.org	0.4.3
				Showing All 5 Rows				

NOTE: Please sort by 'Load Order' to change plugin load ordering.
NOTE: SYSTEM plugins can not be ordered.

What just happened?

You installed the Thold plugin, thereby enabling you to set thresholds on the values of the RRD data and send out alerts if your thresholds are breached.

Configuring Thold

As with most complex plugins, Thold comes with its own configuration tab on the Cacti settings page. Let's look at the various options for Thold.

General options

The **General** settings area contains some very basic options. The following image shows their default values:

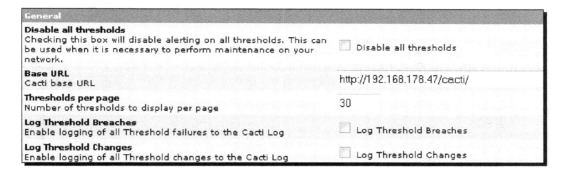

Most of these settings are self explanatory, but you may be wondering what the **Base URL** option is used for. By default, it should be pointing to the URL of your Cacti installation, based on what Thold thinks it is. This value will be used when a threshold alert is sent out as a link to the graph. You should check this URL to make sure it's accurate.

Default Alerting Options

The **Default Alerting Options** area lets you define syslog reporting as well as some exemptions and triggers. Look at the following screenshot showing the default values:

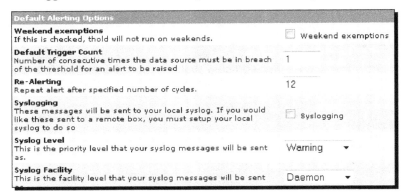

Default Emailing Options

The default **Emailing Options** section lets you define the appearance of alert emails as well as the generic content of these emails. Look at the following image for the default values:

There are two fields that need some special explanation; **Dead Hosts Notifications** and **Dead Host Notifications Email**. By default, Cacti doesn't immediately mark a host as being down if it was unreachable. If you look at the **Poller** tab and scroll down to the bottom of that page, you will see the following settings:

Host Up/Down Settings	
Failure Count The number of polling intervals a host must be down before logging an error and reporting host as down.	2
Recovery Count The number of polling intervals a host must remain up before returning host to an up status and issuing a notice.	3

This means that Cacti will try to poll the host twice before marking it as down, while waiting 3 polling cycles before marking the host as being recovered. Based on the default poller interval of 5 minutes, the total time these values represent are 10 and 15 minutes respectively.

As Thold uses the internal Cacti mechanism, a dead host notification will also be sent out after 2 polling cycles.

You've also seen that Thold accepts an e-mail address that should receive the dead host notification message. As there's no such field on an individual device basis, then the e-mail address entered here will receive dead host notification messages for all devices configured in Cacti. In a multi-tenant environment, this may not be what you want, so make sure you understand the options.

Default Baseline Options

Thold has the ability to trigger alerts by doing some baseline analysis. The default baseline options define the time ranges and triggers to take into account when calculating a threshold breach. The default values can be seen in the following screenshot:

Default Baseline Options	
Baseline notifications Enable sending alert for baseline notifications	☑ Baseline notifications
Default Baseline Trigger Count Number of consecutive times the data source must be in breach of the calculated baseline threshold for an alert to be raised	2
Baseline reference in the past default This is the default value used in creating thresholds or templates.	86400
Baseline time range default This is the default value used in creating thresholds or templates.	10800
Baseline deviation percentage This is the default value used in creating thresholds or templates.	15

Using Thold

Now that you have installed and configured the Thold plugin, let's move on and assign Thold permissions to a user and create some thresholds.

Assigning permissions and setting up an e-mail address

First, you'll have to assign permission for Thold to a user. For alerting to work properly, you should also define an e-mail address for the user.

Time for action – give permission to a user

1. Logon to Cacti as a user with administrative rights.

2. Click on the **Console** tab and go to **Utilities | User Management**.

3. Click on the user to whom you want to provide access, to the plugin.

4. Add an e-mail address for the user in the new **Email Address** field:

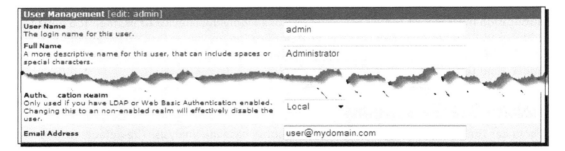

5. On the **Realm Permissions tab**, tick the checkbox next to **Configure Threshold Templates**, **Configure Thresholds** and **View Thresholds** as seen in the following screenshot:

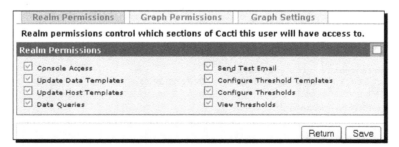

6. Click on the **Save** button.

What just happened?

You just gave a user permission to create threshold templates, individual thresholds, and to view the thresholds within Cacti.

Creating a threshold

Thresholds can be set on a per data source basis, but this can be tedious in large environments so, thankfully, the plugin provides an easy way of creating thresholds using a shortcut icon on the graph view pages.

Time for action – creating your first threshold – Part 1

1. Logon to Cacti as the user you changed in the previous step.

2. Click on the **Graphs** tab and go to a host or graph.

3. On the right of the graphs, there are a number of small icons. Click on the one showing a small document with a checkmark in it, as seen in the following screenshot:

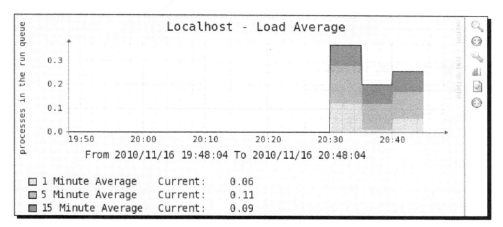

4. On the next page, select **Create a new Threshold** from the drop-down box and click on the **go** button as shown in the following screenshot:

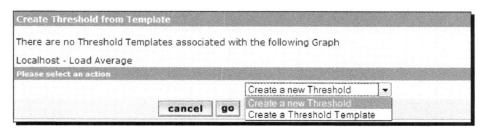

5. On the next page, the **Host** and **Graph** drop-down boxes should already be filled in. Now select **load_15min** as the **Data Source** for which you want to create a threshold. The next image displays the information for the **Localhost – Load Average** graph:

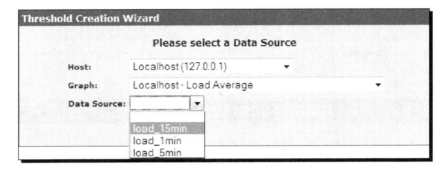

6. Click on the **Create** button.

7. You'll now see a page where you can define the threshold for the specific data source you've selected. Let's stop here for a moment and look at this page in more detail.

The threshold creation page

The threshold creation page can be divided into three main parts:

- ◆ Basic and mandatory settings
- ◆ Threshold setup
- ◆ Alert setup

Depending on the number of data source items that make up the graph, you will also see a tab at the top for alternating between them.

Basic and mandatory settings section

In the **Basic and Mandatory Settings** section you can define some functionality for Thold. If this threshold is based on a threshold template, which we are going to go over a bit later, then you can enable or disable the propagation of settings from the parent template here. Look at the following screenshot for the definition of each field:

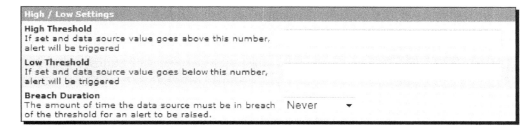

Data Source Item [load_15min] - **Current value:** [0.0701]

Template settings

Template Propagation Enabled
Whether or not these settings will be propagates from the threshold template.
☐ Template Propagation Enabled

Mandatory settings

Threshold Name
Provide the THold a meaningful name
Localhost - Load Average [load_15min]

Threshold Enabled
Whether or not this threshold will be checked and alerted upon.
☑ Threshold Enabled

Weekend Exemption
If this is checked, this Threshold will not alert on weekends.
☐ Weekend Exemption

Disable Restoration Email
If this is checked, Thold will not send an alert when the threshold has returned to normal status.
☐ Disable Restoration Email

Threshold Type
The type of Threshold that will be monitored.
High / Low Values ▼

In this section, you can also change the **Threshold Type** which can be one of the following:

◆ **High / Low Values**: The threshold is breached if the value is above or below these numbers.

◆ **Baseline**: A time range from the past is used to calculate acceptable minimum and maximum values. The threshold is breached if the values deviate by this amount, in percent.

◆ **Time Based**: Similar to the high/low threshold, a time-based threshold is defined by setting high and low numbers. In order to trigger the threshold, it must be breached x number of times within the last y minutes (for example, 2 times within the last 30 minutes).

The type of threshold you choose here changes the content of the following section.

Threshold setup section

This section provides fields for setting up the actual threshold. Depending on the **Threshold Type** you chose earlier, this section changes.

The following screenshot displays the section seen when you choose the **High / Low Values** type:

High / Low Settings

High Threshold
If set and data source value goes above this number, alert will be triggered

Low Threshold
If set and data source value goes below this number, alert will be triggered

Breach Duration
The amount of time the data source must be in breach of the threshold for an alert to be raised.
Never ▼

As mentioned earlier, **High / Low Values** thresholds are the simplest type. A value has to be at fault for a consecutive number of times (**Breach Duration**) for an alert to be issued.

The **Baseline** threshold type provides more fields for you to fill in, as shown in the following screenshot:

Baseline Settings

Baseline monitoring
When enabled, baseline monitoring checks the current data source value against a value in the past. The available range of values is retrieved and a minimum and maximum values are taken as a respective baseline reference. The precedence however is on the "hard" thresholds above.

☑ Baseline monitoring

Reference in the past
Specifies the relative point in the past that will be used as a reference. The value represents seconds, so for a day you would specify 86400, for a week 604800, etc.

Time range
Specifies the time range of values in seconds to be taken from the reference in the past

Baseline deviation UP
Specifies allowed deviation in percentage for the upper bound threshold. If not set, upper bound threshold will not be checked at all.

Baseline deviation DOWN
Specifies allowed deviation in percentage for the lower bound threshold. If not set, lower bound threshold will not be checked at all.

Baseline Trigger Count
Number of consecutive times the data source must be in breach of the baseline threshold for an alert to be raised.
Leave empty to use default value (**Default: cycles**)

As not all data sources can be defined with a fixed threshold limit, the **Baseline** threshold provides an automated way of creating a threshold for these kinds of data sources.

Let's assume that you have a system with an average load of 5% at working hours from Monday to Friday and, due to backups and/or heavy reporting functions running at night, it goes up to 15%. If you now set a high threshold of 15%, then you would probably not notice an unusual load during working hours, when a virus outbreak increases the average load to 10%.

This is where the **Baseline** threshold will come in handy. By setting the reference point for the threshold to the value from a week ago and choosing a decent, but not too large time range, you can define a dynamic threshold by using the **Baseline deviation UP** and **Baseline deviation DOWN** fields. The **Baseline** threshold will then alert you when the average load increases to, for example, 10% during work hours but will also alert you during the night when the average load increases beyond 15%.

You can take care of smaller usage spikes by also defining a **Baseline Trigger Count**.

The last threshold type available is the **Time Based** threshold so let's look at its settings:

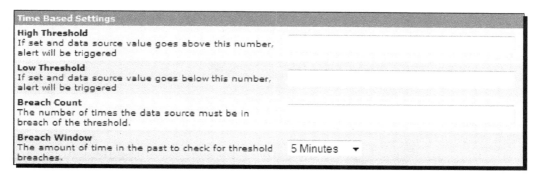

As described earlier, **Time Based** thresholds have fixed high and low threshold values but in contrast to the simple **High / Low Values** type, this one is able to check for the number of threshold breaches within a specific time range.

When would you use this? Let's assume you are counting the number of failed logins of the root user to your system. As it sometimes happens, you type in the wrong password, and you do not want to be alerted for every single failed login, so you set the **High Threshold** to 2. If someone tries to login to your system twice within the last 5 minutes, then you will get an alert. However, if someone tries to login to your system 288 times in the last 24 hours, or on average once every 5 minutes, then you will never get an alert.

Time Based thresholds will allow you to define a case which would cause the threshold to alert if the value is breached 2 times (**Breach Count**) during the last 60 minutes (**Breach Window**). In the example with the failed logins you will now get an alert telling you that someone tried to logon 7 times during the last 60 minutes.

Alert setup section

The alert section allows you to define the recipients of the alert. As you have already set up an e-mail address for a user, it should appear in the **Notify accounts** list.

The **Re-Alert Cycle** field allows you to enable e-mail alerts to be sent out regularly as long as a threshold is breached. This will remind those responsible that there is an ongoing issue to be resolved.

In case you have external users in need of this information, or have systems that create tickets or take action on an alert, you can define some extra e-mail addresses in the **Extra Alert Emails** box.

The following screenshot shows the alert section and a description of the fields:

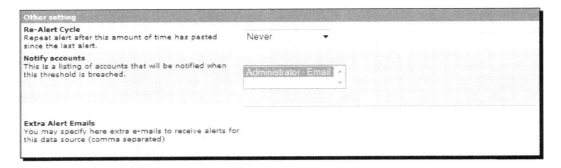

Now let's get back to work and continue with the definition of the threshold.

What just happened?

You just walked through the first steps of creating a threshold. You selected the host and graph for which you're going to create a threshold as well as the data source which will be monitored for threshold breaches.

Time for action – creating your first threshold – Part 2

1. You are now going to define a **High / Low Values** threshold, so select **High / Low Values** as the **Threshold Type**.

2. Look at the sample graph at the top of the page and set a good **High Threshold** which is relatively near or just below the maximum limit of your graph. This will allow you to check the functionality of the alerting later on. In the following graph example the **High Threshold** value should be set to 0.3:

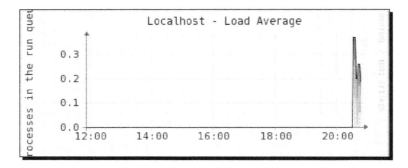

3. Select **5 minutes** as the **Breach Duration**.

4. Leave the **Data Type** to **Exact Value**.

5. Select the account that shows up in the **Notify accounts** field.

6. Click on the **Save** button.

What just happened?

You've finished creating your first threshold. By selecting a high threshold value that's near your normal average load, you should receive an alert e-mail when there's a high load on your system.

As you may have noticed, you skipped the **Data Type** field, leaving it to the default value. What's the purpose of this field? Depending on the data source type you can use different methods for extracting a value from the data source. Remember when you created the graph templates? You sometimes had to use a CDEF to turn bits into bytes or make numbers negative. This same principle applies here. The values returned from the data source are not always the same values you displayed on the graph and, for some of these data sources, you had to use a CDEF to make them appear as you want.

You can also choose to convert values to a percentage compared to another data source. An example of this would be memory calculations, where you may want to set a threshold of the free memory available as a percentage of the total system memory. You can, of course, use a fixed low value with the minimum free memory, but this threshold will only be valid for a limited number of systems. Defining these thresholds as a percentage will be much better when defining threshold templates which will apply to a large set of dissimilar systems with different memory footprints.

Testing the threshold

Now that you have defined a threshold, how can you test if everything is working? On Linux systems you can use a stress test application. Let's look into how to install and use the stress tool from freshmeat.net (http://freshmeat.net/projects/stress/).

Time for action – installing the stress tool

1. Logon to your CentOS Linux system as the root user.

2. Change to the tmp directory:

   cd /tmp

3. Download the stress tool:

   wget http://packages.sw.be/stress/stress-1.0.2-1.el5.rf.i386.rpm

4. Install the package with the `rpm` command:

```
rpm -Uvh stress-1.0.2-1.el5.rf.i386.rpm
```

5. Run a stress test for 60 seconds:

```
stress --cpu 8 --io 4 --vm 2 --vm-bytes 128M --timeout 60s
```

6. Go back to Cacti and look at the average load graph. It should show a much higher average load than when you setup the threshold:

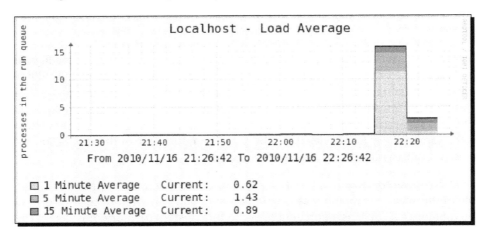

7. Check your e-mail account for the threshold alert.

8. In case you did not receive an e-mail, check the configuration of the settings plugin. There may be a misconfiguration or missing entry there.

Viewing threshold breaches

As you have already created your first threshold, and forced it to breach by using the stress tool, let's now look how you can view these breached thresholds.

Time for action – viewing breached thresholds

1. Logon to Cacti as a user with **View Thresholds** permissions.

2. You should be presented with a page listing all threshold breaches like the one shown in the following screenshot:

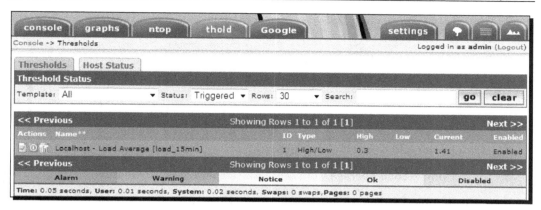

3. Click on the second button with the red background and the white circle in it to disable the threshold:

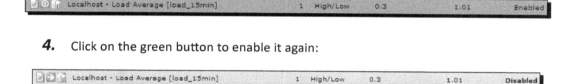

4. Click on the green button to enable it again:

| | Localhost - Load Average [load_15min] | 1 | High/Low | 0.3 | | 1.01 | Disabled |

5. You can edit the threshold by clicking on the first icon, or view the graph for the threshold by clicking on the last icon.

What just happened?

You just looked at the threshold page which is available to all users with **View Thresholds** permissions. Depending on the other permissions you have, not all icons will appear.

Creating threshold templates

Now that you have created a single threshold, let's look into creating a threshold template with baseline support for the average load threshold.

Time for action – creating your first threshold template

1. Logon to Cacti as a user with administrative rights.

2. Go to the **Console** tab and click on **Threshold Templates** under the **Templates** section.

3. You should see an empty table as seen in the following screenshot:

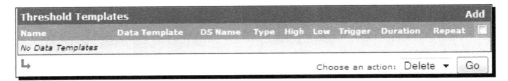

4. Click on the **Add** link to the top right.

5. Select **Unix – Load Average** from the **Data Template** drop-down box.

6. Select **10min (10 Minute Average)** from the **Data Source** box as seen in the following screenshot:

7. Click on the **create** button.

8. On the next screen, change the **Threshold Type** to **Baseline**.

9. In the **Baseline monitoring** section, enable **Baseline monitoring** by ticking the checkbox.

10. Add **10** for the **Baseline deviation UP**.

11. Add **10** for the **Baseline deviation DOWN**.

12. Leave everything else in this section to the default values as shown in the following screenshot:

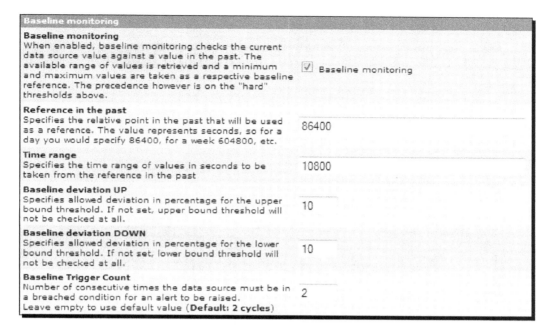

13. Change the **Re-Alert Cycle** and **Notify accounts** to suit your needs.

14. Click on the **Save** button to save your template.

15. Go back to the **Template Thresholds** page under the Template section and check the table for the existence of your new template:

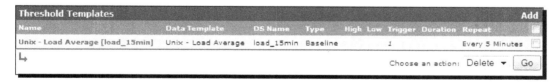

What just happened?

You just created your first baseline based threshold template. As you may have noticed, the data source you selected was the 10min average data source, but the DS Name on the table shows load_15min as the name. This is because the data template for the **Unix – Load Average** assigns the **10min – 10 Minute Average** output field to the **load_15min** internal Data Source Name.

Assigning threshold templates

Now that you have created a template for the Load Average threshold, you can assign this template to the previously created load average threshold for your localhost device.

Time for action – assigning a threshold template

1. Logon to Cacti as a user with administrative rights.

2. Go to the **Console** tab and click on **Thresholds** under the **Management** section.

3. You should see a table with all your currently defined thresholds as shown in the following screenshot:

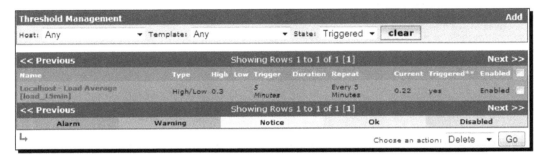

4. Check the checkbox to the right of the **Load Average** threshold.

5. Choose **Delete** from the drop-down box at the bottom and click on the **Go** button. This will make sure that this threshold does not exist any more, as existing thresholds cannot be migrated to ones based on a template.

6. Click on the graphs tab and select the host where you created the **Load Average** threshold earlier.

7. Click on the Create Threshold icon next to the **Load Average** graph.

8. From the following screen, select the **Unix – Load Average [load_15min]** template as seen in the following screenshot:

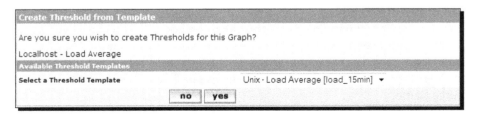

9. Click on **yes** to save your selection.

10. Go to the **Console** tab an click on **Thresholds** under the **Management** section.

11. Change the **State** to **Any** at the top of the page.

12. Click on **Localhost - Load Average [load_15min]** to open the threshold definition page.

13. The **Template Propagation Enabled** checkbox should be checked and all other fields disabled as seen in the following image:

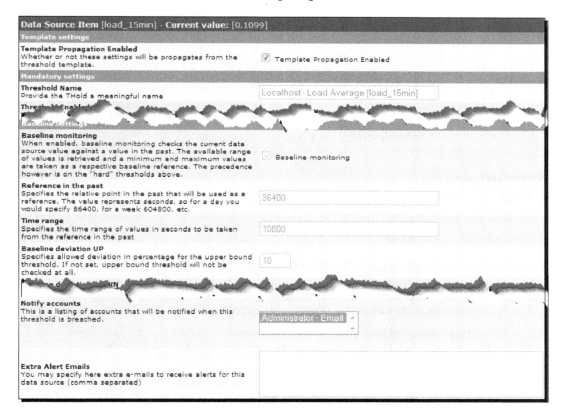

What just happened?

You just assigned your first threshold template to a data source. Every time you change the base threshold template, the changes will propagate to the assigned thresholds. Please note that the notification e-mail recipients are also stored in the template, so for different alert recipients, you will need to create different templates.

Pop Quiz – A few questions about Chapter 10

1. When are baseline thresholds best used?

    a. When performance values stay the same

    b. When performance values vary between different days

    c. To identify performance issues

2. Where do you define the alert e-mail addresses?

    a. In the user management screen

    b. In the alert setup screen

    c. In both screens

3. What happens if you change the notification e-mail address in a threshold template?

    a. Nothing happens

    b. The notification e-mail address gets propagated to the actual thresholds

    c. A confirmation e-mail is sent out to that address

Summary

You have learned quite a lot about thresholds, baselines, and other parts of the Thold plugin.

Specifically, you have covered:

◆ Installing and configuring the Thold plugin

◆ Creating a threshold via the graph view page

◆ The differences between the three threshold types

◆ Creating a baseline based threshold template

◆ How to assign this template to a data source

You should now be able to create a set of thresholds and templates to monitor your network and receive alerts when performance issues occur. In the next chapter, you're going to learn how to create reports containing specific Cacti graphs and how to send them to your customers using scheduled e-mail.

11
Enterprise Reporting

You have created a solid base of graphs, so it's now time to see how you can create reports and send them to your users. This chapter is going to show you how to define reports with the free Nectar and the commercially supported CereusReporting plugins.

In this chapter we are going to:

◆   Provide an overview of Nectar and CereusReporting
◆   Describe the process of creating a report
◆   Schedule reports to be sent via e-mail
◆   Describe the advanced reporting features of CereusReporting

It's time for reporting!

Overview of Nectar and CereusReporting

Why do you need a reporting solution in the first place? Although Cacti is capable of exporting graphs to an FTP server, it does not provide the ability to create on-demand reports or to send out a collection of graphs using an e-mail system. This missing feature is fulfilled by the Nectar and CereusReporting plugins. Let's look at these plugins in more detail.

Nectar

Nectar is the "true" descendant of the "reports" plugin which, in the early days of Cacti, had the ability to e-mail graphs and text on a scheduled basis. As support and development of the "reports" plugin was abandoned some time ago, one of the Cacti developers created a new plugin called **Nectar**. Nectar is capable of creating reports containing the Cacti graphs and some text and sending these graphs as inline images within e-mails.

Nectar supports:

◆ Scheduling report generation

◆ Basic formatting of the reports using HTML and CSS code

◆ Sending of reports based on Cacti graphs via e-mail

Nectar is based on the GPL License. At the time of writing Nectar's latest published version is 0.30.

CereusReporting

The CereusReporting plugin is a complete new development for the 0.8.7 version of Cacti. It is a commercial product which offers a free Express Edition for on-demand report generation.

CereusReporting allows the creation of PDF and HTML based reports and supports report scheduling and mail delivery of these reports.

CereusReporting offers the following features:

◆ On-demand PDF report generation for users

◆ Reports containing text, titles, chapters, and HTML code

◆ Support for Report Templates for customer-specific reports

◆ Support for Availability/SLA reports

◆ Support for the DSSTATS plugin

◆ Support for Smokeping graphs

◆ Commercial support

There is a lot more functionality available, such as the integration of Zenoss reports, depending on the edition.

At the time of writing, there are two editions available, a free Express Edition and a Corporate Edition. The latest published Version is 1.51.

Nectar

Let's look into Nectar, and how to create and schedule reports using this plugin. You can get the latest version of Nectar from the plugin documentation page here: http://docs.cacti.net/plugin:nectar. This example is going to use version 0.30.

Time for action – installing Nectar

1. Logon to your Cacti installation as root.

2. Change to the `plugins` directory of your Cacti installation:

    `cd /var/www/html/cacti/plugins`

3. You can download the latest version:

    `wget -O nectar-v0.30.tgz` http://docs.cacti.net/_media/plugin: nectar-v0.30.tgz

4. Extract the plugin using the `tar` command:

    `tar -xzvf nectar-v0.30.tgz`

5. Now you can login to your Cacti web interface and install/enable the plugin from the **Plugin Management** page.

6. You should now be able to see the **nectar** tab at the top as shown in the following screenshot:

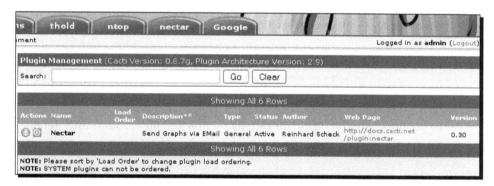

What just happened?

You have just installed and enabled the Nectar plugin for your system. You can now go on and create and schedule reports once you have set the correct realm permissions for your user.

Report generation

Now that you have installed the Nectar plugin, let's look into how to create your first report.

Time for action – create your first Nectar report

1. Logon to your Cacti web interface.

2. Click on the **nectar** tab.

3. You should see an empty table. Click on the **Add** link to the top right.

4. You will see a new page where you can define your nectar report. Enter **My New Report** as the **Report Name** and check the **Enable Report** checkbox.

5. Within the **Email Frequency** section, check the **Next Timestamp for sending Mail Report** field and choose the date/time when you want your first report to be sent out.

6. Select **Day(s)** as the **Report Interval** so your report will be sent out daily at the same time at which you scheduled your first report, as seen in the following screenshot:

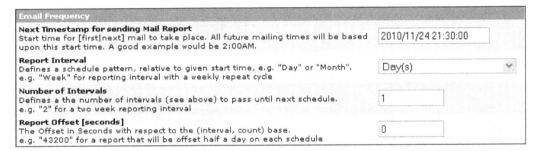

7. Go to the **Email Sender/Receiver Details** section and fill in your e-mail details.

8. Once you are done, click on the **Create** button.

What just happened?

You have just created your first report. This report is still empty as you have yet to add report items to it.

Important note:

Check the regional settings for your MySQL database. Some instances actually use "-" as the date separator, and not "/."

Time for action – adding report items

1. You should now see several new tabs as seen in the following screenshot:

2. Click on the **Items** tab.

3. A new page opens with an empty table. Click on the **Add** link to the top right of the table.

4. As seen in the following screenshot, the new page offers several drop-down boxes to choose from. Select **Graph** as the **Type** and select one of your existing graphs to be added to the report:

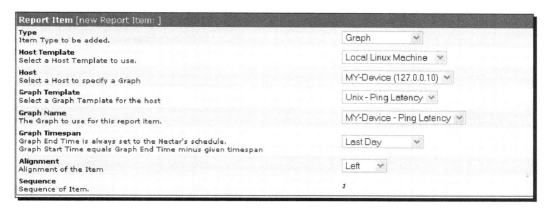

5. Once you select an item from each drop-down box, you will see the graph being displayed underneath. Click on the **Save** button to continue.

6. The table should now list your previously added graph.

7. Click on the **Preview** tab to see a preview of your report.

8. On the **Events** tab you can see the next dates and times when your report will be generated and sent out.

9. In order to test your report, click on the **Send Report** link to the far right of the tabs. An e-mail similar to the one shown in the following screenshot will be sent to you:

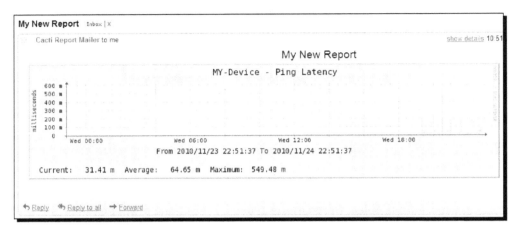

What just happened?

You just added a graph item to your report and scheduled it to be sent via e-mail on a regular basis. The e-mail contains the Cacti graphs as inline images and can be forwarded to other people.

CereusReporting

CereusReporting is the new name of the nmidCreatePDF plugin. It was introduced with version 1.0 and refers to the name of a Cacti species, underlining the close relationship to the Cacti performance monitoring tool.

CereusReporting allows the creation of PDF reports and comes as a free Express Edition as well as a commercial Corporate Edition. Commercially available modules with additional functionality can be enabled for the Express Edition. These modules include report scheduling and mailing as well as other more advanced features.

The Express Edition also supports the nmidSmokeping plugin for adding Smokeping graphs to the PDF report.

Installation

The Express and Corporate Edition share the same code, so let's install the Express Edition now. This installation assumes that you are using Cacti 0.8.7g with PIA 2.9 installed.

You can get the latest version from the CereusReporting project page here:

`http://redmine.nmid-plugins.de/projects/nmidcreatepdf/files`. This example is going to be based on the v1.50.86 version.

Time for action – installing CereusReporting

1. Logon to your Cacti installation as root.

2. Change to the `plugins` directory of your Cacti installation:

```
cd /var/www/html/cacti/plugins
```

3. Download the latest version:

```
wget http://www.network-outsourcing.de/uploads/CereusReporting_
v1.50.86_ionCube_full.tgz
```

4. Extract the plugin using the `tar` command:

```
tar -xzvf CereusReporting_v1.50.86_ionCube_full.tgz
```

5. Change into the newly created directory, nmidCreatePDF:

```
cd nmidCreatePDF
```

6. Change the ownership of the files to your webserver and Cacti:

```
chown -R apache.cactiuser *
```

7. CereusReporting uses a threaded approach for creating the graphs. Therefore you are now going to download the extension responsible for it:

```
wget http://redmine.nmid-plugins.de/attachments/download/231/
parallelGraphRetriever_linux32bit.zip

unzip parallelGraphRetriever_linux32bit.zip

chown apache.cactiuser parallelGraphRetriever

chmod +x parallelGraphRetriever
```

8. In case you do not yet have the `php-gd` and `php-mbstring` modules installed, do it now:

```
yum install php-gd php-mbstring
```

9. The CereusReporting plugin is encrypted with the IonCube software. In order to load the plugin, you need to install the PHP loader. For PHP Version 5.1, the following commands will install the required module:

```
cd /tmp
wget http://downloads2.ioncube.com/loader_downloads/ioncube_
loaders_lin_x86.tar.gz
tar -xzvf ioncube_loaders_lin_x86.tar.gz
cp ioncube/ioncube_loader_lin_5.1.so /usr/lib/php/modules/
```

10. You now have to tell PHP to load this module:

```
echo "zend_extension=/usr/lib/php/modules/ioncube_loader_lin_
5.1.so " > /etc/php.d/aaa_ioncube.ini
```

11. Restart the webserver so it loads the new module:

```
/etc/init.d/httpd restart
```

12. Now logon to your Cacti web interface and enable the plugin.

13. You should now be able to see the **Cereus** tab at the top as shown in the following screenshot:

What just happened?

You have just installed and enabled the CereusReporting Express Edition along with the basic requirements. This edition allows you to create simple on-demand reports as well as creating pre-defined reports. Do not forget to give the appropriate realm permissions to your users.

Plugin configuration

Before creating your first report, you will need to configure the CereusReporting plugin. There are several basic settings which are essential for the plugin to work properly. Let's set up the plugin now.

Time for action – configure CereusReporting

1. Go to **Configuration** | **Settings**.

2. Select the **NMID** tab.

3. Enter **Cacti Report** as the **Report Title**.

4. Enter **provided by your IT department** in the **Report Subtitle** field.

5. Enter `images/urban-software_logo.png` as your **Report Logo**. The logo needs to be readable and writeable by your webserver and the Cacti user.

6. Check the **Print Header/Footer to PDF** box.

7. Enter the URL of your Cacti web interface to the **Cacti Host/Server URL** field.

8. Enter `/usr/bin/php` for your **PHP binary path**. On a Linux system, you can check where your PHP binary is by issuing the following command on the CLI:

```
which php
```

9. Enter **archive** as the **Archive Directory**.

10. You can leave the rest of the settings as they are. Your settings should now look as shown in the following screenshot:

Cacti Settings (NMID)	
NMID - CereusReporting - General - EXPRESS Edition - License Expiry Date : never	
Report Title The title of the report. This will only be displayed if the selected tree item is not a header.	Cacti Report
Report Subtitle The default sub-title of the report. Eg. 'Provided by your Support Team'	provided by your IT department
Report Footer The default footer of the report.	
Print Header/Footer to PDF Enables/Disabled the printing of the Header and Footer. Should be disabled when using a CoverPage/Template.	☑ Print Header/Footer to PDF
Report Logo The company logo you want to be displayed on the PDF report. The default logo is images/default_logo.png. Needs to be a PNG file.	images/urban-software_logo.png
Use 'HOSTNAME(IP)' in host only reports Displays 'Report for host hostname(a.b.c.d)' instead of the default report title	☑ Use 'HOSTNAME(IP)' in host only reports
Graphs link back to cacti A click on a graph in the PDF Report links back to the cacti page for that graph	☑ Graphs link back to cacti
Cacti Host/Server URL The Cacti Host/Server URL to be used in the graph links	http://192.168.178.47/cacti/
WebService URL for nmidSmokeping graphs only. Url to the webservice: http://path /to/plugins/nmidWebService/webservice.php?wsdl	
PHP binary path Path to the php binary. To use the default php installation in the system path, just enter 'php' here.	/usr/bin/php
Archive Directory Archive directory for storing the PDF Reports.	archive
GZip binary path Path to the GZip binary. Archived reports will be gziped if this is set.	/bin/gzip
Scheduler being used The poller is fine for small reports, but it is still recommended to use cron or windows scheduling.	Poller ▾

11. Click on the **Save** button.

What just happened?

You just defined the basic settings for the CereusReporting plugin.

Report generation

The CereusReporting plugin is able to create instant PDF reports from the graph tree view page as well as creating a pre-defined report collection.

On-demand report generation

On-demand reports can be enabled for every user to create instant PDF reports while viewing the Cacti graph tree view pages.

Time for action – creating an on-demand report

Logon to your Cacti web interface.

1. Click on the **graphs** tab. You should notice the new toolbar:

2. Non-admin users will not see the **Add to Report** button and the drop-down box next to it.

3. Select a host for which you want to generate a report.

4. Click on the PDF icon to the far right. After a short time you should be presented with a download dialog. Please note the filename displayed there:

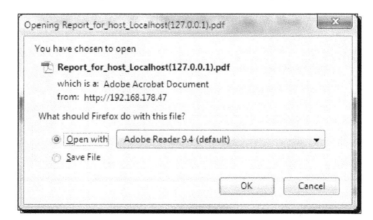

5. When you select a host, the report name will always have the same format as shown in the previous picture. If you click on a sub-tree item and hit the **Include Sub-Leafs** box, the report name will have the name you entered on the settings page.

What just happened?

You just created your first instant PDF report using the CereusReporting plugin. The graphs included within the report show the exact timeframe which you selected in the Cacti tree view page. You are able to select single graphs by clicking on the small checkbox next to each graph, or create a report of a whole subtree by enabling the checkbox next to the PDF icon.

Let's now look at how you can create a pre-defined report.

Pre-defined report generation

Pre-defined reports are a collection of graphs from one or more hosts which can also come from different Cacti trees. This allows you to add graphs from a specific type (for example, hard disk space on servers) to one report.

Time for action – creating a pre-defined report

1. Go to the **console** tab.

2. Click on **NMID | Manage Reports**.

3. An empty table will be shown. Click on the **Add** link at the top right of that table.

4. On the new page, enter **Interface Report** as the **Report Name**.

5. Enter a short **Report Description** of the report. This description will be shown at the beginning of the final PDF report.

6. Select **1 Day** as the **Default Report Timespan**.

7. Keep the rest to their default entries.

8. Click on the **Save** button. You will be redirected back to the report overview table as shown in the following screenshot:

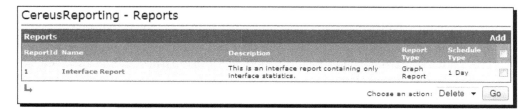

CereusReporting - Reports					
Reports					**Add**
ReportId	**Name**	**Description**	**Report Type**	**Schedule Type**	
1	Interface Report	This is an interface report containing only interface statistics.	Graph Report	1 Day	
⤷			Choose an action:	Delete ▾	Go

9. Click on the **graphs** tab.

10. Select a host entry from your Cacti tree.

11. Select the checkbox next to each interface graph as seen in the following screenshot:

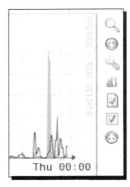

12. Select the **Interface Report** from the drop-down box at the toolbar:

13. Click on the **Add to Report** button.

14. Now click on the **Cereus** tab at the top.

15. You will see a list of pre-defined reports as seen in the following screenshot:

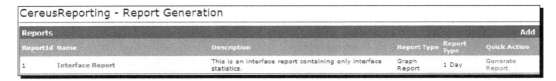

16. Click on the **Generate Report** link next to your **Interface Report**.

17. You will see some information about your report and be able to select a start and end time for your report data. The start and end time is always based on the **Default Report Timespan** which you defined for that particular report as seen in the following screenshot:

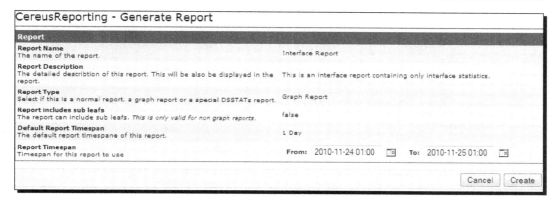

18. Click on the **Create** button to create your report. The report will contain all the graphs which you added previously as well as the report description you defined. The following screenshot shows part of the first page of such a report:

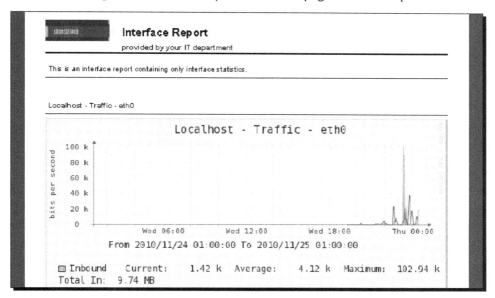

What just happened?

You just created your first pre-defined PDF report. You can use this kind of report to group similar graphs into one report for easier comparison.

Scheduling a report

Let's look into how you can schedule a report to be sent out via e-mail. For this, you will have to request a trial license for the scheduling module.

Time for action – scheduling a pre-defined report

Logon to your Cacti web interface.

1. Go to **NMID | Manage Report Schedule**.

2. On the empty table, click on the **Add** link which is at the top right. A new page will appear.

3. Enter **Daily Interface Report** as the **Schedule Name**.

4. Select the previously defined **Interface Report** as the **Report** to be scheduled.

5. Enter **This is a daily interface report** for the **Report Schedule Description**.

6. Select **daily** as the **Recurring frequency**.

7. Set the **Report Schedule** to 00:00 hours of the next day.

8. Enter your e-mail address in the **Report Recipients** list.

9. Enable all checkboxes on this **Report Schedule** as seen in the following screenshot:

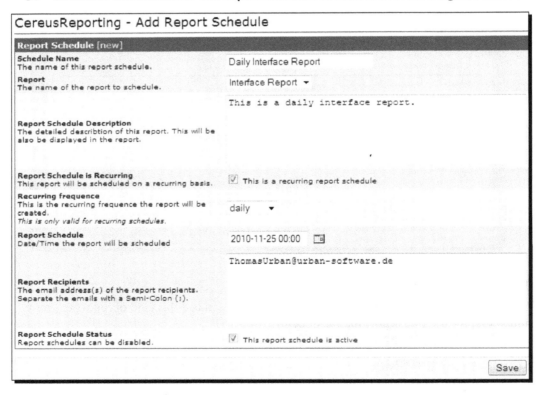

10. Click on the **Save** button.

11. You will be redirected to the **Report Schedules** table. Here you should see your new report schedule, as seen in the following screenshot:

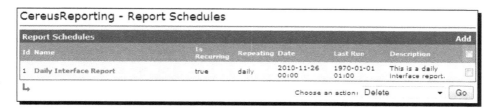

What just happened?

You just scheduled your first report. You will receive the report once the initial date/time has passed.

Report Backup and Restore

Once you create large reports, you may want to create a backup for them. The Express Edition of CereusReporting already includes a Backup and Restore feature, which creates XML-based backup files of your reports.

Time for action – Backup and Restore a pre-defined report

Logon to your Cacti web interface.

1. Go to **NMID | Backup/Restore**.

2. Check on the checkbox next to the **Interface Report** as seen in the following screenshot:

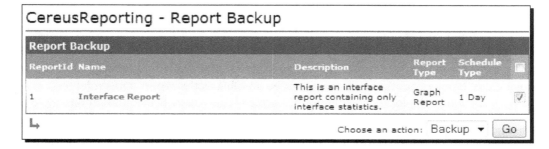

3. Click on the **Go** button at the top to create a backup file.

4. A new table will be displayed at the bottom of the page as seen in the following screenshot:

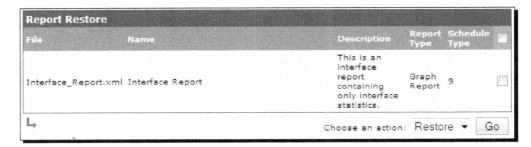

5. Check on the checkbox next to the **Interface_Report.xml** file.

6. Click on the **Go** button at the bottom to restore the report. The CereusReporting plugin never overwrites existing reports, but will create a new report with the same data as the original one, as seen in the following screenshot:

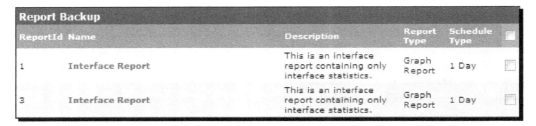

What just happened?

You just created a backup of your **Interface Report** and also restored it. The XML backup file contains all the necessary information to fully restore the report, including:

- General Report settings
- Defined Report Items
- Defined Report Schedules

Moving the report to another system will not be possible as the report items refer to the item IDs within the local Cacti database. Normally these IDs will be different on other systems.

Report scheduling and polling performance

The report generation requires some performance. Depending on the report type, size, and report generation settings, the scheduled report generation can have a negative impact on the polling time when being run by the poller.

Using the poller mode is fine for relatively small reports, but should be avoided when running large reports.

In order to reduce the performance impact of report generation, the CereusReporting plugin provides the ability to run the report generation as a cron job.

Let's look at how you can enable such a cron-based report generation.

Time for action – setup of a cron-based report generation

1. Logon to your Cacti server.

2. Create a new file in /etc/cron.d for running the report generation:

   ```
   vi /etc/cron.d/reportScheduler
   ```

3. Add the following one line to this file:

   ```
   */1 * * * * cactiuser /usr/bin/php /var/www/html/cacti/plugins/
   nmidCreatePDF/cron_pdf_scheduler.php > /dev/null 2>&1
   ```

4. Save the file by hitting *ESC* and entering *x*.

5. Now logon to your Cacti web interface.

6. Go to **Configuration** | **Settings**.

7. Click on the **NMID** tab.

8. Select **Cron** as the **Scheduler being used**.

9. Click on the **Save** button.

What just happened?

You just changed your scheduler from the poller-based version to a cron-based one. This will allow the Cacti poller to concentrate on polling performance data while the operating system deals with the report generation.

Advanced reporting features of CereusReporting

CereusReporting has some advanced reporting features such as the ability to create Top10 like charts using the DSStats plugin or creating availability reports for devices. This section provides you with an overview of these advanced features.

mPDF Report Engine

The mPDF Report Engine is an advanced reporting engine capable of adding bookmarks or Unicode support to PDF files. In order to use more advanced features like the report template support, you will have to install and select the mPDF report engine.

DSSTATS Reports

The DSSTATS Reports feature allows the creation of graphical charts for the raw data provided by the DSSTATS plugin. The DSSTATS or Cacti Data Source Statistics Plugin tracks the peak and average values for all data sources. It does not store all the data from the RRD files, but you will be able to retrieve the values for hourly, daily, weekly, monthly, and yearly time periods.

The DSSTATS Reports are using simple SQL queries to generate pie, bar, or simple line charts which can be added to a PDF report.

A simple example of such a DSSTATS chart is shown in the following screenshot:

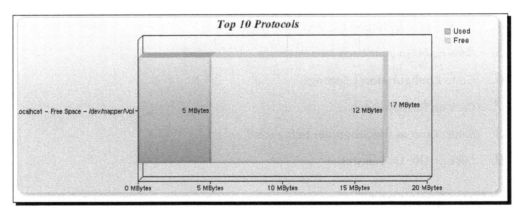

Availability reports

A new feature introduced with the release of the 1.0 version is the ability to create Availability reports. Device availability is calculated using the Cacti internal polling statistics. The following functionality is provided with this feature:

- ◆ Ability to define a global or host-based SLA time frame (for example, 8h x 5 days SLA report)
- ◆ Global and/or per host definable SLA

An example for the availability chart with a 8x5 defined SLA time frame can be seen in the following screenshot:

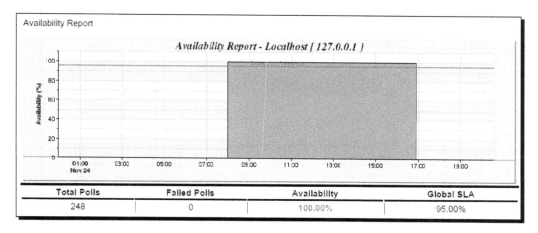

Smokeping reports

CereusReporting allows the integration of Smokeping graphs by utilizing the free nmidSmokeping plugin.

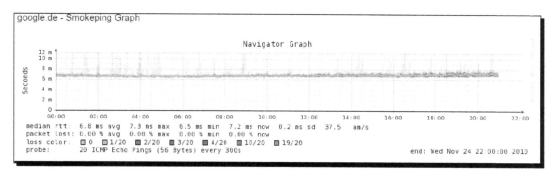

Mobile client support

Using the BlackBerry client for Cacti, it is also possible to add graphs to pre-defined reports through the BlackBerry mobile device. You can therefore change reports while not being in the office or having access to a computer.

Report templates

You can create your own report templates by using your favorite word processor and exporting your corporate or customer-specific report design to a PDF file. The PDF file can be used to create the look and feel of the PDF reports as seen in the following screenshot:

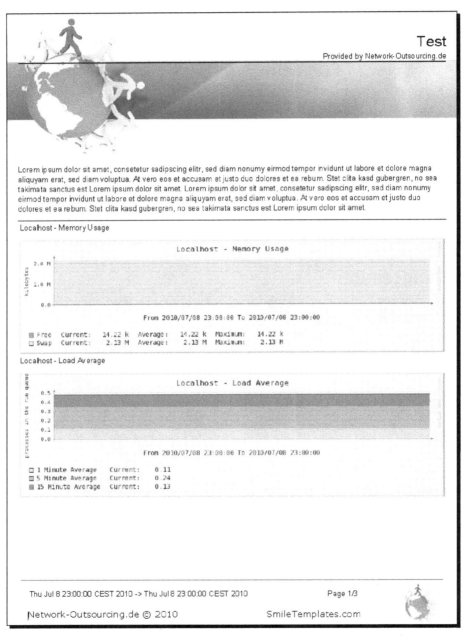

Pop Quiz – a few questions about Chapter 11

1. What type of reports can you generate using Nectar?
    a. An HTML report
    b. A CSV report
    c. An HTML e-mail containing the report
    d. All of the above types

2. How can you disable the report in Nectar?
    a. By going to the nectar tab
    b. By editing the report
    c. By disabling the nectar plugin

3. What plugins and extensions does the CereusReporting plugin support?
    a. The Smokeping tool
    b. The DSSTATS plugin
    c. Availability reports
    d. All of the above

Summary

In this chapter, you have learned how to create HTML and PDF based reports to send out to your colleagues, management, or customers. You have seen two different plugins capable of creating, scheduling, and mailing reports.

Specifically, you have covered:

- Installing the Nectar plugin
- Installing the CereusReporting plugin
- Creating a custom report with Nectar
- Scheduling a report using Nectar
- Creating an instant PDF report with the CereusReporting plugin
- Creating pre-defined reports using the CereusReporting plugin
- Creating a report schedule with the CereusReporting plugin
- Performance considerations when creating large reports

You should now be able to define new reports and schedule these reports to be sent out to a list of e-mail recipients. Now, you not only have a performance monitoring solution, but a performance reporting solution as well! In the next chapter, you're going to learn how to use the Cacti CLI and the autom8 plugin to automate your Cacti instance.

12

Cacti Automation for NOC

In a NOC environment, adding users and managing devices and graphs can become a time consuming job. With the availability of the Cacti CLI, most of these manual tasks can be automated, but selecting and creating meaningful graphs for devices still involves quite some effort. This chapter will show you how to use the CLI to automate device management and how to create rules for adding graphs to a device using the new Autom8 plugin.

In this chapter we are going to:

- ◆ Provide an overview of Cacti automation
- ◆ Describe the process of using the CLI to add permissions, devices, and trees
- ◆ Install and use Autom8

Let's automate Cacti!

Overview of Cacti automation

The automation of the many administrative Cacti tasks can be done using either the Cacti CLI, Autom8, or both. Let's look into the different functionalities which the Cacti CLI and Autom8 have to offer.

The Cacti CLI

The Cacti CLI was the first tool to automate the different Cacti tasks. As its name suggests, it is a CLI-based set of PHP files which interact with the Cacti core functions and database. The Cacti CLI can be used to create scripts for integrating external tools such as an asset management tool into Cacti. NOC environments usually have a central inventory management system holding detailed device information, and the Cacti CLI will help you import devices into Cacti using this information. What else does the Cacti CLI offer you?

Users

Cacti users can be created using the CLI by copying an existing user with a new userID. You've already done this in Chapter 4 when you imported a list of users into Cacti.

Permissions

When you create a user, the user has the same realm permissions as the template user had during the copy or import process. If you want to give additional permissions to a user, you can use the Cacti CLI to do so. Unfortunately, only the adding of permissions is supported, as the Cacti CLI does not allow the removal of permissions.

Trees

A special CLI script exists for managing the Cacti tree. You can add a new tree, or add different items to an existing tree, using the Cacti CLI.

Devices

As already mentioned, you can use the Cacti CLI to add new devices to Cacti. This is especially useful if you want to import a lot of devices.

Graphs

As you can add devices to Cacti using the CLI, it also provides an interface for adding graphs to a device.

Overview of Autom8

Autom8 allows you to automate tree items and graph creations based on device and graph details. The automation can be defined as rules which are triggered when a new device or graph is created. Let's look at the different aspects of this automation.

Trees

Autom8 doesn't create trees itself, but can create tree items, such as headings, or add host items to an existing tree. This function lets you automatically organize newly created devices and graphs without manual interaction. The Autom8 rules can also be applied to existing devices.

Graphs

Graph rules automate the addition of graph templates to devices. They are applied whenever a device is added or when the index information (for example, for SNMP interfaces) is re-indexed. Graph rules can be created based on any of the graph data query fields, such as the operating status of an interface (**ifOperStatus**).

Using the Cacti CLI

Let's look at how you can use the Cacti CLI to manage user permissions and examine some of the basic administrative tasks.

Adding permissions

When copying a user, the user permissions of the original user are copied to the new user. If you want to add further permissions to the new user, you can use a special script from the Cacti CLI.

Time for action – adding permissions to a user

1. Logon to your Cacti system.

2. Change to the Cacti CLI directory:

   cd /var/www/html/cacti/cli

3. Execute the following command:

   php add_perms.php

4. You'll see a short overview of the available options for this command:

   ```
   # php add_perms.php
   Add Permissions Script 1.0, Copyright 2004-2010 - The Cacti Group

   A simple command line utility to add permissions to tree items in Cacti

   usage: add_perms.php [ --user-id=[ID] ]
       --item-type=[graph|tree|host|graph_template]
       --item-id [--quiet]

   Where item-id is the id of the object of type item-type
   List Options:
       --list-users
       --list-trees
       --list-graph-templates
       --list-graphs --host-id=[ID]
   #
   ```

5. As you can see, this tool requires the **user-id** so let's get a list of all available users:

   php add_perms.php --list-users

6. You'll see displayed a list of all users together with their user IDs:

```
# php add_perms.php --list-users
Known Users:
id       username        full_name
1        admin    Administrator
3        guest    Guest Account
4        thurban  Thomas Urban
5        Test     User
6        _CustomerA_user Template User for Customer A
7        user1    User Name1
8        user2    User Name2
9        user3    User Name3
10       user4    User Name4

#
```

7. Now let's assume you want to give access to a specific tree. The command for this is:

```
php add_perms.php --user-id=[ID] --item-type=tree --item-id=[TREEID]
```

8. You already have the ID for the user so let's get the TREEID with the following command:

```
php add_perms.php --list-trees
```

9. As with the users list, you will see a list of the Cacti trees available together with their IDs:

```
# php add_perms.php --list-trees
Known Trees:
id       sort method                  name
1        Manual Ordering (No Sorting)  Default Tree
2        Manual Ordering (No Sorting)  Customer A

#
```

10. Now you are able to give access to a user. Let's give access of the **Customer A** tree to **user1**:

```
php add_perms.php --user-id=7 --item-type=tree --item-id=2
```

11. When executed, you will not get any confirmation back:

```
# php add_perms.php --user-id=7 --item-type=tree --item-id=2
#
```

12. You can check the User Management page of that user for the result:

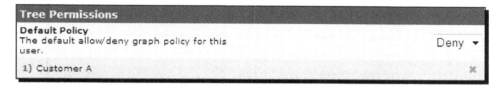

What just happened?

You just added permissions to an existing user to allow the viewing of a specific Cacti tree. In combination with an access request system where users can request access or additional permissions to a system, this script can be used to automate the process for adding the requested permission to Cacti. By using this script Cacti administrators are able to reduce their workload by automating the task of adding permissions to an existing user.

Adding a Cacti tree

Although manually adding a Cacti tree does not involve a lot of work, managing the items underneath, however, does.

Time for action – adding a Cacti tree

1. Logon to your Cacti system.

2. Change to the Cacti CLI directory:

```
cd /var/www/html/cacti/cli
```

3. Execute the following command:

```
php add_tree.php
```

4. You will see the different options for this command:

```
# php add_tree.php
Add Tree Script 1.0, Copyright 2004-2010 - The Cacti Group

A simple command line utility to add objects to a tree in Cacti

usage: add_tree.php  --type=[tree|node] [type-options] [--quiet]

Tree options:
    --name=[Tree Name]
    --sort-method=[manual|alpha|natural|numeric]

Node options:
    --node-type=[header|host|graph]
    --tree-id=[ID]
    [--parent-node=[ID] [Node Type Options]]

Header node options:
    --name=[Name]

Host node options:
    --host-id=[ID]
    [--host-group-style=[1|2]]
    (host group styles:
    1 = Graph Template,
    2 = Data Query Index)

Graph node options:
    --graph-id=[ID]
    [--rra-id=[ID]]

List Options:
    --list-hosts
    --list-trees
    --list-nodes --tree-id=[ID]
    --list-rras
    --list-graphs --host-id=[ID]
#
```

5. As you can see you can add trees, hosts, or even single graphs to a tree or sub-tree. Let's add the `localhost` device to a tree. Use the following command to retrieve a list of hosts:

```
php add_tree.php --list-hosts
```

6. Use the following command to get a list of existing trees:

```
php add_tree.php --list-trees
```

7. Now get a list of the nodes from a tree:

```
php add_tree.php --tree-id=2 --list-nodes
```

8. You will see a list of the existing nodes for that tree as shown in the following screenshot:

```
# php add_tree.php --list-trees
Known Trees:
id      sort method                  name
1       Manual Ordering (No Sorting)  Default Tree
2       Manual Ordering (No Sorting)  Customer A

# php add_tree.php --tree-id=2 --list-nodes
Known Tree Nodes:
type      id      parentid      title      attribs
Header    8       N/A      Country A      Manual Ordering (No Sorting)
Header    9       8        Site A  Manual Ordering (No Sorting)
Host      10      9        192.168.178.40  Graph Template

#
```

9. Now let's add the `localhost` device to **Site A**:

```
php add_tree.php --type=node --node-type=host --tree-id=2 --
parent-node=9 --host-id=1
```

10. This will add the `localhost` device (`--host-id=1`) to the `Site A` node (`--parent-node=9`) under the **Customer A** tree (`--tree-id=2`).

11. You will see a confirmation once the item has been added as shown in the following screenshot:

```
# php add_tree.php --type=node
Added Node node-id: (11)
#
```

What just happened?

You just added a device to a sub-tree within Cacti. This can be used to automatically add new devices to the correct sub-trees. You will later see how this can be achieved easily using the Autom8 plugin.

Adding a device

Let's look into how you can use the Cacti CLI to automatically import a bunch of devices, but first let's look at the CLI commands which you will need for the import process.

Time for action – adding a single device to Cacti

1. Logon to your Cacti system.

2. Change to the Cacti CLI directory:

   `cd /var/www/html/cacti/cli`

3. Execute the following command:

   `php add_device.php`

4. You will see a list of all available options. Here you can see a short summary of these:

```
# php add_device.php
Add Device Script 1.0, Copyright 2004-2010 - The Cacti Group

A simple command line utility to add a device in Cacti

usage: add_device.php --description=[description] --ip=[IP] --template=[ID] [--notes="[]"] [--disable]
    [--avail=[ping]] --ping_method=[icmp] --ping_port=[N/A, 1-65534] --ping_retries=[2]
    [--version=[1|2|3]] [--community=] [--port=161] [--timeout=500]
    [--username= --password=] [--authproto=] [--privpass= --privproto=] [--context=]
    [--quiet]
```

5. Let's assume that you are using a global SNMP community which you have defined in the General section on the Cacti settings page. Then you can add a device using the following syntax:

   `php add_device.php --ip="192.168.178.53" --description="myCLIDevic e" --template=1`

6. This will add a `"Generic SNMP-enabled host"` to Cacti as seen in the following image:

```
# php add_device.php --ip="192.168.178.53" --description="myCLIDevice" --template=1
Adding myCLIDevice (192.168.178.53) as "Generic SNMP-enabled Host" using SNMP v1 with community "public"
Success - new device-id: (4)
#
```

What just happened?

You just added a new device using the Cacti CLI. You can now build an import script for adding a list of devices into Cacti.

Importing a list of devices into Cacti

Let's now look at the import script. The following code is parsing a special import file containing the device description, IP, SNMP version, community, and host template:

```php
$import_file = $_SERVER["argv"][1];
$dir = dirname(__FILE__);

print "Cacti Device Import Utility\n";
print "Import File: ". $import_file . "\n";

/* Check if the import file exists */
if ( file_exists( $import_file ) ) {
   print "\nImporting Devices...\n";
   // read in the import file
   $lines = file( $import_file );
   foreach ($lines as $line)
   {
      // cycle through the file
      $line = rtrim ($line); // remove the line ending character
      $data = preg_split("/;/",$line);  // split at the ";"
      $device_description = $data[0];
      $device_ip = $data[1];
      $device_snmp_version = $data[2];
      $device_snmp_community = $data[3];
      $device_template = $data[4];
      // Check if the device template is a number
      // and if not, set the template to a generic device template
      if ( preg_match("/^\d+$/",$device_template) == 0 ) {
        $device_template = 1; // Generic SNMP-enabled device
      }
      // Build the command
      $command = "php $dir/add_device.php ".
                 "--ip=\"$device_ip\" ".
                 "--description=\"$device_description\" ".
                 "--version=$device_snmp_version ".
                 "--community=$device_snmp_community ".
                 "--template=$device_template";
      $return_code = `$command`;
      print $return_code;
   }
}
else {
  die("Error: Import file [$import_file] does not exist!\n\n");
}
```

As you can see, this import script is using the existing `add_device.php` tool for actually adding the device to Cacti. The import script only wraps the system call to this tool within a **foreach** loop, which cycles through every entry of the import file.

So instead of adding every single device into Cacti, you can use a single text file containing the basic information about your devices. Let's have a look at this import file:

```
myDevice;192.168.0.11;2;public;1
myOtherDevice;192.168.0.12;2;public;
```

Each line of this import file contains the following data:

```
description;ip;SNMP version;SNMP community;host template
```

The available host templates can be displayed with the following command:

php add_device.php --list-host-templates

You can import a device list saved as `devicelist.txt` with the following line:

php import_devices.php devicelist.txt

You will see the following output on the command line:

```
# php import_devices.php devicelist.txt
Cacti Device Import Utility
Import File: devicelist.txt

Importing Devices...
Adding myDevice (192.168.0.11) as "Generic SNMP-enabled Host" using SNMP v2 with community "public"
Success - new device-id: (7)
Adding myOtherDevice (192.168.0.12) as "Generic SNMP-enabled Host" using SNMP v2 with community "public"
Success - new device-id: (8)
#
```

As you can see, by using the Cacti CLI and some additional scripting, you can integrate external inventory databases with Cacti.

Adding a graph to a device

Although adding a graph to a device is also possible using the CLI, it is recommended to use the Autom8 plugin for this task.

Autom8 – true Cacti automation

Using the capabilities of the CLI to add devices to Cacti, you can use Autom8 to automatically create graphs for that device and add it to a Cacti tree.

Installation

The installation of Autom8 is divided into 2 sections, the basic plugin installation and the patching of some of the Cacti files. Let's start with the basic plugin installation.

Time for action – installing the Autom8 plugin

1. Logon to your Cacti installation as the root user.

2. Change to the plugins directory of your Cacti installation:

   ```
   cd /var/www/html/cacti/plugins
   ```

3. Download the Autom8 plugin. You can find the download link at http://docs. cacti.net/plugin:autom8. Unfortunately v0.33 is not compatible with Cacti 0.8.7g so we have to use a beta version available from the Autom8 thread in the Cacti forums (http://forums.cacti.net/viewtopic.php?f=19&t=36493):

   ```
   wget -O autom8-v0.35b6.tgz  http://forums.cacti.net/download/file.
   php?id=21363
   ```

4. Extract the plugin:

   ```
   tar -xzvf autom8-v0.35b6.tgz
   ```

5. Do not yet install and enable the plugin.

What just happened?

You just finished the first part of the Autom8 installation. As the Autom8 plugin also needs some additional functionality for some of the core Cacti files, you will now need to follow the next step of patching these core Cacti files.

Patching the Cacti files

Now that you have extracted the plugin, you can continue with adding the required functions to the core Cacti files by applying the patches provided.

Time for action – patching the Cacti files

1. Change into the main Cacti directory:

   ```
   cd /var/www/html/cacti
   ```

2. Do a dry-run to check the provided patch file. As you have PIA 2.9 installed you will see several errors. PIA 2.9 contains most of the patches already:

   ```
   patch -p0 -N --dry-run < plugins/autom8/patches-087g/cacti087g_
   autom8.patch
   ```

3. Now apply the patch with the following command:

```
patch -p0 -N < plugins/autom8/patches-087g/cacti087g_autom8.patch
```

4. Check the `.rej` files for any errors. As already mentioned, most of these files complain about the patch already being applied as seen in the following console output of the patch command:

What just happened?

You just added the required functions to the core Cacti files. As you already have PIA 2.9 installed, most of these functions were already added when you installed PIA 2.9. Therefore, the patching process complains about previously applied patches.

Autom8 rules

Autom8 uses rules which are triggered by special events such as:

- Adding a new device to Cacti
- Re-Indexing the device

Rules are based on any item of the hosts table, so you can even use the new fields which have been added with the CbEnhancedInfo plugin you created earlier!

Tree rules

Let's have a look at creating a tree rule using some of the fields of the cbEnhancedInfo plugin.

Time for action – adding a new Tree Rule

1. Logon to the Cacti web interface with administrator privileges.

2. Go to **Templates | Tree Rules**.

3. You will see the following table with some default entries:

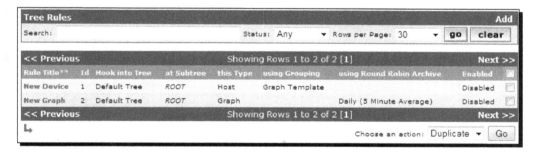

4. Click on the **Add** link to the top right of that page.

5. You should now see the new **Tree Rule Selection**.

6. Enter **Country A** as the **Name**.

7. Select **Customer A** as the **Tree**.

8. Select **Host** as the **Leaf Item Type**.

9. Select **Graph Template** as the **Graph Grouping Style**.

10. The form should look like the following screenshot:

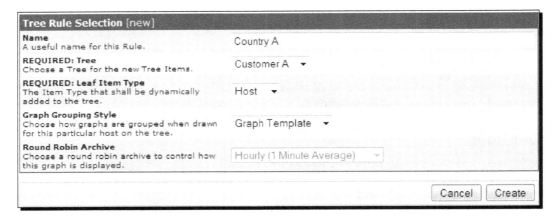

11. Click on **Create**.

12. Some additional tables and fields should now appear, as shown in the following screenshot:

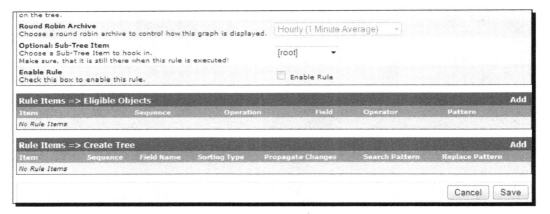

13. Click on the **Add** link of the **Rule Items => Eligible Object** table.

14. You can now create a new **Rule Item**.

15. Select **HOST: ebEnhancedInfo_country** as the **Field Name**.

16. Select **contains** as the **Operator**.

17. Enter **Country A** as the **Matching Pattern**. This can also be a regular expression depending on the **Operator** being used.

18. Your new **Rule Items** should now look like the following screenshot:

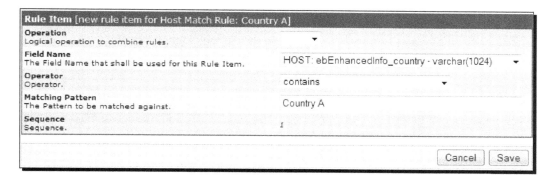

19. Click on the **Save** button.

20. Now you should define the action part, so click on the **Add** link to the top right of the **Rule Items => Create Tree** table.

21. On this new **Rule Item**, select **Alphabetic Ordering** as the **Sorting Type**.

22. Select **HOST: ebEnhancedInfo_country** as the **Header Type**.

23. Enter **.*** as the **Matching Pattern** so your new rule appears as shown in the following screenshot:

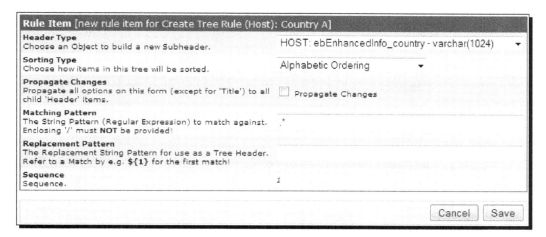

24. Click on the **Save** button.

25. On the main **Tree Rule Selection**, you will need to change some of the items now.

26. Select **Country A** as the **Sub-Tree Item**.

27. Check the checkbox next to **Enable Rule**.

28. Click on the **Save** button. Your **Tree Rule** should look identical to the following screenshot:

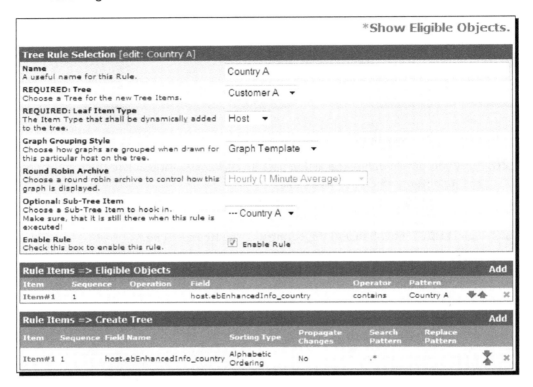

29. If you have defined the country field in a host to match Country A, you will see that host when you click on the **Show Eligible Objects** link at the top of that page:

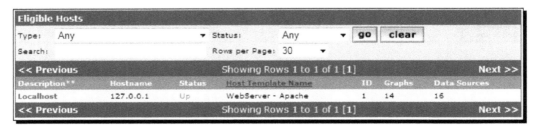

What just happened?

You just created your first **Tree Rule**. Now every time you add a new device or re-index a device that contains **Country A** in the country field, that host will be added to the **Country A** Cacti tree.

Let's look at how you can manually apply this new rule to existing devices.

Time for action – applying an Autom8 rule to devices

1. Go to **Management | Devices**.

2. Select the devices to which you want to apply the new Autom8 rule.

3. Select **Apply Autom8 Rules to Device(s)** from the action drop-down box as seen in the following sceenshot:

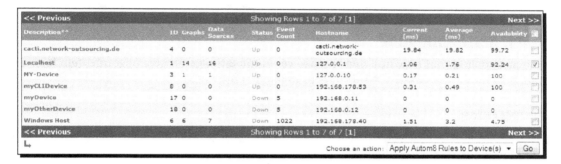

4. Click on the **Go** button.

5. On the following confirmation dialog press the **Continue** button.

6. Now go to **Management | Graph Trees**.

7. Click on the **Customer A** tree.

8. You should see your device appearing under the **Country A** item as seen in the following screenshot:

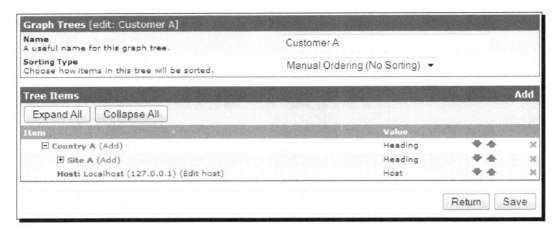

What just happened?

You just applied your new tree rule to a device. Autom8 then created a new tree item for that host under the **Country A** sub-tree, as defined in the rule.

Graph rules

Let's have a look at how you can use Autom8 to create an **In/Out Bits (64-bit Counters)** graph for interfaces which are **ifOperStatus** up.

Time for action – adding a Graph Rule

1. Go to **Templates | Graph Rules**.

2. Click on the **Add** link to the top right of the table.

3. Enter **IfOperStatus - UP - 64bit** as the **Name**.

4. Select **SNMP – Interface Statistics** as the **Data Query** as seen in the following screenshot:

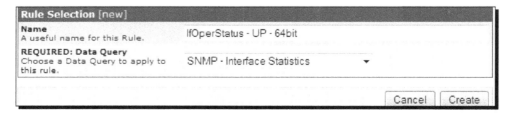

5. Click on the **Create** button.

6. Select **In/Out Bits (64-bit Counters)** as the **Graph Type**.

7. Check on the checkbox next to **Enable Rule**.

8. Add some **Rule Items => Eligible Hosts**, so your rules look as shown in the following screenshot:

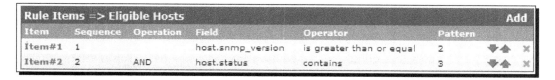

9. Now click on the **Add** link on the **Rule Items => Create Graph** table.

10. Select **ifOperStatus – Status** as the **Field Name**.

11. Select **contains** as the **Operator**.

12. Enter **up** as the **Matching Pattern**.

13. Click on the **Save** button.

14. Your new graph rule should now look like the following screenshot:

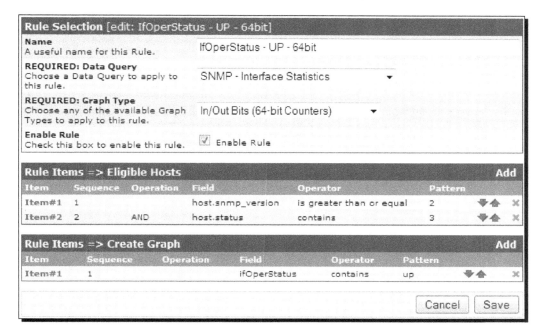

What just happened?

You just created a new graph rule for adding traffic graphs with 64-bit counters to any interface that is up. You can use the links at the top right of the graph rule screen to check which hosts and interfaces match your selection.

You can now apply this rule by going back to the device management screen and applying the Autom8 rule as you did with the tree rule you created earlier.

Further information

This chapter only provides a very short overview of the possibilities of Autom8. If you look into the `plugins` directory of Autom8, you will notice a PDF file there. This is the manual for Autom8 which contains further information, as well as other examples for creating rules. Of course, you're also encouraged to go to the Cacti forum for further information or help.

Pop Quiz – Let's test your knowledge about Chapter 12

1. What file and which parameters do you need to call to add a new Cacti tree?

   a. `php add_tree.php --function=new --type=tree --name="New Cacti Tree"`

   b. `php add_tree.php --type=tree --name="New Cacti Tree"`

   c. `php create_tree.php --type=tree --name="New Cacti Tree"`

2. What is the number for the up status of a device?

   a. 1

   b. 2

   c. 3

3. What rule do you need to create to have all Cisco devices within a sub-tree?

   a. You can use the SNMP description

   b. You can use the host template name

   c. You can use both of the above

Summary

In this final chapter you have learned how to automate parts of Cacti.

Specifically, you have covered:

◆ Using the CLI to add realm permissions to a user

◆ Importing devices using the CLI and some custom code

◆ Installing the Autom8 plugin

◆ Creating a tree rule for automatically putting devices into the correct Cacti tree

◆ Creating a graph rule for adding 64-bit counter traffic graphs to all interfaces which are up and are using SNMP version 2

You should now be able to automate most of the common Cacti tasks by using the Cacti CLI and the Autom8 plugin.

The information you've learned throughout this book allows you to install and manage your own Cacti instance. You've read how to extend Cacti with readily available plugins and how to create your own plugins. With the reporting and automation functionality added, you're able to offer a full set of automated services to your customers.

In the following appendices, you will see that extending Cacti is not limited to the local installation, but that you're also able to access and use Cacti with mobile devices.

Mobile Access / Administration

With the popularity of Smartphones and BlackBerry devices increasing daily, mobile administration and access has become more and more important. There are several options available ranging from a mobile enhanced web page to pure mobile clients.

In this appendix, you're going to:

- ◆ Get an overview of mobile solutions for Cacti
- ◆ Take a quick look at the iPhone client—iCacti
- ◆ Install the nmidWebService plugin to add a SOAP interface to Cacti
- ◆ Install, configure, and use the BlackBerry client—BBCacti
- ◆ Familiarize yourself with the mobile web interface—the mobile client

Let's get mobile with Cacti!

Overview of mobile solutions for Cacti

There are several mobile clients and solutions available for Cacti.

iCacti—the iPhone/iPad client

The iCacti client is a pure iPhone and iPad client which allows end users to view the Cacti graphs on a remote server using their iPhone or iPad device. The current version 2.1 doesn't provide additional plugin support.

The iCacti client is available from the iTunes store.

BBCacti—the BlackBerry client

The BlackBerry client allows end users to view Cacti graphs on their mobile devices. They're able to browse the Cacti tree and select a specific time range to look at.

The following features are supported by this mobile client:

- Uses a SOAP WebService when connecting to the Cacti server
- Has the ability to view graphs with user-defined time frames
- Allows users to view threshold breaches when using the Thold plugin
- Provides a list of downed hosts
- Supports adding graphs to a report using the CereusReporting plugin
- Allows for mobile access to be enabled on a per-user basis

The BlackBerry client needs the nmidWebService plugin to be installed and configured.

The following screenshot shows an example of a graph on a BlackBerry Storm device:

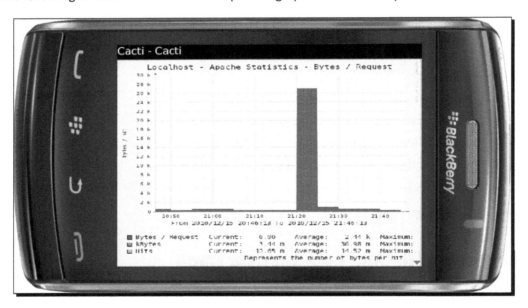

The BBCacti client is available from the author's homepage.

nmidMobileClient—the Windows mobile client

The nmidMobileClient uses the nmidWebService SOAP interface when connecting to the Cacti server for retrieving tree and graph information. An example graph from the nmidMobileClient can be seen in the following screenshot:

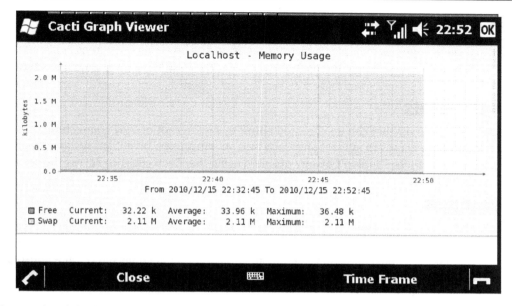

The nmidMobileClient supports the following features:

- Addition of one or more Cacti instances
- Browsing the Cacti Tree
- Viewing Cacti graphs

Unfortunately, at the time of writing, this client is still under development.

The mobile plugin—mobile enhanced Cacti web page

The mobile plugin is a small add-on which provides a simplified web page for some basic Cacti information such as down hosts and breached thresholds, as can be seen in the following screenshot:

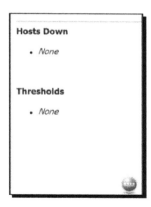

The iPhone/iPad client

The iCacti client supports multiple Cacti instances as well as browsing Cacti trees. It allows the user to view graphs and change the time frame of the graphs using some pre-defined values.

Requirements

Besides a Cacti server that can be accessed either by an Internet or VPN connection, users also need to have access to at least one Cacti tree. As most users on a Cacti system already have this access, there shouldn't be any problem using the iCacti client to access the server.

Advantages

The client doesn't require any special software or plugin to be installed on the Cacti server. With the 2.x version, access requirements for mobile users have been reduced to the normal Cacti access and console access isn't needed any more. Earlier versions did require console access, therefore the client was only useable by Cacti administrators.

Disadvantages

Cacti administrators aren't able to limit mobile client access to some specific users as the iPhone client uses the Cacti web page like any normal browser does.

Support

Some support is provided through the Cacti forums and via e-mail. Please make sure to read the feedback posted by some of the existing iCacti users.

BBCacti—the BlackBerry client

BlackBerry devices are widely used in business environments and are usually able to connect to internal systems without the need to create separate VPN connections. The BBCacti client allows end users to view graphs or manage reports using the familiar BlackBerry interface.

Requirements

The BlackBerry client requires the installation of the nmidWebService plugin on the Cacti server. The plugin provides various functions to the BBCacti client, such as retrieving the contents of Cacti trees and authenticating users against the configured mechanisms. Changes on the Cacti system (for example, updating to a new version) do not necessarily require an update to the BlackBerry client, but just the adaption of the nmidWebService plugin to the new version.

Installing the nmidWebService plugin also allows Cacti administrators to allow or deny mobile access to Cacti by using a realm permissions setting.

The BBCacti version is currently only compatible with versions 4.x and 5.x of the BlackBerry OS, but support for 6.x is coming soon.

Advantages

The BBCacti client is able to support plugins such as Thold or CereusReporting by utilizing the built-in functionality of the nmidWebServices' SOAP interface. By using this SOAP interface, updates to Thold or other plugins does not require a client update on the BlackBerry. There's also no need for any special user access requirements for mobile users.

BlackBerry devices are usually able to connect to internal systems using the BlackBerry Enterprise Server.

Disadvantages

The BlackBerry user interface isn't as good looking as the iPhone/iPad one. BlackBerry devices usually don't have large displays, which makes the graphs small and of lower quality. In addition, the installation of the nmidWebService plugin can be difficult as it requires a particular PHP module to be compiled and installed.

The nmidWebService plugin

The nmidWebService plugin provides a SOAP interface to Cacti by using the WSO2 WebService Framework for PHP. Using a SOAP interface to connect to Cacti allows clients and remote systems to use a standardized way of retrieving and delivering data to and from the Cacti system.

Let's look into installing the nmidWebService plugin and the WSO2 WebService Framework for PHP on your CentOS system.

Time for action – installing the WSO2 WebService framework

1. Logon to your Cacti server.

2. Change to the `tmp` directory:

   `cd /tmp`

3. Download the WSO2 plugin:

   ```
   wget http://dist.wso2.org/products/wsf/php/2.1.0/wso2-wsf-php-src-
   2.1.0.tar.gz
   ```

4. Install some required packages:
   ```
   yum install php-devel php-xml libxml2-devel
   ```

5. Extract the `tar.gz` file:
   ```
   tar -xzvf wso2-wsf-php-src-2.1.0.tar.gz
   ```

6. Change to the new directory:
   ```
   cd wso2-wsf-php-src-2.1.0
   ```

7. Run configure to automatically generate the make files:
   ```
   ./configure
   ```

8. This will take some time to complete. Once finished, start the build process:
   ```
   make
   ```

9. If the build process finished successfully, install the binaries:
   ```
   make install
   ```

10. Create a file to tell PHP to load the new module:
    ```
    echo "extension=wsf.so" >> /etc/php.d/wsf.ini
    ```

11. Check if the module loads by issuing the following command:
    ```
    php -m
    ```

12. The newly added module should be listed in the output.

13. Restart the web server so it loads the new extension:
    ```
    /etc/init.d/httpd restart
    ```

What just happened?

You just installed the WSO2 WebService Framework for PHP which is required for the nmidWebService plugin to work correctly. This framework provides some WebService functionality which the native PHP-SOAP module is not able to provide.

Installing the nmidWebService plugin

Now that you've installed the basic requirement for the nmidWebService plugin, let's look at how to install and configure the plugin itself.

Time for action – installing the nmidWebService plugin

1. Change to the Cacti plugins directory:

   ```
   cd /var/www/html/cacti/plugins
   ```

2. Download the nmidWebService plugin:

   ```
   wget http://redmine.nmid-plugins.de/attachments/download/292/
   nmidWebService_v09b.tgz
   ```

3. Extract the plugin:

   ```
   tar -xzvpf  nmidWebService_v09b.tgz
   ```

4. Change to the new directory:

   ```
   cd nmidWebService
   ```

5. Make the `tmp` directory writeable by the web server:

   ```
   chown apache.cacti tmp
   ```

   ```
   chmod 775 tmp
   ```

6. Edit the `webservice_wso.wsdl` file and change all references for `cacti.network-outsourcing.de` to your server.

7. Install and enable the nmidWebService plugin from the Cacti web interface:

			Showing All 9 Rows					
Actions	Name	Load Order	Description**	Type	Status	Author	Web Page	Version
⊕ ⊠	Autom8		Automate Cacti Tasks	General	Active	Reinhard Scheck	http://docs.cacti.net/plugin:autom8	0.35b6
⊕ ⊠	CbEnhancedInfo		cbEnhancedInfo	General	Active	Thomas Urban	n/a	1.00
⊕ ⊠	Settings		Global Plugin Settings	System	Active	Jimmy Conner	http://cactiusers.org	0.7
⊕ ⊠	NmidCreatePDF		NMID CereusReporting Plugin	General	Active	Thomas Urban	http://www.urban-software.de	1.51
⊕ ⊠	NmidWebService		NMID WebService Plugin	General	Active	Thomas Urban	http://www.urban-software.de	0.9b
⊕ ⊠	Ntop		NTop Viewer	General	Active	Jimmy Conner	http://cactiusers.org	0.2
⊕ ⊠	Nectar		Send Graphs via EMail	General	Active	Reinhard Scheck	http://docs.cacti.net/plugin:nectar	0.28
⊕	Superlinks		SuperLinks	Old PIA	Active	Howard Jones	http://wotsit.thingy.com/haj/cacti/superlinks-plugin.html	0.8
⊕ ⊠	Thold		Thresholds	General	Active	Jimmy Conner	http://cactiusers.org	0.4.2
			Showing All 9 Rows					
NOTE: Please sort by 'Load Order' to change plugin load ordering.								
NOTE: SYSTEM plugins can not be ordered.								

8. Go to the Cacti settings page and click on the **NMID** tab. Look for the **NMID – WebService** section within that tab.

9. Enter **guest** as the **WebService Password**:

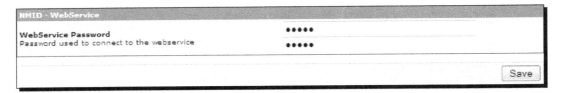

10. Click on **Save**.

What just happened?

You just installed and enabled the nmidWebService plugin. By setting a WebService password, this will allow you to use the BBCacti client to connect to your Cacti server.

BBCacti installation

The BBCacti client can be installed using the BlackBerry Desktop software which is available free from the BlackBerry site at: `http://de.blackberry.com/services/desktop/`.

The latest version of BBCacti can be downloaded using the following URL:

`http://www.network-outsourcing.de/uploads/nmidMobileClients/BBCactiClient_latest.zip`.

You'll also need to request a trial license from the following page:

`http://www.network-outsourcing.de/Products/bbcacti/bbcacti_trialrequest.html`.

Time for action – installing the BBCacti client

1. Download the latest version from the URL provided at the start of this section.

2. Extract the archive to your desktop.

3. Start the BlackBerry desktop software and connect your BlackBerry device to your PC.

4. Once the BlackBerry is connected, click on **Applications**. You'll see a list of available software for your device, as well as an import button at the top-right:

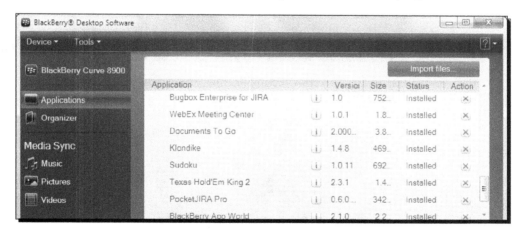

5. Click on the import button and select the BBCactiClient.alx file extracted from the previous step.

6. The list should now contain the BBCacti application as seen in the following screenshot:

7. Click on the **Apply** button at the bottom-left of the screen to install the BBCacti application.

8. You'll see a dialog with a progress bar installing any updates as well as the application. Wait until it finishes. Your device may reboot during the process.

What just happened?

You just installed the Cacti client for BlackBerry to your mobile device. By default the installation directory for the BBCacti client icon is the download folder, so an icon should be displayed there. Now, let's look at how to configure the client.

BBCacti configuration

Before you begin, write down the basics of your Cacti server. This example will use the following information:

◆ Cacti Name: myCacti Server

◆ Cacti URL: `http://192.168.178.53/cacti/plugins/nmidWebService/`

◆ Password: `guest`

Let's start.

Time for action – configuration of BBCacti

1. Click on the BBCacti icon to start the application:

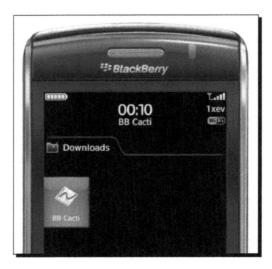

2. You'll be asked to enter an **Activation Code**. Enter the trial key which you received:

3. You'll see a confirmation box once the **Activation Code** has been accepted:

4. The application will close once the **OK** button has been clicked. Restart it to continue the configuration process.

5. The application will ask for the details of your Cacti installation. Enter the information you wrote down earlier and click on the **Save** button:

6. Again the application will close to store the information to the device. If you change the data later, or add a new Cacti server, the BBCacti client won't close again.

7. At the next start, the application will ask for a Cacti username and password. You can use any Cacti user to whom you've granted the permissions to use the mobile client interface:

8. Once logged in, you'll be presented with a screen allowing you to browse the Cacti tree, view threshold breaches, or look at a list of currently down hosts:

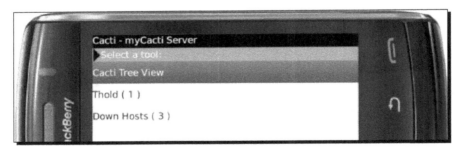

What just happened?

You just activated your trial license and configured the BBCacti application to go to your Cacti installation using the nmidWebService plugin, and the configured WebService password. You also used an existing Cacti user to logon to your system.

Time for action – using the BBCacti client

1. Select the **Cacti Tree View**. You'll be presented with the list of available trees as seen in Cacti:

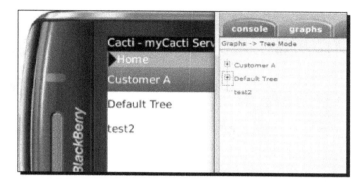

2. The **Thold** page seen after the login shows you a list of graphs which have thresholds that are breached. You can directly select and view the graph from the **Thold** page.

3. The **Down Hosts** list is just a simple list of hosts currently marked as **down** by Cacti.

4. Drill down the **Cacti Tree View** and select your localhost device:

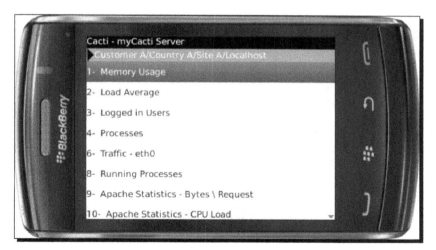

5. Select the **Load Average** graph. A loading icon should appear. Wait until the graph loads:

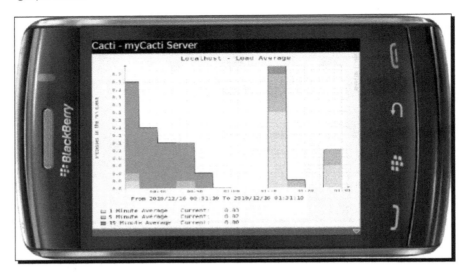

6. You can change the timeframe by clicking on the trackball or using the default BlackBerry menu. You can select any of the pre-defined timeframes or define a custom one:

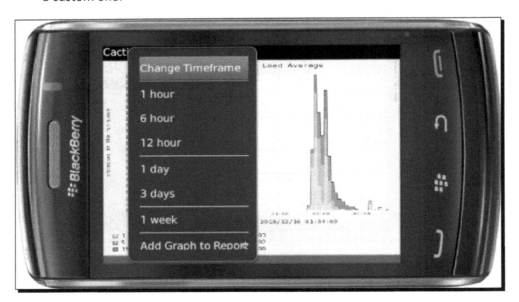

What just happened?

You just connected to your Cacti server and looked at your first graph on your BlackBerry device. You're now able to browse the graphs on your server and limit access to the mobile client interface using the normal Cacti user management system. You're also able to look at graphs with threshold breaches without searching the Cacti tree for the correct graph.

The mobile plugin

The mobile plugin provides a fast way of accessing the threshold and down hosts' data using any mobile device capable of running a web browser. Older mobile devices with limited functionalities and no application support are still capable of viewing the threshold data and a list of down hosts by using the mobile plugin.

Time for action – installing the mobile plugin

1. Logon to your Cacti installation.

2. Change to the plugins directory:

```
cd /var/www/html/cacti/plugins
```

3. Download the mobile plugin from http://docs.cacti.net/plugin:mobile:

```
wget -O mobile-latest.tgz 'http://docs.cacti.net/_media/plugin:
mobile-latest.tgz?id=plugin%3Amobile&cache=cache'
```

4. Extract the mobile plugin:

```
tar -xzvf  mobile-latest.tgz
```

5. Rename the mobile-0.1 directory:

```
mv mobile-0.1/ mobile
```

6. Enable the plugin from the Plugin Management page:

\multicolumn{9}{c}{Showing All 10 Rows}
Actions	Name	Load Order	Description**	Type	Status	Author	Web Page	Version
⊙ ⊡	Autom8		Automate Cacti Tasks	General	Active	Reinhard Scheck	http://docs.cacti.net /plugin:autom8	0.35b6
⊙ ⊡	CbEnhancedInfo		cbEnhancedInfo	General	Active	Thomas Urban	n/a	1.00
⊙ ⊡	Settings		Global Plugin Settings	System	Active	Jimmy Conner	http://cactiusers.org	0.7
⊙	Mobile		Mobile Cacti	Old PIA	Active	Jimmy Conner	http://cactiusers.org	0.1
⊙ ⊡	NmidCreatePDF		NMID CereusReporting Plugin	General	Active	Thomas Urban	http://www.urban-software.de	1.51
⊙ ⊡	NmidWebService		NMID WebService Plugin	General	Active	Thomas Urban	http://www.urban-software.de	0.9b
⊙ ⊡	Ntop		NTop Viewer	General	Active	Jimmy Conner	http://cactiusers.org	0.2
⊙ ⊡	Nectar		Send Graphs via EMail	General	Active	Reinhard Scheck	http://docs.cacti.net /plugin:nectar	0.28
⊙	Superlinks		SuperLinks	Old PIA	Active	Howard Jones	http://wotsit.thingy.com /haj/cacti/superlinks-plugin.html	0.8
⊙ ⊡	Thold		Thresholds	General	Active	Jimmy Conner	http://cactiusers.org	0.4.2
\multicolumn{9}{c}{Showing All 10 Rows}

NOTE: Please sort by 'Load Order' to change plugin load ordering.
NOTE: SYSTEM plugins can not be ordered.

What just happened?

You just installed the mobile plugin. If you now browse to your Cacti web interface using an older mobile device, you'll be presented with a list of down hosts and breached thresholds. The mobile plugin doesn't provide any further functionality such as viewing graphs.

Summary

In this appendix you've learned some further information on how to access your Cacti installation with mobile devices. As you've seen, there are different methods by which to access a Cacti system remotely. Clients for Android and other tablet devices will likely be developed in the future, so you'll be able to choose from a variety of systems and use the one that best suits your needs.

Specifically, you've covered:

- ◆ Installing the nmidWebService plugin
- ◆ Installing and configuring the BlackBerry Client BBCacti
- ◆ Installing and enabling the mobile plugin
- ◆ How to use the BlackBerry client to view Cacti graphs

You should now know about the options for accessing Cacti with mobile devices and the different functions and techniques for retrieving data from the Cacti system.

B
Online Resources

Cacti website

The main Cacti website provides the latest patches as well as lots of other useful information. You can visit it at: http://www.cacti.net.

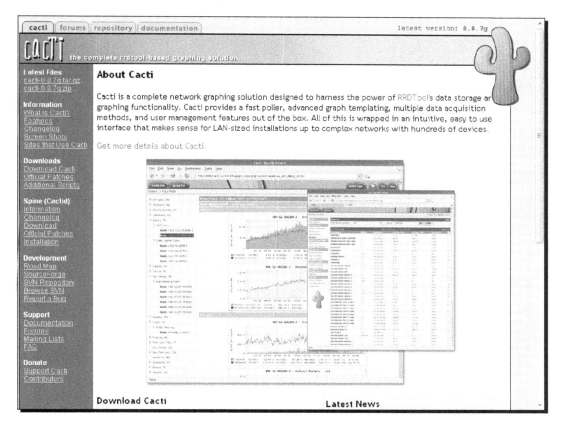

Spine

Spine is a high performance poller which, by far, exceeds the performance of the original `cmd.php`. You can find the latest spine version at:

`http://www.cacti.net/spine_download.php.`

Plugin Architecture

The Plugin Architecture provides additional functionality to Cacti. You won't be able to use any plugins without installing it. The upcoming Cacti version 0.8.8, which is still under development, is going to include the Plugin Architecture. You can download the latest Plugin Architecture at:

`http://www.cacti.net/downloads/pia/.`

Cacti documentation

The Cacti community, as well as Cacti developers, provide lots of documentation for Cacti, the available plugins, scripts, and templates. You can access the Cacti documentation site at:

`http://docs.cacti.net/.`

Cacti forum

The main source for support and information is the Cacti forum. You can find it at:

`http://forums.cacti.net/.`

Cacti bug reporting

If you find a bug in Cacti, and the community in the forums can confirm it, you should post a bug ticket in their tracker at:

`http://bugs.cacti.net/.`

Cacti plugin hooks overview

You can find a list of available hooks provided by the Plugin Architecture and their description at the following page:

`http://docs.cacti.net/plugins:development.hook_api_ref.`

Cacti Users' site

The Cacti Users' site provides some additional plugins, as well as the CactiEZ ISO images. CactiEZ allows you to install a full Cacti system with the Plugin Architecture, as well as having several plugins already installed and configured. You can find the Cacti Users' site at:

```
http://www.cactiusers.org/.
```

Howie's stuff

Howie, an active user from the forums, provides the well-known Weathermap plugin for Cacti. You can find his page at:

```
www.network-weathermap.com.
```

RRDTool

RRDTool provides the basis for data storage within Cacti. You can find more information on it at:

```
http://www.mrtg.org/rrdtool/.
```

Tobi Oetiker

Of course, when talking about RRDTool, the creator of this and many other useful tools, Tobi Oetiker, should also be mentioned. You can find his homepage at:

```
http://tobi.oetiker.ch/hp/.
```

RRDTool, Cacti, and time zones

You should always have your Cacti server run in UTC time. There's a good article about why you should do so at:

```
http://www.vandenbogaerdt.nl/rrdtool/timezone.php.
```

Xing German Cacti group

There's a German speaking Cacti group on `Xing.com`. Look here for more:

```
https://www.xing.com/net/pri1c981ex/cacti
```

LinkedIn Cacti Group

Of course there's also a Cacti group on LinkedIn:

```
http://www.linkedin.com/groups?home=&gid=968927
```

NMID plugins and CereusReporting

The CereusReporting plugin as well as the NMID plugins have their own pages. You can find more information at:

```
http://www.network-outsourcing.de/
```

Further Information

The Round Robin Database Tool

Cacti uses RRDtool to store and graph its performance data. RRD files store data in a fixed size file using a **First In**, **First Out** (**FIFO**) methodology and in order to aggregate data, different **Round Robin Archives** (**RRA**) are defined within a single RRD file. These RRAs usually consist of daily, weekly, monthly, and yearly archives but can be freely defined.

The RRD file architecture

The principle of an RRD file is shown in the next figure. We have defined three Round Robin Archives—one storing 5 minute polling data, one storing 20 minutes (4 * 5 minute polling data) aggregated data, and another storing hourly (12 * 5 minute polling data) aggregated data.

In this example, the data step is defined as 5 minutes (300 seconds) so updates to the RRD file should happen every 5 minutes. During each update, the data is being written to the first archive. After 20 minutes have passed, the first data set is aggregated and written to the second archive so that it contains an overall view of the 20-minute period. Once a full hour has passed, the first data set is once again aggregated and written to the hourly archive, providing a broader view.

Each RRA is limited to a specific amount of data points, after which the data that has been written first will be overwritten by the newest data. This methodology ensures that the RRD files do not grow in size beyond their initial state. The disadvantage of this is the loss of detailed data once the RRA overwrites it:

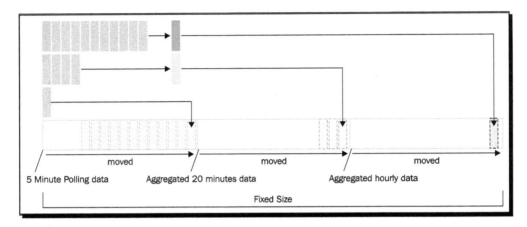

Let's take the example and look at the corresponding `rrdtool` command:

```
rrdtool create test.rrd --step 300 \
DS:data:GAUGE:600:U:U              \
RRA:AVERAGE:0.5:1:16               \
RRA:AVERAGE:0.5:4:16               \
RRA:AVERAGE:0.5:12:16
```

The `--step` flag sets the heartbeat in which data is supposed to come in. In the example it is 5 minutes (`300` seconds), which is the default for RRD files. This file contains one data source (DS) called `data`, which is defined as a gauge. Since we don't want to limit the data entering the archive based on a minimum or maximum value, it is set to `U`. The `600` defined here is the time in seconds allowed to pass between two updates before the specific data point is set to unknown.

The file contains three round RRAs. The first one stores 16 data points, so a total of 80 minutes of data is stored.

The second archive stores 16 data points, which are each an aggregated average of the last four data polls. This gives a total amount of 320 minutes, or five hours. This also means that this archive has already lost some detailed information as each data point in it only represents a 20-minute timeslot, but we can view data going much further back.

The last archive also contains 16 data points, but this time one data point is an aggregated average of the last 12 polls. Therefore, each data point in the archive represents one whole hour, but allows us to keep data from 16 hours earlier.

As can be seen in this example, if you go beyond the previous 80 minutes, you will lose the data granularity, as aggregation kicks in.

The default RRA definitions of Cacti are:

◆ Daily (5-minute Average)
◆ Weekly (30-minute Average)
◆ Monthly (2-hour Average)
◆ Yearly (1-day Average)

As the default polling interval for Cacti is five minutes, the daily data will have the most detailed data. Unfortunately, the Daily 5-minute Average RRA will only keep this detailed data for 2 days, after which you will lose the detailed information. This can be changed in Cacti, but will also increase the RRD file size significantly.

There are many more options available during the RRD file creation. If you are interested in learning more, you will find some links and references in the previous appendix.

SNMP: The Simple Network Management Protocol

When it comes to network management protocols, the **Simple Network Management Protocol (SNMP)** is probably one of the best known. It is commonly used in networks and several applications internally support SNMP for monitoring purposes.

In this section, we will only provide a short overview of SNMP because its full workings are beyond the scope of this book.

The Management Information Base

SNMP stores information in a virtual database called a Management Information Base (MIB). The database is hierarchical (tree-structured) and entries are addressed through object identifiers (OID). The following SNMP table output shows this structure:

```
.1.3.6.1.2.1.25.3.8.1.1.1 = INTEGER: 1
.1.3.6.1.2.1.25.3.8.1.1.2 = INTEGER: 2
.1.3.6.1.2.1.25.3.8.1.2.1 = STRING: "/"
.1.3.6.1.2.1.25.3.8.1.2.2 = STRING: "/boot"
.1.3.6.1.2.1.25.3.8.1.3.1 = ""
.1.3.6.1.2.1.25.3.8.1.3.2 = ""
.1.3.6.1.2.1.25.3.8.1.4.1 = OID: .1.3.6.1.2.1.25.3.9.23
.1.3.6.1.2.1.25.3.8.1.4.2 = OID: .1.3.6.1.2.1.25.3.9.23
.1.3.6.1.2.1.25.3.8.1.5.1 = INTEGER: readWrite(1)
.1.3.6.1.2.1.25.3.8.1.5.2 = INTEGER: readWrite(1)
.1.3.6.1.2.1.25.3.8.1.6.1 = INTEGER: true(1)
.1.3.6.1.2.1.25.3.8.1.6.2 = INTEGER: false(2)
```

The number to the left represent the OIDs, the data to the right are the actual values of that OID. If you look at the OIDs to the left, you can see the actual tree structure:

```
.1.3.6.1.2.1.25.3.8.1.
                      \--1
                        \--1
                        \--2
                      \--2
                        \--1
                        \--2
```

Generally an organization that has an SNMP agent will publish an MIB-Module for their product and this is used on the management station to map the OIDs to human readable equivalents and perform some basic sanity checks on the format of data returned.

SNMPv1

SNMPv1 is the original SNMP protocol defined in the late 1980s. One of the main design goals for SNMP was to keep it simple and easy to implement. Due to this decision, SNMPv1 gained widespread commercial relevance and today most manageable network equipment supports at least SNMPv1.

By keeping it simple on the agent (network equipment) side, more complex tasks were left to the clients.

SNMPv1 had 5 core protocol data units (PDUs) for getting and setting data as well as sending out alerts. These are:

- GetRequest
- GetNextRequest
- SetRequest
- Response
- Trap

The GetRequest and GetNextRequest units are used to retrieving data from an agent but they can only retrieve one data point at a time, so retrieving interface statistics on a large network device requires many GetRequests or GetNextRequests to be sent to the device.

With the SetRequest unit, data can be set on the device. This is typically used to change configurations (e.g. on Cisco routers/swtiches), or for sending commands to a network device (e.g. ping).

The Response unit is sent by the SNMP agent to the management station as a response to a Get or Set request.

Traps are initiated from the SNMP agent to send immediate alerts to the defined management station. They include information about:

- ◆ Who is sending the trap
- ◆ What occurred
- ◆ When it occurred
- ◆ Additional information as OID/value pairs

Cacti itself does not handle SNMP traps. There are several plugins available for adding this functionality to Cacti.

Security

SNMPv1 does not have any encryption and only uses a community string to identify the management station, and even then it is transmitted in clear text. As a result, SNMPv1 is a very insecure protocol because SetRequests can be used to reconfigure network equipment if improperly configured.

Modern network equipment allows the definition of access lists for requests to the SNMP agent which should be used in order to reduce security issues.

SNMPv2 / SNMPv2c

SNMPv2 addresses some of the shortcomings of the SNMPv1 protocol by introducing two new protocol data units: GetBulkRequests and InformRequest.

The GetBulkRequest unit allows a single GetRequest to retrieve numerous OIDs from an SNMP agent without the need to send several GetRequests. This is particularly useful for retrieving large amounts of objects such as a list of all interfaces of a network device.

The Inform unit addresses the unreliability of the Trap unit, which sends a unidirectional trap. In contrast to this, Informs provide a mechanism to send reliable events from the agent to the management station, which is then acknowledged with a response so that the notification is confirmed by the agent.

With SNMPv2 there was also an update to the MIB definition, which was enhanced to support more data types such as IPv6 addresses, Octet strings and 64-bit counters.

Security

Although SNMPv2 was also supposed to address the security deficits of SNMPv1, it still uses un-encrypted communication, secured only by a community string and access control lists. This is also reflected by the additional "c" in SNMPv2c.

SNMPv3

SNMPv3 does not add new operations or enhancements to the MIB, but addresses the security problems of SNMPv1 and SNMPv2c. It can be seen as SNMPv2c plus additional security, as it allows message encryption and strong authentication of senders.

SNMP support in Cacti

Cacti supports all three versions of the SNMP protocol which allows legacy equipment to be monitored alongside the latest devices.

MRTG – Multi Router Traffic Grapher

You have probably already heard of MRTG, but what are the differences between Cacti and MRTG? MRTG has been around for some time with Version 1 being released in 1995, about 6 years before the first version of Cacti.

MRTG provides the ability to gather network performance data on a scheduled basis, and a fast graphical view of network use with historic data for comparison is available.

Both use RRD files to store performance data and also use a web interface to display the graphs. The major difference between MRTG and Cacti is the feature-rich web application that Cacti offers. The whole configuration for the system is done using the Cacti web interface whereas MRTG only offers text-based configuration files.

In contrast to MRTG, Cacti also offers granular user rights management, which allows administrators to allow or deny access to whole graph trees or even individual graphs. This enables Cacti to be multi-client aware. MRTG itself doesn't have such a system, which reduces the ability to use it in multi-client environments, as would be needed by network outsourcing centers.

Where to get support?

There are several options for getting support for Cacti or the numerous add-ons and plugins.

Cacti forums

The Cacti forums are the primary source for support, finding solutions or getting add-ons and plugins. The Cacti community is very active, with most developers posting on the forums daily.

You will find helpful HowTos and lots of information on plugins, templates, and monitoring different kinds of hosts.

You can find the Cacti forums at `forums.cacti.net`.

Mailing list

The Cacti community also provides a mailing list for announcements and e-mail support. The mailing list is also monitored by the Cacti community.

The mailing lists can be found at `http://www.cacti.net/mailing_lists.php`.

Commercial support

Cacti is open source and the main development team does not offer commercial support for it. There are, however, a few companies such as GroundWork Open Source or Bayside Networks that offer commercial support for Cacti, or have specially integrated Cacti versions available.

In addition, some of the plugin developers offer commercial support for their plugins.

Pop Quiz Answers

Chapter 1:

Installing Cacti

1	2	3
a	b	c

Chapter 2:

Using Graphs to Monitor Networks and Devices

1	2	3
c	c	c

Chapter 3:

Creating and Using Templates

1	2	3
c	a	c

Chapter 4:

User Management

1	2	3
d	a	d

Chapter 5:

Data Management

1	2	3
c	c	c

Chapter 6:

Cacti Maintenance

1	2	3
c	c	c

Chapter 7:

Network and Server Monitoring

1	2	3
c	a	a

Chapter 8:

Plugin Architecture

1	2	3
c	a	b

Chapter 9:

Plugins

1	2	3
	a	b

Chapter 10:

Threshold Monitoring with Thold

1	2	3
b	b	a

Chapter 11:

Enterprise Reporting

1	2	3
c	a	d

Chapter 12:

Cacti Automation for NOC

1	2	3
b	c	c

Index

remote script 105, 106
remote SSH data input method
  creating 105
  data input method, creating 112, 113
  data template, creating 114
  graph, adding to device 114
  graph template, creating 114
  local script 106
  remote script 105
  SSH keys, creating with PuTTY Key Generator
      110, 111
  SSH public key authentication 109
repair_database.php script 138
repair_templates.php script 137
report
  graph item, adding to 245, 246
report, generating
  CereusReporting plugin used 250
  Nectar plugin used 243
reporting solutions, Cacti
  CereusReporting 242, 246
  Nectar 241, 242
  need for 241
report items
  adding 245, 246
report templates 260
resource directory 121
Response unit 308
restore process
  about 128
  Cacti config.php file, restoring 130-132
  Cacti database, restoring 128
  Cacti files, restoring 128, 130
returnData array 108
Round Robin Archives (RRA) 305
Round Robin Database Tool. *See* RRDtool
rra directory 121
RRD file architecture 305-307
RRD file check
  automating 135, 136
RRD files
  listing 133, 135
RRDTool
  about 303, 305
  URL 303
rrdtool graph command 65
RRDtool graph function 54

RRDtool graphs 32
rtrim command 90

S

scripts directory 121
SetRequest unit 308
settings plugin
  about 174, 184
  functions 184
  installing 174, 175
  removing 176, 177
setup.php file 172, 180, 187, 189
Simple Network Management Protocol. *See*
      SNMP
single device
  adding, to Cacti 270
Smokeping reports feature 259
SNMP
  about 307
  Cacti support 310
  Management Information Base 307, 308
  setting up, on Cisco devices 143, 144
  SNMPv1 308
  SNMPv2 / SNMPv2c 309
  SNMPv3 310
SNMP-based data templates
  about 57
  creating 55-57
snmp-server commands 143
SNMP access
  configuring, on CISCO PIX Firewall 145
  configuring, on Cisco Switch 142-144
  setting up, for VMware ESXi 4 147, 148
  setting up, on VMware ESX 3.5 148, 149
SNMP based data query
  rebuilding 99
  XML data file, building 99
snmpd daemon
  restarting 115
SNMP Server feature
  enabling 150, 151
SNMPv1
  about 308
  protocol data units 308
  security 309
SNMPv2 / SNMPv2c
  about 309

protocol data units 309
security 309
SNMPv3 310
snmpwalk command 101
Spine
about 302
URL 302
Spine poller
installing, under CentOS 5 system 16-18
installing, under Windows 22
SSH keys
creating, with PuTTY Key Generator 110, 111
SSH public key authentication 109
stress tool
installing 233, 234
threshold, testing 233, 234
superlinks plugin
about 184
configuring 185, 186
functions 184
installing 185
using 185, 186

T

table list view page
creating 202
data, deleting 203, 204
data, retrieving 204-207
data, sorting 204-207
tar command 126
template permissions 79
template repository 72
templates
about 53
data templates 54
exporting 71
graph templates 54
host templates 54
importing 68, 70
template user
about 83
missing packages, installing 83, 84
Thold
about 166, 167, 222

breached thresholds, viewing 234, 235
configuring 223
e-mail address, setting up 226, 227
installing 222, 223
permissions, assigning to users 226, 227
threshold, creating 227-233
threshold monitoring 221
threshold templates, assigning 238, 239
threshold templates, creating 235, 237
Thold, configuring
default altering options 224
default baseline options 225
default email options 224, 225
general options 223
threshold
creating 227-233
testing 233, 234
threshold creation page
about 228
alert setup section 231
basic and mandatory settings section 228, 229
threshold setup section 229, 230
threshold line
adding, to graph 61, 62
threshold monitoring 221
threshold setup section 229, 230
threshold templates
assigning 238, 239
creating 235, 237
time zones
URL 303
Tobi Oetike
about 303
URL 303
top_graph_header_tabs 182
top_header_tabs 182
Traps unit 309
tree_after hook 188, 201, 202
tree rules, Autom8
about 264
adding 275-279
trees, Cacti CLI
about 264
adding 267-269
tree view page
data, presenting on 201, 202

Thank you for buying
Cacti 0.8 Beginner's Guide

About Packt Publishing

Packt, pronounced 'packed', published its first book "*Mastering phpMyAdmin for Effective MySQL Management*" in April 2004 and subsequently continued to specialize in publishing highly focused books on specific technologies and solutions.

Our books and publications share the experiences of your fellow IT professionals in adapting and customizing today's systems, applications, and frameworks. Our solution based books give you the knowledge and power to customize the software and technologies you're using to get the job done. Packt books are more specific and less general than the IT books you have seen in the past. Our unique business model allows us to bring you more focused information, giving you more of what you need to know, and less of what you don't.

Packt is a modern, yet unique publishing company, which focuses on producing quality, cutting-edge books for communities of developers, administrators, and newbies alike. For more information, please visit our website: www.packtpub.com.

About Packt Open Source

In 2010, Packt launched two new brands, Packt Open Source and Packt Enterprise, in order to continue its focus on specialization. This book is part of the Packt Open Source brand, home to books published on software built around Open Source licences, and offering information to anybody from advanced developers to budding web designers. The Open Source brand also runs Packt's Open Source Royalty Scheme, by which Packt gives a royalty to each Open Source project about whose software a book is sold.

Writing for Packt

We welcome all inquiries from people who are interested in authoring. Book proposals should be sent to author@packtpub.com. If your book idea is still at an early stage and you would like to discuss it first before writing a formal book proposal, contact us; one of our commissioning editors will get in touch with you.

We're not just looking for published authors; if you have strong technical skills but no writing experience, our experienced editors can help you develop a writing career, or simply get some additional reward for your expertise.

open source
community experience distilled

Cacti 0.8 Network Monitoring

ISBN: 978-1-847195-96-8   Paperback: 132 pages

Monitor your network with ease!

1. Install and setup Cacti to monitor your network and assign permissions to this setup in no time at all

2. Create, edit, test, and host a graph template to customize your output graph

3. Create new data input methods, SNMP, and Script XML data query

4. Full of screenshots and step-by-step instructions to monitor your network with Cacti

Zabbix 1.8 Network Monitoring

ISBN: 978-1-847197-68-9   Paperback: 428 pages

Monitor your network hardware, servers, and web performance effectively and efficiently

1. Start with the very basics of Zabbix, an enterprise-class open source network monitoring solution, and move up to more advanced tasks later

2. Efficiently manage your hosts, users, and permissions

3. Get alerts and react to changes in monitored parameters by sending out e-mails, SMSs, or even execute commands on remote machines

4. In-depth coverage for both beginners and advanced users with plenty of practical, working examples and clear explanations

Please check **www.PacktPub.com** for information on our titles

www.ingramcontent.com/pod-product-compliance
Lightning Source LLC
Chambersburg PA
CBHW080152060326
40689CB00018B/3947